John L. Esposito (Ed.)

Religion and Violence

This book is a reprint of the special issue that appeared in the online open access journal
Religions (ISSN 2077-1444) in 2015 (available at:
http://www.mdpi.com/journal/religions/special_issues/ReligionViolence).

Guest Editor
John L. Esposito
Georgetown University
Washington

Editorial Office
MDPI AG
Klybeckstrasse 64
Basel, Switzerland

Publisher
Shu-Kun Lin

Assistant Editor
Jie Gu

1. Edition 2016

MDPI • Basel • Beijing • Wuhan

ISBN 978-3-03842-143-6 (Hbk)
ISBN 978-3-03842-144-3 (PDF)

© 2016 by the authors; licensee MDPI, Basel, Switzerland. All articles in this volume are Open Access distributed under the Creative Commons Attribution license (CC-BY), which allows users to download, copy and build upon published articles even for commercial purposes, as long as the author and publisher are properly credited, which ensures maximum dissemination and a wider impact of our publications. However, the dissemination and distribution of physical copies of this book as a whole is restricted to MDPI, Basel, Switzerland.

Table of Contents

List of Contributors V

Preface VII

Jocelyne Cesari
Religion and Politics: What Does God Have To Do with It?
Reprinted from: *Religions* **2015**, *6*(4), 1330-1344
http://www.mdpi.com/2077-1444/6/4/1330 1

Mark LeVine
When Art Is the Weapon: Culture and Resistance Confronting Violence in the Post-Uprisings Arab World
Reprinted from: *Religions* **2015**, *6*(4), 1277-1313
http://www.mdpi.com/2077-1444/6/4/1277 16

Virginie Andre
Violent Jihad and Beheadings in the Land of Al Fatoni Darussalam
Reprinted from: *Religions* **2015**, *6*(4), 1203-1216
http://www.mdpi.com/2077-1444/6/4/1203 55

John O. Voll
Boko Haram: Religion and Violence in the 21st Century
Reprinted from: *Religions* **2015**, *6*(4), 1182-1202
http://www.mdpi.com/2077-1444/6/4/1182 69

C. Christine Fair
Explaining Support for Sectarian Terrorism in Pakistan: Piety, Maslak and Sharia
Reprinted from: *Religions* **2015**, *6*(4), 1137-1167
http://www.mdpi.com/2077-1444/6/4/1137 90

John L. Esposito
Islam and Political Violence
Reprinted from: *Religions* **2015**, *6*(3), 1067-1081
http://www.mdpi.com/2077-1444/6/3/1067 122

Arie Perliger
Comparative Framework for Understanding Jewish and Christian Violent Fundamentalism
Reprinted from: *Religions* **2015**, *6*(3), 1033-1047
http://www.mdpi.com/2077-1444/6/3/1033 137

Mark Juergensmeyer
Entering the Mindset of Violent Religious Activists
Reprinted from: *Religions* **2015**, *6*(3), 852-859
http://www.mdpi.com/2077-1444/6/3/852 153

List of Contributors

Virginie Andre: Alfred Deakin Institute for Citizenship and Globalisation, Deakin University, 221 Burwood Highway, VIC 3125 Burwood, Australia.

Jocelyne Cesari: Senior Research Fellow and Professor of the Practice of Religion, Peace, and Conflict Resolution; Berkley Center for Religion, Peace and World Affairs, Georgetown University, 3307 M St NW, Washington, DC 20007, USA.

John L. Esposito: Prince Alwaleed Bin Talal Center for Muslim-Christian Understanding Georgetown University, Washington, DC 20057, USA.

C. Christine Fair: Edmund A. Walsh School of Foreign Service, Georgetown University, 3600 N. St., Washington, DC 2007, USA.

Mark Juergensmeyer: Department of Sociology and Global Studies, University of California, Santa Barbara, Santa Barbara, CA 93106, USA.

Mark LeVine: Department of History, University of California, Irvine, Krieger Hall 220, Irvine, CA 92697-3275, USA; Center for Middle Eastern Studies, Lund University, Finngatan 16, 223 62 Lund, Sweden.

Arie Perliger: Department of Social Sciences, United States Military Academy, 607 Cullum Road, Lincoln Hall, Rm. 120. West Point, NY 10996, USA.

John O. Voll: Alwaleed Center for Muslim-Christian Understanding, Georgetown University, Washington, DC 20016, USA.

Preface

Religion and Violence

Understanding the relationship of religion to violence, domestic and global, has become increasingly critical in the 21st century. Violent conflicts in which religion is a factor exist among all the major World religions (Judaism, Christianity, Islam, Hinduism and Buddhism) and have occurred across the globe: Nigeria, Sudan, Egypt, Syria, Iraq, Myanmar/Burma, Sri Lanka, Thailand, India, Iraq, Iran, China, Syria, Pakistan, Malaysia, Indonesia, Israel, Palestine, Afghanistan, Central Asia…

The Pew Research Center reported (2014) that religious conflict abroad was increasing. A high level of social hostilities involving religion reached a six-year peak in 2012. Thirty-three percent of the 198 countries and territories included in the study had high religious hostilities in 2012, up from 29% in 2011 and from 20% in 2007. Religious hostilities increased in every major region of the world except the Americas. The sharpest increase was in the Middle East and North Africa, which still are feeling the effects of the 2010–2011 political uprisings known as the Arab Spring. There also was a significant increase in religious hostilities in the Asia-Pacific region, where China edged into the "high" category for the first time. The PEW report concluded that there was an increase in "social hostilities involving religion", noting that this is not necessarily saying that religion is the primary driver.

All religions have a transcendent and a "dark side". Religion is about a transcendent (divine, absolute or ultimate) Being or Reality. It enables believers or practitioners to achieve levels of self-transcendence. All have been sources of ultimate meaning, compassion, peace and social justice as well as inspired religious leaders and social movements (non-violent and violent of liberation from oppression and tyranny; a religiously legitimated ideological alternative to the established order, a form of liberation, resistance, guerrilla warfare, violence and regional or global terror. Whether these are authentic uses of religion, or the hijacking of a religious tradition and legitimate or illegitimate use of violence in defensive or offensive conflicts and wars, has been a contentious point in the past and today.

Religion and Politics: Mainstream and Extremist

The last decades of the 20th century witnessed an increase of religiosity in personal piety and religious observances, ethnic and national identity, and in politics and the public square. Governments and their opponents, mainstream and militant, appealed to religion, embraced by religiously legitimated movements in the name of Judaism, Christianity, Islam, Buddhism, Hinduism, and Sikhism. Religious rhetoric, symbols, and ideology/theology replaced or buttressed secular ideologies and nationalisms, an ideological alternative to the established order, a form of liberation that justified liberation and resistance, violence, national, regional and transnational terrorism.

Religion and Violence

Religiously motivated or legitimated violence and terror adds the dimension of divine or absolute authority, buttressing the authority of governments, movements and leaders, providing moral certitude and justification, motivation and obligation, and heavenly reward that enhance recruitment and a willingness to fight and die in a sacred and cosmic struggle. For religious extremists/terrorists, their theological worldview is not simply an ideological and political alternative but an imperative. Since it is God's command, implementation must be immediate, not gradual, and the obligation to implement it is incumbent on all true believers. Those who remain apolitical or resist—individuals or governments—are no longer regarded as true believers but rather non-believers or heretics, enemies of God, against whom all true believers must wage a holy war. Acts normally forbidden—such as stealing, murder, and terrorism—are seen as required in a cosmic war between good and evil, between the army of God and the forces of Evil/Satan.

This volume looks at the worldviews and mindsets of religious activists and violent extremists with links to Judaism, Christianity, Islam, Buddhism and Sikhism. It raises and addresses critical questions about the primary drivers and catalysts for so-called religious violence. What is the role of religion in motivating and legitimating acts of violence and terrorism? What roles do religious scriptures, texts, beliefs, and leaders play? How important are political, economic and social contexts and grievances in creating the conditions that have radicalized individuals and led to the formation of Jewish, Catholic, Protestant, Muslim and Jewish movements or fundamentalist groups (Christian Identity and abortion clinic bombers, Zionist, HAMAS, Al Qaeda, ISIS and others) in the United States, Israel and Palestine, the Middle East, Myanmar, Japan and in Northern Ireland? Is religion, or are political contexts, the primary driver? Is there a significant link between the two? How have the ideology/or theology and nature of religious militant groups and their violence evolved in the context of globalization and new technologies?

For decades religion was not seen as a significant topic or variable in modernization and international relations. Many spoke of the choice in the Muslim world as being Mecca or mechanization. Jocelyn Cesari notes that religion was the "black hole" of international relations scholarship, and the political influence of religion both nationally and internationally, from Hindu and Buddhist nationalism to political Islam, ignored.

As a result, in the last decades of the 20th century, Iran's Islamic revolution in 1978–1979 and the reemergence of religion in politics, not only in Islam but all the major World Religions, accompanied by the greater appeal to religion by governments and mainstream and extremist opposition, challenged the conventional wisdom.

In "Religion and Politics: What Does God Have to Do With It?" Cesari challenges the tendency since the 9/11 attacks by Al Qaeda and the "war on global terrorism" and the threat posed by ISIL to view violence committed in the name of God as a "different" kind of violence, that triggers more "absolute" and radical manifestations than its secular counterparts. She maintains that the most extreme cases of violence in the name of religion are actually closely associated with specific forms of politicization of religion initiated by "secular" state actors and/or institutions.

Cesari argues that the "hegemonic" status granted to a religion by the state is often associated with greater political violence, building on research conducted in Egypt, Turkey, Iraq, and Pakistan. Hegemonic status, differentiated from the established or dominant religion, refers to the institutional absorption of religious institutions, personnel and norms within state institutions. This absorption creates an unprecedented conflation between national, civic and religious identity, distinct from the level of belief and religiosity of individuals. This hegemonic status of the religion is often correlated with lack of democracy. These results open up a new perspective on the relations between religion and political violence, shedding light on the unique interactions between religion and national identities that cannot be deciphered in the religious tradition as such.

Mark Juergensmeyer in "Entering the Mindset of Violent Religious Activists" argues that while the rise of ISIS, Jewish extremism, or the outbreak of Christian Islamophobia can be explained by external political and social factors, these analyses are flawed since they do not adequately explain the role of religion Al Qaeda and the post 9/11 war on global terrorism and, most recently, ISIL in acts of violence that appear to be justified by faith. Drawing on extensive personal interviews globally, Juergensmeyer discusses the mindsets of a diverse group of Protestant, Catholic, Christian, Muslim, and Buddhist activists and extremists and his conclusions. Though religious scriptures and beliefs may be a part of their worldview, he argues that they are not the causes, but rather the vocabulary through which social and political issues are framed and enunciated.

Arie Perliger, believing that most scholars and studies of religion and terrorism focus on Islam, thus ignoring its significant presence, has written, "Comparative Framework for Understanding Jewish and Christian Violent Fundamentalism." In it, he analyzes Christian Identity and the Religious-Zionist movements, as breeding grounds for the emergence of violent apocalyptic fundamentalisms. While terrorism is often perceived as the weapon of the weak, these individuals and groups belonged to communities belonging to the dominant religions in their respective societies. Members of Jewish-Zionist and Christian Identity movements perceived themselves as branches of Judaism and Christianity.

Pakistan provides another example where religion, piety and a desire for some form of sharia, are often attributed to religious extremism and support for sectarian (Sunni-Shiah) violence. Pakistan's domestic Islamist terrorists have long targeted religious minorities, including Hindus and Christians, as well as other Muslims such as Shia, Barelvi and Ahmedi whom they regard as heretics or non-Muslims.

In contrast to the conventional wisdom, Fair finds, based on an analysis of major national survey of Pakistanis, that the piety index and dimensions of sharia are not as significant as the particular school of Islam espoused, ethnicity, and key demographics which are the most consistent predictors of support for sectarian violence.

The global threat of Al Qaeda post 9/11 and ISIL, increased Sunni–Shia conflicts, and violence in the Middle East and Pakistan challenge governments in the region and globally. Muslim extremists and many Western experts and observers speak of a clash of civilizations or a culture war in Muslim–West relations. The religiously based ideology, discourse, symbols and violence raise questions about the relationship of Islam to violence and terrorism. John Esposito, in "Islam and Political Violence", addresses these questions in the context of development of global jihadist movements, in particular Al Qaeda and ISIL, their roots, causes, ideology and agenda. Among the key questions explored are: Is Islam a particularly violent religion? Critics cite Quranic passages, doctrines like jihad and events in Muslim history as strong indicators and proof that Islam is the primary driver of Muslim extremism and terrorism. What do the Quran and Islamic law have to say about violence, jihad and warfare? What are the primary drivers of terrorism in the name of Islam today? These questions are addressed in the context of development of global jihadist movements, in particular Al Qaeda and ISIL, their roots, causes, ideology and agenda.

Boko Haram in Nigeria provides an important example of the combination of religion and violence in the twenty-first century. It is both a movement that employs religiously justified violence and a significant representative of new types of modern terrorism. John Voll in Boka Haram: Religion and Violence in the 21st Century discusses how Boko Haram is the heir to a long jihad tradition in West Africa, following well-established patterns of older militant Muslim groups. However, Voll maintains, Boko Haram also departs significantly from those patterns, shaping itself in the context of twenty-first century, exhibiting characteristics of a new style of religious terrorism that is more like the so-called Islamic State than even an older type of terrorist organization such as Al Qaeda.

The Pattani Muslim resistance movement in southern Thailand dates back to Siam's (modern day Thailand) annexation and subjugation of the Sultanate of Pattani. It offers another example of the transformation of a militant movement in the 21st century. Virginie Andre, in "Violent Jihad and Beheadings in the Land of Al Fatoni Darussalam" (Islamic Land of Pattani), examines the long-standing Muslim separatist conflict of Southern Thailand and the contemporary revival and transformation of the Pattani struggle. Andre traces the evolution of a traditional ethno-nationalist insurgency now led by a new generation of militants, inspired by the Islamic ideologies and global religious consciousness, example and actions, of transnational Muslim militant movements such as Al Qaeda and ISIL. Thus, an ethnic Muslim struggle for the "liberation of the Republic" has been transformed into a glocalised neo-jihad to "liberate an Islamic land", a Cosmic war whose new forms of extreme violence have never been witnessed before in the Pattani struggle.

The Arab uprisings and revolutions in Egypt, Tunisia, Libya, Yemen, Syria and elsewhere in 2010–2011 and the intervening years have produced, as Mark Levine notes in "When Music is the Weapon: Culture and Resistance Confronting Violence in the post-Uprisings Arab World", some of the most politically as well as aesthetically powerful and innovative art. While the role of social media has received a great deal of attention, the role of music, poetry, theatre, graffiti and related visual arts as a weapon against violence have not. Citing examples from Egypt, Tunisia and Morocco to Syria and Yemen, Levine documents the ways in which the Arab uprisings were motivated and enabled by a wide range of cultural production and performance "banners featuring photos of martyrs, walls covered by graffiti, musicians playing, drummers drumming, poets rhyming, activists chanting, rappers rapping, and documentaries filmed and screened on makeshift white sheets, 'replaying' the events of the day."

Levine also discusses the extent to which Islamists who came to power through democratic elections, Egypt's Muslim Brotherhood and Tunisia's Ennahda, also recognized the importance of art. The Muslim Brotherhood's Freedom and Justice Party declared: "art is a significant form of expression which sends an influential message to its audience. Following the January revolution it is imperative we embrace the changes and blend with it." The Brotherhood supported theater, music and art in support of the revolution, declaring that, "anyone who has any kind of creative artistic act can participate with us and help shape the conscience of the nation."

In Tunisia, Ennahda's leader, Rachid Ghannouchi, strongly opposed the prosecution actors and artists arrested for allegedly indecent or anti-government art and condemned ultra conservative Salafis for their attacks on artists or patrons of theaters and other artistic events.

The case studies in this volume, Religion and Violence, demonstrate how, since the late 20th century, religious worldviews and vocabulary have provided the framework through which mainstream religious communities as well as religious extremists and terrorists have rooted, justified and legitimated their beliefs and actions. A major bone of contention is the relationship of religion to violence and terrorism. "New atheists" like Sam Harris, Richard Dawkins, Daniel and Christopher Hitchens as well as some policymakers, experts and pundits insist that religion itself or specific religions like Islam is the primary cause. Others emphasize the primacy of political, economic and social contexts and that militant extremists use religion to legitimate their acts of violence and terror and to motivate and recruit followers.

As we look to the future, major polling data and reports from Gallup, PEW and others indicate that religion will continue to be a major source of faith and guidance for many in their personal lives and in their societies, affecting domestic and foreign politics and policies. At the same time, the repressive policies of authoritarian regimes and failure of global powers and the international community to address widespread and legitimate political grievances will perpetuate conditions that feed the growth of militant movements and religion and violence.

John L. Esposito
Guest Editor

Religion and Politics: What Does God Have To Do with It?

Jocelyne Cesari

Abstract: Since 9/11, and even more so with the atrocities committed by ISIS in Iraq and Syria, violence in the name of God is predominantly perceived as a "different" kind of violence, which triggers more "absolute" and radical manifestations than its secular counter parts. In its first part, this article will challenge this so called exceptionalism of religious violence by questioning the neat divide between politics and religion that makes any forms of interactions between the two illegitimate or dangerous. It will look specifically at state actions *vis-à-vis* religions since the inception of the nation-state and show that the most extreme cases of violence in the name of religion are actually closely associated with specific forms of politicization of religion initiated by "secular" state actors and/or institutions. It argues that the "hegemonic" status granted to a religion by the state is often associated with greater political violence, building on research conducted in Egypt, Turkey, Iraq, and Pakistan.

Reprinted from *Religions*. Cite as: Cesari, J. Religion and Politics: What Does God Have To Do with It? *Religions* **2015**, *6*, 1330–1344.

1. Introduction

More than a decade after 9/11, it cannot be said anymore that religion is the "black hole" of international relations scholarship (hereafter IR). In fact, one of the unexpected consequence of this tragic event has been to put religion firmly on the agenda of IR. Most of the post-9/11 literature is actually an attempt to explain "the secularizing silence" [1], scholars attributing this neglect to the nature of Westphalian state system created in 1648, and the consequential influence of secular principles on international affairs. In this regard, the discipline has for a long time lagged behind the concrete political influence of religion both nationally and internationally, from Hindu and Buddhist nationalism to political Islam.

The end of the Cold War and the emergence of religiously motivated political groups on the international scene, however, have dramatically changed this perception among scholars of international affairs. It has been the work of Samuel Huntington, first presented in a 1993 article in *Foreign Affairs* and subsequently elaborated in his 1996 book *The Clash of Civilization and the Remaking of World Order*, which has dominated the discourse on culture as an element in international conflicts [2]. Huntington argues that Islam is uniquely incompatible with and antagonistic to the core values of the West (such as equality and modernity). This argument resurfaces in most current analyses of international affairs and globalization, notably in terrorism studies since 9/11. However, as social sciences has abundantly proven, civilizations are not homogenous, monolithic players in world politics with an inclination to "clash", but rather consist of pluralistic, divergent, and convergent actors and practices that are constantly evolving [3]. Thus, the "clash of civilizations" fails to address not only conflict between civilizations but also conflict and differences within civilizations. In particular, evidence does not exist to substantiate

Huntington's prediction that countries with similar cultures are coming together, while countries with different cultures are coming apart.

The cultural divide is thus envisaged as the primary cause of international crises. Admittedly, the "Huntingtonian" position is based on a premise that cannot be simply dismissed: that identity and culture play a decisive role in international relations. Additionally, Huntington's argument can be situated within the current trend of researchers attempting to understand the scope of the political revolts against the Western-dominated international order [4]. However, *what* culture and *what* Islam are being spoken of here? The idea of a monolithic Islam leads to a reductionism in which the conflicts in Sudan, Lebanon, Bosnia, Iraq, and Afghanistan are imagined to stem collectively and wholly from the domain of religion. It is, moreover, ironic that the role of religion, so long ignored or neglected in International theory is, is now exaggerated and decontextualized in an ahistorical perspective, which has elicited its fair share of criticism from scholars of religions.

Another issue with the recent scholarship on religion and international affairs, is that it focuses primarily on Islam and terrorism. This contributes to the misleading perception, so dominant in world affairs, that the scope and reach of terrorism in the name of God has grown out of control, that this violence is inspired by the specifics of the Islamic tradition and resilient to usual forms of compromise or negotiation.

This paper challenges this approach on religion and international relations by suggesting that the relevance of religion is not in the content of the Islamic tradition per se but in the interactions between religious and political actors, institutions, and ideas. In this regard, limiting Islam to beliefs or texts proves to be a dead end as the text can lead to very opposite political mobilizations. Instead, looking at belonging and behaving and the ways they are interconnected with belief helps us solve the puzzle of apparently very secular projects leading to political battles over Islamically correct social behaviors, which are currently happening in Turkey, Egypt or Tunisia. In other words, the social and political visibility of Islam is not caused by an increase in personal beliefs or religiosity. People are not stronger believers than they used to be, but their identification to Islam has certainly shifted, creating a collusion between political and Islamic belongings that facilitate political mobilization. Hence, the question is not on the nature of the religion but more on how historical processes and cultural transformations inform the tensions between religion and politics or between secular and religious, which are at play everywhere. Such a perspective requires a *"longue durée"*, historicized analysis that drastically challenges the rational choice centered theories that still dominate the International Relations discipline.

In sum, we will take into account the long-standing processes of mutual interactions between religion and politics to demonstrate the following:

(1) the politicization of religion in Muslim countries can be traced back to the building of the nation-state and the active role of "secular rulers" in reshaping the Islamic tradition as we will show through the case studies of countries often considered as the most secular: Iraq (under Saddam), Egypt, Turkey, Pakistan and Tunisia.
(2) the outcome of the absorption of Islam by the nation-state is what we call "hegemonic Islam" that is defined by exclusive legal, political and cultural privileges granted to one religion over all the others.

(3) Hegemonic forms of Islam in particular and of religion in general are conducive to more domestic and international political violence.

The politicization of religion cannot solely be found in the study of religious doctrines, which is often the bias at play in most of the analyses of political Islam [5]. In fact, the politicization of Islam has not affected so much theology or doctrines (except in the case of the Islamic Republic of Iran with the introduction of the *vilayet a faqih* concept, *i.e.*, the political guidance of the ayatollahs). However, it has certainly changed the identifications to the Islamic tradition by mingling it with national belonging. More to the point: in most Muslim-majority countries, political Islam is not the monopoly of Islamic parties but also a foundational element of the national and civic identity. Although most of the founders of Muslim-majority countries were secularized, they nevertheless included Islam in the state system, spurring its politicization by turning it into a modern national ideology, which operates as a common denominator for all political forces, secular or otherwise. As such, political Islam should be understood in a broader context that goes beyond Islamist ideology or Islamic parties. I therefore argue that both the state and the Islamists have been instrumental in politicizing Islam. In this broader sense, political Islam includes the nationalization of Islamic institutions and personnel under state ministries and the use of Islamic references in law and national education.

2. Nationalism and Pan-Islamism: Responses to the Western Concepts of Nation and State

After the symbolic inclusion of the Ottoman Empire into the Westphalian Order at the treaty of Paris that ended the Crimean war in 1856 [6], the gradual insertion of Muslim countries into the international order in the first half of the twentieth century was the result of three disparate factors: the end of the Ottoman Empire; the growing popularity of local nationalist movements in urban centers such as Cairo, Tunis, Baghdad, and Damascus; and the emergence of states under colonial power. The political and cultural resistance the imperialism of Western powers took two different but intertwined forms: Pan-Islamism and Pan-Arabism [7].

Pan-Islamists considered the universal Islamic community (Ummah) as the true basis and source of modern political unity and took as model the life and teachings of the Prophet Mohammed as well as his first four successors. In the waning days of the Ottoman Empire, the Pan-Islamism movement was fueled by the threat of European incursions into Egypt and Tunisia in 1798 and 1881. These actions by European states influenced reformers, such Jamal al-Din al-Afghani (1838–1897) and his disciple, Muhammad Abduh (1849–1905), who both called for *al-Wahda al-Islamiyya* (Muslim Unity) against Western imperialism in their journal *al-Urwa al-Wuthqa* (The Firmest Bond) ([7], p. 61). Consequentially, these intellectuals redefined the Caliphate as the community of all Muslim believers under the Prophet-Muhammad's vice-regent, in an attempt at buttressing the Empire's claims of legitimacy in the international system ([7], p. 33)[1]. In this way, Pan-Islamism resisted the idea of the Nation-State by becoming an alternate ideological approach

---

[1] In the pre-modern Islamic tradition, the Ummah is the totality of territories under the rule of the caliphate, which includes multiple religions, ethnicities and languages. In this regard, the idea of a caliphate for Muslims only, is modern and directly related to the engagements of Muslim thinkers with Western concepts of nation and nationalism.

for the political community in Ottoman territory, making it a trans-national geopolitical tool ([7], p. 60). At the end of the Second World War, a rethinking of the feasibility of political Pan-Islam gradually led to a search for alternative propositions, more adapted to the intense nation-building that was taking place at the time. The political goal of a neo caliphate was therefore replaced by more national-centered Islamic parties and movements. It was also after the Second World War that Pan-Islamism took on a categorically anti-Western rhetoric, which was not significant at the inception of the movement.

Reaching its height the in 1960s, Pan-Arabism started around the same time as Pan-Islamism. Rather than religion, it centered on a unified linguistic and cultural community. With the growing use of print media, the movement saw its rise in conjunction with Arabic poetry and literature during the *al-Nahda* renaissance in the late 19th and early 20th centuries [8]. This "awakening", like Pan-Islamism, was in response to the domination of Western cultural norms. Once the Ottoman Empire started to crumble and Pan-Arabism gained the support of the British power [9], the competition with Pan-Islamism intensified [10]. Both movements however, shaped the resistance to European political imperialism either through the lens of Islamic terminology for Pan-Islamists or through Arab culture for Pan-Arabists. The brief historical account below of national resistance in Egypt, Syria, Iraq, Pakistan, Turkey, and Tunisia is illustrative of the tensions but also the cross-pollination between the two movements.

In Egypt, Mohammad Abduh (1849–1905), reinterpreted the basic Islamic principles of his mentor and "founder" of Pan-Islamism, al-Afghani, to argue that while Islamic principles were consistent with modern Western rules of power and rationality, an intellectual battle, rather than an actual war, should be waged to fight Western imperialism [11]. In turn, one of Abduh's followers, Shaykh Rashid Rida (1865–1935), founder of the journal *al-Manar*, called for the unity of all Muslims under the banner of a reconstituted caliphate [12]. This modern approach to the caliphate as governance for Muslims only, influenced Hassan al-Banna (1906–1949), the founder of the Muslim Brotherhood. Borrowing from Abduh and Rida, al-Banna believed that Islam rather than the nation was the best tool for intellectual resistance to the Western project [13]. This anti-nationalist agenda was most prevalent with the alliance between the Muslim Brotherhood and King Faruq (1936–1952) who supported Pan-Islamist ideals instead of the nationalist and secular Wafd party. However, in the decades leading to the Second World War, the Muslim Brotherhood's ideology came in conflict with both King Faruq and nationalist groups. The conflict continued long after the monarchy's fall with Gamal Abdel Nasser (1956–1970) rise to power which marks the supremacy of nationalism over Pan-Islamism.

In Syria, the Ba'ath Party's created by Michel Aflaq (1910–1989) and Salah Bitar (1912–1980) in 1956 was the direct outcome of the influence of Pan-Arabism which promoted the ideal of a global Arab Nation, and translated in short-lived attempts such as the unification of Egypt and Syria into the United Arab Republic (1958–1961) [14]. A similar story to Syria was playing out in neighboring Iraq, where the Ba'ath Party gained power [15], which eventually led to the rise of Saddam Hussein in 1979 and the creation of Iraq into a unified Arab nation [16]. To this effect, Saddam penned policies emphasizing Arab unity, such as the Arab National Charter in 1980, which attempted to increase Arab cooperation towards common regional goals. At the same time, these Arab nationalists took control and deeply reshaped Islamic institutions and teaching.

As for Pakistan, although it was initially conceived as a political refuge for Muslims; Pan-Islamism itself was not the main source of inspiration that led to its partitioning from the Indian subcontinent. Prior to the calls for independence from British-ruled India, several Pan-Islamist movements, led by poet-philosopher Mohammad Iqbal (1877–1938) and Muhammad Ali Jinnah (1876–1948), gained widespread support in the subcontinent. Before the entrance of Iqbal and Jinnah to the Pan-Islamist stage, Sayyid Ahmad Raza Khan Barelvi (1856–1921) created a populist Islamic revivalist movement in the late 1800s. Officially named the *Ahl e Sunnat wa Jama'at*, Barelvi's ideals had both Sunni and Sufi origins and was popularly known for its more "liberal" ideology in Islam. For example, the movement championed the belief of intercession between the Divine and humans, a belief challenged by the more puritan Wahhabis and Deobandis [17]. Following this trend was the pro-Ottoman Khilafat movement, led by Maulana Mohammad Ali (1878–1931) and Maulana Shaukat Ali (1873–1938), who, during a conference in Karachi in July 1921, swore allegiance of all Indian Muslims to the Ottoman Empire [18]. The Khilafat movement quickly lost its momentum once the caliphate was abolished in 1924. The fall of the Khilafat movement set the stage for Iqbal and Jinnah to campaign for a Muslim state separate from Hindu hegemony in India. This goal would eventually become the highest ideal and course of action set by Iqbal in 1930 and adopted by Jinnah with the creation of the Muslim League [19].

Turkey's history of nation building was set around the tensions and conflict within the Ottoman Empire between Pan-Islamic and Pan-Arabist camps. By the time Western political ideas were penetrating different parts of the empire, the last of the Ottoman Sultans, Abdulhamid II (1876–1909), used Pan-Islamic ideas to promote imperial unity and maintain political control by contrasting Islamic identity to Western values [20]. As Kemal Karpat suggests, "religious" activities were used to "nationalize" the millets [21] of the Ottoman dynasty. For Abduhamid, these religious activities buttressed his position as Caliph to those who saw Islam as a significant personal identity. Towards the end of Abdulhamid's reign, the Young Turk Movement (beginning in 1908) emerged as a political alternative to Pan-Islamism. Young Turks, such as Ahmet Riza (1859–1930), were best known for their attempts to combine Islam with Western ideals rather than pitting them against each other. Riza's attempts were an "anti-clerical struggle to refashion Islam as a private matter and as a rational belief comparable with modernization" [22]. In this sense, Riza and the Young Turks were not anti-Islam, rather they were against the religious nature of the Caliphate. With multiple independence movements sprouting up throughout the empire (Armenia, Greek, *etc.*), the Young Turks attempted to consolidate their hold on the Turkish areas by spreading the idea of a Turkish nation and promoting a form of Islam where prayers and sermons were performed in Turkish ([20], p. 305). Once the empire collapsed at the end of World War I, the Young Turks were in a position to take control of former Ottoman provinces and establish what is today modern Turkey.

In Tunisia, allegiance to the Ummah, manifested by a pervasive loyalty to the caliphate, was seen as a way to resist reforms initiated by the modernist elite under French control, such as

Mohammad as-Sadiq Bey (1859–1881). Pan-Islamist resistance against the urban Westernized elites lasted from 1864 to 1881, immediately after the country became a protectorate under France with the Treaty of Bardo [23]. In the wake of the First World War, Islamic belonging persisted with the creation of the Destour Party in 1920, headed by Sheik Abdelaziz Taalbi (1920–1934), a man who spoke little French and a student of Rida and Afghani [24]. The Destour Party drew its membership from the educated elite who distinguished themselves by being fluent in Islamic and Arab cultures rather than those who drew their references from the French. Ironically, the Destour Party was the precursor to the Neo-Destour Party, established in 1934 which led the nationalist movement under Habib Bourgiba (1957–1987). The main difference between the old and new Destour Party was the connection between Islam and nationalism with the Neo-Destour Party ultimately imposing nationalism over Pan-Islamism. However, while Bourguiba was widely known for his secular beliefs and the dismantling and minimizing of the *ulama* and other Islamic institutions, he was often referred to as *al-Mujahid ul-Akbar* (the great warrior), and relied heavily on Islamic institutions and symbols to mobilize in masses in the anticolonial jihad [25]. For example, during the fight for independence from France, Bourghiba often held meetings in Mosques and Sufi zawiyas and urged the public to pray five times a day for the national martyrs [26]. This is in stark contrast with his policies after achieving independence in 1956, which included the Personal Status Law of 1957 that abolished *Shari'a* courts, banned the *hijab,* and restricted polygamy. This brought to the forefront Tunisia's French influences and secular-nationalist identity overpowering its Arab-Islamic identity.

In sum, in all nationalist movements, Islam was used as a rallying cry against colonial powers. However once Independence was achieved, Islam was painted as a symbol of the past while Westernization was seen as more representative of the newly independent country's future. At the same time, it was not possible for secular rulers to remain indifferent to the Islamic dimension of their new nations.

3. Nation-Building and Framing New Norms: The Creation of Hegemonic Islam

The nation-building process in the Muslim world saw a decisive rearrangement of the society-state-religion nexus. During the Caliphate era, religious institutions were not subservient to political power and most scholars of political history [27,28] argue that separations of labor and hierarchies of power between temporal and spiritual establishments were generally well organized and established by the tenth century. This does not mean that there were not "official" *Ulama* working in conjunction with the political rulers, similarly to the modern era. The major difference, however, was that in pre-modern time, religious authorities and institutions were not financially and organizationally dependent on the political power.

The Caliphs also acknowledged the cultural and religious diversity of the empire, although not so much as to translate into an egalitarian society for all religions and ethnicities. For example, the *Ummah* was established as the totality of the territories and people under the Caliphate rule, which included an extensive collection of ethnic, cultural, and linguistic groups including Muslims, Christians, Jews, Zoroastrians, Bahais, and Druze. This is in stark contrast of what one would see as the original successor of the community that followed the message of the Prophet Mohammad.

In reality, the Caliphate's power was limited by geography and governed in a way comparable to any secular dynasty charged with ruling multiple ethnic and religious groups [29]. This gap between the ideal community following the model of the Prophet and the political reality manifested itself in the distinction between *Shari'a* and *Syar* established by the juris consulates. While *Shari'a* referred to laws that apply to Muslims, *Syar* refers to laws applying to non-Muslims both living under the Caliphate and at the international level [6][2]. In contrast, the modern idea of the *Ummah* refers to a spiritual, community distinguished by those following Islam. In other words, the *Ummah* is now defined as a kind of extra-territorial citizenship for Muslims, regardless of where they live [30]. This new concept has become very pervasive in modern theological thinking.[3]

The collapse of the Ottoman Empire marks the end of the Islamic rule over different religious, ethnic, and linguistic communities. Nation-building in the wake of the Empire's fall, systematically omitted and in some cases, eradicated, particular ethnic, religious, and linguistics groups in hopes of creating a nation defined by a single religion and language. This homogenization had a direct influence on the politicization of religion. More generally, with the advent of the modern Nation-State, the relationship between religion and politics had been redefined everywhere. Creators of new Nation-States outside of the Western world had to contend with a major challenge: to what degree the "core" collective identity of the new country should be replaced by the Western institutions and technologies necessary to strengthen the state as a whole both militarily and economically? [31]. In the case of post-Ottoman Nations, the emergence of new political norms in concert with nationalism generally resulted in state projects that made use of Islamic terminology or vocabulary (Ummah/Jihad) or were articulated within an Islamic framework in order to anchor the nation-state project the vernacular mindset [32]. To put it differently, Islamic references or norms were applied to "localize" the nation-building process and legitimize state actors and policies, the outcome of which was the redefining of Islam within state institutions. The pruning and grafting of these new political norms on the pre-existing ones happened at four levels:

(1) The inscription of Islam in the Constitution as religion of the country or religion of the state;
(2) The Nationalization of Institutions, clerics and places of worship of one particular trend of Islam (for example Sunni over Shia);
(3) Redefinition and adjustment of Sharia to the modern legal system as well as inclusion of Islamic references into civil law (marriage/divorce) as well as restriction of freedom of speech (blasphemy/apostasy), based on the prescriptions of that particular brand of Islam;

---

[2] The concept of *Syar* was developed in the early centuries of Islam by Al-Shaybānī (748–805) and later codified by Al-Sarakhsī (d. 1101): "The *syar*…describes the conduct of the believers in their relations with the unbelievers of enemy territory as well as with the people with whom the believers had made treaties, who may have been temporarily (*musta'mins*) or permanently (*dhimmīs*) in Islamic lands; with apostates, who were the worst of the unbelievers […] and with rebels."

[3] Yusuf al Qaradawi, in the context of the Palestinian national movement. Qaradawi sees the *Ummah* as a transnational and compulsory alliance of Muslims that excludes non-Muslims. "Supporting the Palestinian people in Gaza is a religious duty on every Muslims individual (from Morocco to Indonesia) according to his capabilities, and no one is exempted from that duty."

(4) Insertion of the doctrine of that religion into the public school curriculum beyond religious instruction, that is in national history textbooks, civic education and so forth.

These four features concur to establish Islam as a hegemonic religion. It is important to note the difference between a dominant religion, an established religion, and a hegemonic religion. A religion is dominant when it is the religion of the majority of a given country. In such cases, the dominant religion continues to impart historical and cultural references considered "natural" and "legitimate". Religious symbols and rituals become embedded in the public culture and the country. Examples of such dominant religions include Protestantism in the United States or Catholicism in France and Poland. An established religion is a church recognized by law as the religion of the country or the state and sometimes financially supported by the state like the Church of Denmark. Usually, the existence of an established church is not incompatible with the legal protection of religious minorities and freedom of speech.

A religion becomes hegemonic, however, when the state grants a certain religious group exclusive legal, economic, or political rights denied to other religions. In other words, *religious hegemony* refers to legal and political privileges granted to a specific religious group, which in most but not all cases is the dominant religion. Most importantly, it also related to *public culture and social identities* fashioned by Islamic references even for citizens who are not Muslims or do not believe.

The unexpected and often unseen consequences of legal privilege are state restrictions and controls over the activities of the official religion. It usually involves:

- A ministry of religious affairs and administration to manage the official religion;
- Government regulation of the use of religious symbols or activities;
- Limitations by state laws and policies on freedom of expression (apostasy law);
- Penalties for the defamation of the official religion (blasphemy law); and
- Government interference with worship (state authorization for building of places of worship. State censure of religious discourses and publications).

All Muslim countries, including Turkey, possess two or four of these features, the exceptions being Lebanon, Senegal and Indonesia (although discriminatory practices do exist). Interestingly, they are also the only ones that qualify as democracies, according to the Freedom House index. The other exceptions are the Muslim countries that were under communist rule and in which religion was banned (see table below).

While democracy can accommodate some forms of state involvement into religions, the hegemonic status granted to one religion is an impediment to democratic life or transition to democracy. Additionally, hegemonic religion is usually correlated with higher levels of violence between citizens as discussed below. In sum, states which give exclusive, rights, privileges, status, and benefits to a single religion are significantly less likely to be democratic. Additionally, Muslim-majority states, especially in the Middle East, are more likely to have hegemonic traits, although these traits are by no means exclusive to these states.

4. Hegemonic Religion and Political Violence

Data on Islam's role in the following domains was methodically collected (see Table 1): (a) the Constitution; (b) the nationalization of clerics and religious institutions; (c) the legal system; (d) the education system. The data covers the period from the creation of each Nation-State to present. According to this systemic review, out of the 45 Muslim-majority countries listed below, 28 score between a 2 and 4 on a four-point scale measuring the hegemony of Islam.

Table 1. Hegemonic features of Muslim states.[4]

	Constitution	Nationalization	Law	Education
Score of 4				
Egypt				
Saudi Arabia				
Pakistan				
Algeria				
Morocco				
Malaysia				
Bangladesh				
Jordan				
Kuwait				
Somalia	√	√	√	√
Qatar				
UAE				
Sudan				
Yemen				
Iran				
Afghanistan				
Libya (under Qadaffi)				
Bahrain				
Comoros				
Brunei				
Mauritania				
Score of 3				
Syria				
Iraq (under Saddam Hussein)		√	√	√
Tunisia				
Oman				
Uzbekistan				

---

[4] A caveat is in order: This table groups countries in a very unusual way (Saudi Arabia/Egypt for example) because it scores only institutional arrangements as they stand today. Therefore, it does not reflect nor contextualize the political and social forces at work in each country that are obviously very different and diverse. For the score of 0, countries (especially former communist countries like Albania) have no history of ties with religion. Others, like Lebanon, provide an example of confessionalism, which proportionally allocates political power and represents the demographic distribution of the recognized religions. Indonesia, Gambia, and Senegal recognize all religions and legally provide education and resources for all religious institutions.

Table 1. *Cont.*

	Constitution	Nationalization	Law	Education
Score of 2				
Tajikistan	-	x	-	√
Turkey				
Score of 1				
Nigeria				
Mali				
Niger	-	-	-	√
Chad				
Kyrgyzstan				
Turkmenistan				
Score of 0				
Albania				
Kosovo				
Guinea				
Kazakhstan				
Azerbaijan	-	-	-	-
Burkina Faso				
Sierra Leone				
Lebanon				
Senegal				
Indonesia				
Gambia				

The four conditions are not individually sufficient to secure the hegemonic status of Islam, and not all of these conditions hold the same weight, especially the inscription of Islam in the Constitution that in some countries can be merely symbolic. However, the conjunction of the nationalization, legal system, and education conditions are probably necessary to secure a hegemonic status. In other words, if Islamic institutions are State institutions, Islamic law is part of the legal system, and Islam is engrained in the curriculum of public schools, Islam has a hegemonic status. In this regard, our research confirms findings that correlate religious instruction with the role of political Islam in most of Muslim majority countries [33].

Other states outside the Muslim world, such as Sri Lanka, Butan or the Dominican Republic can also be defined by two or three traits of the hegemonic religion. It happens that they are also low on the democracy index and high on political violence and social hostility. Other research, beside our own, shows that state restrictions on religion increase social and political violence [3]. The Pew Forum surveys confirm that government and social restrictions of religion lead to higher levels of religious persecution and violence across *all* countries independent of the religious tradition. They also corroborate that the highest degree of persecution happens in countries with sociopolitical monopoly of religion or monopolistic social pressures [34], or what we call hegemonic Islam. The monopoly or quasi monopoly situation covers 90% of Muslim-majority countries and further converges with the data produced by Jonathan Fox and Shmuel Sandler on the Government Involvement in Religion, where Muslim-majority countries score the highest [35,36]. In other words, Muslim majority countries are not distinctive when it comes to higher levels of religious persecution and violence *vis-à-vis* government and social restriction. Instead, these studies in conjunction with one another point to a different reason for increased religious violence in Muslim majority countries, which is the existence of a total monopoly or quasi monopoly over religion, regardless of the specific religion. This means that the issue of religious violence is not with Islam, but with the treatment of religion in general by the government and society.

The correlation of state-religions interactions with politicization of religion and increased probability of political violence in the name of God, obliges us to revisit the divide between religion and politics and secular and religious.

5. Conclusions

With no doubt, the work of Talal Asad or Michel Connolly has strongly questioned the definition of religion as a set of beliefs and demonstrated that this understanding, far from being universal, is the direct outcome of the historical evolution of Christianity in the West [37].

In fact, our incursion in Muslim territories shows that the belonging and the behaving are equally important in the politicization of religion. The distinction between believing, belonging and behaving has been made by sociologists to understand modern forms of religiosity. These three dimensions have historically been systematically linked or associated in the definition of a person's religiosity. They respectively refer to beliefs, religious practices and collective identity and have been for a long time defined as simultaneously part and parcel of a person's religiosity. However, recent sociological analyses have shed light on the increasing disjunction of these three dimensions and apprehended this disjunction as modern forms of religiosity [38,39]. Thus, a person can believe without automatically behaving and belonging; can belong without believing or behaving; or can behave without believing or belonging.[5]

In Muslim countries, the transformation brought by the nation-state has primarily transformed the belonging of citizens to Islam by a fusion of religious and national identifications. We have mentioned how from national historiography to civil law, the political socialization has introduced the belonging to the hegemonic form of Islam as synonymous to belonging to the nation. For this reason, what was traditionally considered religious, like belief in God is now politically discussed in public cases that address apostasy or blasphemy. It is important to stress that this politicization of religious belonging shapes the modern public space. One can argue that Islamic belonging was also key in defining the pre modern public space: after all, transgressions to Islamic beliefs in public space were sanctioned by death. But this punishment was ultimately in the hands of the Ulemas, not of the political authority. By contrast, the modern state, not the Ulemas, has taken on

---

[5] In *Genealogies of Religion*, Talal Asad describes the status of religion in medieval society as very different from the place what it is that religion holds in the modern age. Christianity during this period, he argues, functioned as a "great cloak" that defined an adherent's entire experience of the world. It possessed an "all-embracing capacity"—a distinctive practice and belief system—that disciplined the religious subject and nurtured certain virtues. Religion was not some essentially distinct form of culture, process of reasoning, or experiential state—that existed apart from other cultural experiences. It encompassed the cultural horizon of the subject's practices and assumptions about the world.

the punishment for apostasy or blasphemy, even in secular countries like Egypt or Pakistan or Tunisia[6]. This state interference is not unique: some European states have maintained until now blasphemy law (most recently, the UK abolished its blasphemy law after 9/11). Nevertheless, the social and cultural secularization has actually rendered these laws obsolete in modern times. While in Muslim countries, the politicization of religion within the nation-state has made them more used and central to the public space than they were in the pre-modern Islamic periods [40].

These public and collective assertions of Islam are different from personal religious practices or beliefs. Actually, an analysis of the disjunctions between belonging and behaving can explain the intriguing and apparently contradictory political changes in Turkey, Tunisia, Pakistan and even Iraq. All started as secular national projects grounded in some Islamic references. It meant that Islam and the nation became combined in the same collective belonging in an effort to counter Islamic transnational projects (Pan-Islamism/Sufism). At the same time, in all these countries, the first national phase resulted in a secularization of citizen's religious practices in terms of dress code, gender relations, and life style. In the last three decades however, these societies have gone through a greater Islamization reflected in the increase of the *hijab*, as well as of Islamically-correct behaviors and speech. Consequentially, the political tensions are not on the belonging anymore, in the sense that Islamists have come to term with the national framework. After all, the past and present claims of Islamic state are evidence of the acceptation of what was initially seen as foreign. Although the most recent iterations of Islamism like al Qaida and now ISIS are in their respective ways attempts to destroy nation-states. What is now at stake is the behaving of believers-citizens and its consequences for women rights, freedom of speech and expression.

Additionally, our research validates what has already been hinted by other scholars, *i.e.*, religious tradition is not a good predictor to explain political violence. This finding speaks to several important debates on issues of religion and politics. For example, Huntington's clash of civilizations mentioned above, has been extensively criticized. In fact, as already discussed above, multiple surveys show that religious hegemony, not religious differences, increases conflicts and the probability of politicization of religion. In the same vein, according to the Pew data, 33 percent of countries dominated by one religion have a high level of religious-based violence, compared to 20 percent of countries where no religion dominates ([3], p. 67).

Finally, unlike what most theories of political development still assert, state involvement in religion is not necessarily an obstacle to democracy but the hegemonic status of religion may be. A worthwhile investigation, outside the scope of this article, would be looking at alternative forms of secularism beyond differentiation of state and religion, and their respective compatibility with democracy.

Conflicts of Interest

The author declares no conflict of interest.

---

[6] In Egypt, there is no blasphemy law, but condemnation for insult to the Prophets is a penal offense, likewise in Tunisia and Turkey. Pakistan is one of the secular country that has introduced in the 1970s blasphemy and apostasy laws punishable by death, like Iran after the Islamic Revolution.

References and Notes

1. Mona Kanwal Sheikh, and Ole Wæver. "Western Secularisms: Variation in a Doctrine and Its Practice." In *Thinking International Relations Differently*. London: Routledge, 2012.
2. Samuel Huntington. *The Clash of Civilizations and the Remaking of World Order*. New York: Simon & Schuster, 1996.
3. Brian J. Grim, and Roger Finke. *The Price of Freedom Denied: Religious Prosecution and Conflict in the Twenty-First Century*. Cambridge: Cambridge University Press, 2011.
4. Adda Bozeman. "The International Order in a Multicultural World." In *The Expansion of International Society*. Oxford: Oxford University Press, 1984.
5. Jocelyne Cesari. *The Awakening of Muslim Democracy: Religion, Modernity and the State*. Cambridge: Cambridge University Press, 2014.
6. Michelle Burgis. "Faith in the States? Traditions of Territoriality and the Emergence of Modern Arab Statehood." *Journal of the History of International Law* 11 (2009): 37–79.
7. Cemil Aydin. *The Politics of Anti-Westernism in Asia: Visions of World Order in Pan-Islamic and Pan-Asian Thought*. New York: Columbia University Press, 2007.
8. Rashid Khalidi. *The Origins of Arab Nationalism*. New York: Columbia University Press, 1991.
9. Mary Wilson. "The Hashemites, the Arab Revolt, and Arab Nationalism." In *The Origins of Arab Nationalism*. New York: Columbia University Press, 1991, pp. 204–31.
10. John Willis. "Debating the Caliphate: Islam and Nation in the Work of Rashid Rida and Abul Kalam Azad." *The Internatonal History Review* 32 (2010): 711–32.
11. Christina Phelps. *Nationalism and Revolution in Egypt*. Stanford: Houton & Co., 1964, p. 116.
12. Dale Eickelman, and James Piscatori. *Muslim Politics*. Princeton: Princeton University Press, 1996, p. 31.
13. Richard Mitchell. *The Society of the Muslim Brothers*. New York: Oxford University Press, 1993, p. 16.
14. Liam Anderson, and Garreth Stansfield. *The Future of Iraq: Dictatorship, Democracy, or Division*? New York: Palgrave Macmillan, 2004, p. 66. Aflaq himself was a secular Christian, however he still considered Islam as an integral component of the Arab nation, of which ideology "whose Spirit is Islam".
15. John Devlin. "The Baath Party: Rise and Metamorphosis." *The American Historical Review* 96 (1991): 1396–407.
16. Felicia Okeke-Ibezim. *Saddam Hussein: The Legendary Dictator*. New York: Ekwike, 2006, p. 9.
17. Kemal Karpat. *The Politicization of Islam: Reconstructing Identity, State, Faith, and Community in the Late Ottoman State*. Oxford: Oxford University Press, 2002, p. 46.
18. Akbar Ahmed. *Jinnah, Pakistan, and Islamic Identity: The Search for Saladin*. London: Routledge, 1997, p. 70.
19. Anwar Hussein Syed. *Pakistan: Islam, Politics, and National Solidarity*. New York: Praeger, 1982, p. 42.
20. Kemal Karpat. *The Politicization of Islam*. Oxford: Oxford University Press, 2001, p. 125.

21 Millets were religious communities regulated by their own civil rules. They were the cornerstone of the Ottoman political system.
22 Umat Azak. *Islam and Secularism in Turkey: Kemalism, Religion and the Nation State*. London: I.B. Tauris, 2010, pp. 5–6.
23 Signed on May 12, 1881 between France and Mohammad as-Sadiq Bey, by which Tunisia became a French protectorate.
24 Clement Henry Moore. *Tunisia since Independence: The Dynamics of One-Party Government*. Berkeley: University of Califormia Press, 1956, p. 27.
25 Michael Brett. "Review of: Habib Bourguiba, Islam and the Creation of Tunisia, in African Affairs." *African Affairs* 87 (1998): 126–28. Interestingly, he was also known as *Combattant Suprême*, which reveals the French connotations of Bourguiba's anticolonial character, while *al-Mujahid ul-Akbar* reflects "the Islamic associations of the other of these ostensibly synonymous terms".
26 Marion Boulby. "The Islamic Challenge: Tunisia since independence." *Third World Quarterly* 10 (1988): 590–614.
27 Hamid Enayat. *Modern Islamic Political Thought*. New York: I.B. Tauris, 2005.
28 Ira Lapidus. *A History of Islamic Societies*, 2nd ed. Cambridge: Cambridge University Press, 2002.
29 Albert Habib Hourani. *Arabic Thought in the Liberal Age, 1798–1939*. Cambridge: Cambridge University Press, 1988, p. 12.
30 Riaz Hassan. *Faithlines: Muslim Conceptions of Islam and Society*. Oxford: Oxford University Press, 2002, p. 94.
31 Prasenjit Duara. *Rescuing History from the Nation: Questioning Narratives of Modern China*. Chicago: University of Chicago Press, 1995. The adjective "core" refers to an essentialized vision of culture and idenity, but most of the time, such essentializations drove political reforms at the time.
32 Amitav Acharya, and Malik Mufti. "How Ideas Spread." In *Sovereign Creations: Pan-Arabism and Political Order in Syria and Iraq*. Ithaca: Cornell University Press, 1996, pp. 239–75.
33 Colin Beck. "State Building as a Source of Islamic Political Organization." *Socioligical Forum* 24 (2009): 337–56.
34 Brian Grim. "Rising Restrictions on Religion: One-Third of the World's Population Experiences an Increase." In *The PEW Forum on Religion & Public Life*. Washington: Pew Research Center, 2011.
35 Jonathan Fox. "Separation of Religion and State in the 21st Century: Comparing the Middle East and Western Democracies." *Quarterly Journal of Economics* 120 (2005): 1331–70.
36 Jonathan Fox. "World Separation of Religion and State into the Twenty First Century." *Comparative Political Studies* 1 (2006): 255–86.
37 Talal Asad. *Genealogies of Religion: Discipline and Reasons of Power in Christianity and Islam*. Baltimore: Johns Hopkins University Press, 1993.

38 Grace Davie. *Religion in Britain since 1945: Believing without Belonging.* Oxford: Blackwell, 1994.
39 Daniele Hervieu-Léger. "Religion und sozialer Zusammenhalt in Europa." *Transit* 26 (2003): 101–19.
40 Ira Lapidus. "The Separation of State and Religion in the Development of Early Islamic Society." *International Journal of Middle East Studies* 6 (1975): 363–85.

When Art Is the Weapon: Culture and Resistance Confronting Violence in the Post-Uprisings Arab World

Mark LeVine

Abstract: This article examines the explosion of artistic production in the Arab world during the so-called Arab Spring. Focusing on music, poetry, theatre, and graffiti and related visual arts, I explore how these "do-it-yourself" scenes represent, at least potentially, a "return of the aura" to the production of culture at the edge of social and political transformation. At the same time, the struggle to retain a revolutionary grounding in the wake of successful counter-revolutionary moves highlights the essentially "religious" grounding of "committed" art at the intersection of intense creativity and conflict across the Arab world.

Reprinted from *Religions*. Cite as: LeVine, M. When Art Is the Weapon: Culture and Resistance Confronting Violence in the Post-Uprisings Arab World. *Religions* **2015**, *6*, 1277–1313.

What to do when military thugs have thrown your mother out of the second story window of your home? If you're Nigerian Afrobeat pioneer Fela Kuta, Africa's greatest political artist, you march her coffin to the Presidential compound and write a song, "Coffin for Head of State," about the murder. Just to make sure everyone gets the point, you use the photo of the crowd at the gates of the compound with her coffin as the album cover [1].

Kuti understood, perhaps earlier and more viscerally than most artists in the global era, that art, and music in particular, is the "weapon of the future" (as he titled his final album) [2] in the struggle against violent, corrupt and repressive regimes. Art is especially important where civil society has little space for protest or to otherwise challenge the power of repressive regimes. His was a seminal late 20th century example of how art both serves as a vehicle and creates spaces for subcultures to become countercultures—how groups of (usually) marginalized young people, drawn together by common cultural tastes (in music, modes of dress, styles of speech, *etc.*) and performances, gradually articulate a powerful oppositional political vision that challenges authoritarian state power. In 1970s and 1980s Nigeria, led by a brutal and even genocidal military dictatorship (the 1967–1970 War in Biafra killed upwards of 3 million Biafrans in the same amount of time the Syrian civil war claimed 200,000 lives) and flush with oil income, Kuti's evaluation of the power of music proved sadly cogent. It could bring together large number of poor Nigerians around an artistic and political vision to challenge an unjust system, but the time where music or art more broadly could encourage a revolutionary momentum that would fundamentally challenge and change the system was—and remains still—in the future for Nigerians, and most of the world as well.Art has always been a handmaiden to revolution and culture its fuel, for no other reason than social and political (inter)action are inherently symbolic and performative, and thus inherently aesthetic and affective. It is impossible to move large masses of people into the streets and convince them to risk everything for the slim chance of changing their future for the better without having a powerful cultural and artistic component to convey the messages in the most affective—that is, emotionally effective—manner possible. But the era of contemporary globalization has significantly augmented the role and power of artistic and cultural production within societies. Contemporary globalization is unique in several respects compared to earlier iterations of global integration. Broadly speaking culture has been the driving force behind contemporary globalization far more so than in previous eras. Political integration has been largely absent outside of the European Union; and even this process is increasingly under threat. Economic integration is often thought of as the hallmark of contemporary globalizaiton; but in truth, the economic aspects of globalization (greater integration into the world economy, foreign direct investment, effective liberalization and privatization policies) have on the global scale been highly skewed as greater wealth has been accompanied by greater inequality and poverty in many areas.

In the MENA region in particular, outside the Gulf countries the kind of broadly distributed economic development that should accompany globalization (as it's been advertised) hasn't occurred nearly to the degree that it's occurred in the advanced economies and top tier developing economies such as China, India, Turkey, or Brazil (the so-called BRICS). In the era of contemporary, neoliberal-driven globalization, "the economy is globalized to the extent it is culturalized," that is, transacted through cultural symbols [3,4] Culture is inherently transnational and translational, colonizing and colonized, othering and othered, part survival strategy and part "expedient" invention that continuously redefines our identities.

Here I understand globalization as inherent to the emergence of the political, economic and cultural/ideological coefficients of what I term the "modernity matrix"—the complex and implicate set of processes composed of capitalism, colonialism/imperialism, nationalism and modernity as a self-referential concept and ideology that began to congeal at the time of the Columbian voyages and opening of the Americas to European conquest in the late 15th and early 16th century, and which have together driven world history since then. The balance, mix and relative strength of the various elements change over time and geography.

If culture has become a "crucial key" (as the United Nations described it) in solving our world's myriad crises, in the dominant neoliberal version of globalization among the most powerful experiences and performances of culture have become depoliticized and commodified at precisely the moment that it has become the defining mechanism of political and economic interaction and the engine of global integration. At the same time, because of the penetrative power of contemporary technologies—particularly satellite television and then the internet—the power of globalization to "disembed" or "deterritorialize" people from their original cultures has become all the more evident, as people all over the world are exposed to an unprecedented array of cultural symbols, products and experiences that transform their identities in profound ways. Some, by virtue of circumstance of personality or both, can experience this process as liberating. For others, fear, anger and violence are the most likely response.

Neoliberalism, the guiding ideology and power apparatus undergirding contemporary globalization, also has had profound economic impact which in many but not all cases resembles the impact of colonialism in centuries past. Specifically, in the developing countries such as those of the Arab world (outside of the small number of wealthy gulf petro-kingdoms and emirates) it has encouraged greater corruption and authoritarian rule as processes of so-called "privatization" or "liberalization" concentrated wealth in the hands of existing (if somewhat broadened) class of elites, undid the advances in human development that were one of the few positive developments of the "authoritarian bargain" of the era of Arab socialism, and weakened the power of citizens to mitigate the worst effects of authoritarian rule even as in principle they should have led to greater space for civil society. The intersection of "really existing neoliberalism" and increasing cultural interpenetration constitute one of the core dynamics of the contemporary era, creating an almost schizophrenic situation in which tens of millions of inhabitants of the region have been caught between competing identities, narratives, languages, dreams, and powers with little room for maneuver.

As the Moroccan fusion band Hoba Hoba Spirit explained why they gave their 2005 album the title *Blad Schizo* (*Schizo Country*): "Because it is a schizophrenic country." Centuries of power wielded by the Makhzen (the name long used to describe the Moroccan European imperialism and now globalization, have made it so. "You have to understand," frontman Reda Allali continued, "even our language is schizo. [Derija, the Moroccan dialect of Arabic, is a mix of Arabic, Berber, French, and its own grammar.] No one else, from the Middle East, Africa, or Europe, understands us. And our politics are twisted as well [5].

The "schizo" nature of globalized culture played a crucial role in the genealogy of the Arab uprisings. In interviews with numerous activists from countries that experienced the most intense protests (for example, Tunisia, Egypt and Bahrain) a narrative has emerged in which the youth generation that instigated the protests began literally to split from the dominant patriarchal, authoritarian culture in the 1990s and early 2000s, with a core group developing an identity through new networks of communication and cultural experience and interaction—as epitomized by the emergence of the internet, but also through the formation of various subcultures (from young Muslim brothers to metalheads) and particularly through their experience in the universities, the cauldron for previous generations' politicization as well. This cultural split, this coming of age of an unprecedented number of young people from the Arab world (Arab countries boasted the largest share of under 30 populations in the world by the 1990s) who were highly educated, multicultural and multilingual, broadly alienated from their broader cultures, and feeling as if the existing systems both provided no hope for the future and that they therefore had little if anything to lose by challenging their governments in increasingly direct ways. As Mohamed-Salah Omri explains for Tunisia, "One key feature of the system during Ben Ali's rule was a duality or parallel existence of two opposing systems of values and cultural production. At the cultural level, everything was double, and just as there was thriving parallel commerce, run largely by the ruling family, as we found out after Ben Ali ran away, there was 'the theater of parallel commerce'…The same goes for poetry, fiction, music, and cinema" [6,7].

1. Radical and Resistance Cultures

African American writer Toni Cade Bambara has declared that "the duty of the radical artist is to make the revolution irresistible." [8]. But art has to be more than just a tool of critique. As the Dalai Lama declared, art must "awaken people to compassion" at the same time it motivates them to revolution [8]. This raises the question, however, of what kind of artistic/aesthetic production makes it impossible not to risk everything for the chance fundamentally to change the system in which one lives. I argue that the key to art, and music specifically, is the return of what Walter Benjamin described as its "aura," which he argues was lost as artistic production and circulation became industrialized, commodified, and commercialized.

With the modern mass production and circulation of art—Benjamin calls it "mechanical" or "technological"—"the aura" that previously had given art such aesthetic, and thus social power by highlighting its singularity and irreplaceable value, disappeared. For Benjamin, the disappearance of the aura of art was a positive development because it allowed for artistic production that no longer ritualistically served existing power structures and thus could enable new and even revolutionary visions of the future.

Benjamin's friend and comrade, Theodor Adorno, was profoundly influenced by the notion of the aura developed in Benjamin's seminal "The Work of Art in the Age of Mechanical (lit. "technological") Reproduction." But Adorno saw the process more negatively: for him, the mass produced, commodified cultural production led to the creation of a "culture industry." Far from challenging the power of capital and its ideologies, the culture industry imposed an artificial aura, the "aura of style," upon cultural production, which had unprecedented power to reinforce the hegemonic ideology of the system (in this case the emerging consumer capitalism). In Adorno's words, this process constituted a "stereotyped appropriation of everything for the purpose of mechanical reproduction that eliminated every unprepared and unresolved discord." [9].

Of course, revolutionary music and art more broadly must highlight, not resolve, discord; it must become "immanently critical," in the same manner that Adorno and his Frankfurt School colleagues imagined philosophy should behave, if it is to enable greater human freedom. But it can't stop with merely highlighting, never mind heightening discord; it has to take the next step and promote a vision, a path and a method to create a new kind of accord between the people who must act in concert if the system is to be seriously challenged.

And here, the rise of new digital technologies have profoundly reshaped the production, dissemination and consumption of art. Professional quality films—both fiction and particularly documentaries—can be shot for very little money by young people, edited on their computers with the latest software and uploaded to the internet where they can be watched by anyone, anywhere, at any time. Artists and poets can put their work on the internet with the same results. Music has been far more democratized than any other art form by the internet by the ability to produce and circulate globally high quality recordings at low or no cost, evading the constraints of both capital and governments. I argue that at least with respect to music (which has particularly affective power for young people) this dynamic has returned the aura to music (or at least these styles of music), allowing it to connect to and move people in the ways necessary to encourage and sustain revolutionary action.

The digital revolution in production and distribution has enabled a return of the aura to music by enabling these two simultaneous processes. "Mechanical" reproduction and commodified distribution necessitated the development a "culture industry" to ensure its widest growth, and with the incorporation of cultural production and distribution into capitalist networks and control, the resultant art as well as its consumption could not help but reinforce the system's ideology, and serve as one of the most powerful weapons in capital's—especially late, post-industrial capital's—ideological and hegemony-producing arsenal.

But with low cost digital production capabilities and products that can be endlessly circulated for free, the necessary link between large-scale circulation and distribution of cultural products and commodification was broken. Specifically, the rise of "DIY" (do-it-yourself) musical scenes like heavy metal, punk, hiphop and other "alt" popular music, involved the creation of subcultures that were inherently (if only latently at the start) subversive and countercultural.

Moreover, these scenes were composed in good measure of "outsiders" and others who were marginalized in their societies, and of members who had high levels of new media-related skills experience organizing at the underground—or at least un(der)-commodified level to spread their music. This dynamic does not only concern music; other arts also have their "DIY" scenes. Finally and most important, these scenes survived and indeed thrived on face-to-face gatherings where music was intensely, viscerally and ritualistically shared, creating shared experiences, and through them solidarities, which strengthened the power of the music.

The combination of dynamics described here is what led to the return of the "aura" of music, by which I mean that music once again served as a "ritualistic" (to use Benjamin's term) condenser and amplifier of solidarities and identities—but it was now, at least potentially, free of servitude to the capitalist market and its attendant political and ideological systems. This aura, which we could see glimpses of during the height of the hippie era and then again with the birth of punk and hip-hop (all three of which were deeply grounded in broader political-economic conflicts), has the power to attract more people and help inspire and disseminate alternative identities and visions of the future of society.

In the advanced capitalist countries of North America, Europe and Asia, such auratic scenes still cannot compete with the hyper-commodified and politically dominant forms of cultural production and distribution generated and controlled by the commercial entertainment industries. But in Middle East, North Africa, and other parts of the developing world, they have greater possibility of encouraging and participating in movements for systemic change and even revolutionary movements.

2. Art without End

The Arab uprisings have motivated, enabled and been accompanied by a wide range of cultural performance, production and experience which can be divided into two broad categories. First are political actions and events which were inherently aesthetic or had very strong aesthetic components. The protests in Tunis, Tahrir Square and so many other locations epitomize this phenomenon. They are what I and my colleague Bryan Reynolds describe as "theater of immediacy," cultural (often, but not necessarily artistic) creation and performance for an intended audience that is not merely emergent—that is, in the process of formation—but "emurgent" (emergent + urgent); developing rapidly and in the context of intense sociopolitical struggle that destabilizes and even reconfigures previously dominant, congealed structures and networks of power and identity. These performances—and here I understand culture to be inherently and always performative—constitute, to borrow a concept from Benjamin, a space and experience in which performance becomes auratic, and so transformative [10].

If protests and other large scale highly charged public political events are inherently cultural and often feature a significant artistic component, artists themselves played an outsize role in the unfolding of the Arab uprisings. Perhaps the most well-known artistic symbols of the Arab uprisings are two musical artists, Tunisian rapper El Général and Egyptian singer Ramy Essam, both of whom I discuss below. But music was not the only artistic form central to the Arab uprisings. Poets and photographers, playwrights and graffiti artists, in their home countries and exile, all played a prominent role. Not only that, the form and content of the art produced by Arab activist artists has continuously changed during the last five years, as conditions on the ground, the political situations, and the goals, dreams and expectations of the artists.

Finally, the artistic production and the theater of protests are of course intimately related. What made Tahrir such a powerful space was all the forms of art—music, graffiti, posters, humor, song, photography, poetry—that occurred within in. The intensity could be overwhelming, chanting with drums next to poetry surrounding by life sizes photographs, many of them grizzly, of the revolution's martyrs, astride hand-drawn cartoons and poetic banners, all within the space of a few meters. It was also "self-perpetuating," as each crackdown by police produced more art—none the more so and longer into the revolutionary era than graffiti, which was the subject of constant warfare between the Egyptian government and protesters for almost three years in the area around Tahrir [11]. Moreover, artists also constantly changed their tone and emphasis as the protests, revolutions and civil wars have evolved, whether from within or outside the countries [12–14].

Many countries attempt to claim pride of place in producing the most innovative and greatest quantify of artistic output since the eruption of the Arab uprisings. Given the sheer size of its population, Egypt likely could lay the most legitimate claim to this position, but as Miriam Cooke argues, given all the violence and suffering Syrians have endured the last five years, they have been the "most artistically and culturally prolific" [15], while Palestine has had longer direct experience confronting the full force of an oppressive regime.

What is clear is that the region has seen a real explosion of creative talent and energy since the self-immolation of Muhammad Bouazizi, in such varied areas as Tunisian rap, Libyan literature, Moroccan experimental theater, Yemeni protest music and Egyptian graffiti [16]. All of these forms have historically "thrived on conflict" while at the same time pushed the boundaries of moral, political and cultural freedom while given vent to the frustrations of the people, especially the youth. The problem that we must explore is to what extent this release mechanism went from having revolutionary power to erase fear, claim public space (especially streets and squares) and set off protests and even uprisings to merely offering a "festivalisation of dissent," as Aomar Boum describes it, containing and dissipating (or at least redirecting) anger and calls for social justice to less threatening ends [17].

Theater, as much as music and poetry, can produce "tarab," that aesthetic quality causing "enjoyment, reciprocation of emotion and communication between performers and audiences." Such intensity of affect is not merely at the core of great art, it's at the core of all revolutionary upsurges, which is yet another reason why all great art is revolutionary and all successful revolutions must have their own art. The question is, how much "tarab" can it have when it is tightly controlled, as for example was theater in Nasser's Egypt, where social realism and critique along Arab socialist principles were the rule [18]. At the same time, we cannot just look at state-sponsored theater even in the 1950s–1970s. There has always been a "decadent" (habit) theater alongside the officially sponsored theater. Its themes were far more varied and complex than the official theater, but it could only have so much impact from the fringes.

3. Delineating Revolution Art

At the height of the Tahrir protests, from 25 January 2011 through late 2012, there was really no place on earth quite like the "Republic of Tahrir" (Gumhuriya at-Tahrir). All the arts were present at one spot or another, a fully immersive sensory explosion that was, quite literally, life-changing. Surrounded by a seemingly numberless ring of 10-foot long banners featuring photos of disfigured martyrs, pavement and walls covered by graffiti (with a new mural or two likely being painted while you watch), musicians playing, drummers drumming, poets rhyming, activists chanting, rappers rapping, documentaries being filmed while others were screened on makeshift white (no doubt Egyptian cotton) sheets, street theater "replaying" the events of the day.

All this in the midst of tens and even hundreds of thousands of people talking, screaming, chanting, debating, blogging, vlogging, facebooking, reporting, calling home to tell loved ones it's okay (or not) to come to the Square, and on and on. And when fighting broke out with the military, security services, police or their various thugs (baltagiyya), we can add generous amounts of tear gas, bird shot, rocks, spears, knives, molotov cocktails, and high velocity bullets to the mix. And on your increasingly smart phone, dozens of new tweets and facebook postings every minute or two from friends, comrades and colleagues reporting the latest arrest, death, meeting or protest or the latest video or story on al-Jazeera or one of the new independent newspapers. And on and on, hour after hour, day after day.

And if it's November, and it's raining hard, and your camping in the Midan and a river seems to be running right under—and through—your tent, and have your computer and guitar or oud with you, and are hungry, and need a bathroom, and the Ultras who are protecting you think everyone they don't know is an informant (which more often than not might well be true) and the street kids you've adopted—more truthfully who've adopted you—are also hungry and cold, well, at least baltagiya are not trying to burn the tents down. Such was life in revolutionary Egypt, an experience that was echoed to various degrees and periods across the Arab world, from Rabat to Sanaa and dozens of cities in between during the uprisings era from early 2011 through 2013, at which point counter-revolutionary and extremist forces had effectively contained and even crushed most of the radical pro-democracy movements.

4. Music: Weapon of the Present

Music may have been the weapon of the future for Fela Kuti, but for Tunisians in late 2010, it was very much the weapon of the present—not merely the soundtrack of the revolution that caught fire in the ashes of Muhammad Bouazizi, but a motivating factor in bringing people into the streets and reshaping their basic political subjectivity, which is a core process of any revolutionary change in a country's social and political structures [19]. Indeed, as captured in an instantly classic photograph of a Libyan "guitar hero" singing and strumming his guitar next to several comrades in the midst of a heated battle with government forces, when necessary today's artists are as courageous as their counterparts in centuries past, when drummers, trumpeters and other musicians marched in step with soldiers, playing their music over the din of the battle in order to encourage their comrades to defy their fear of death and march headlong into unimaginable violence [20].

The most famous exemplar of the role of music in the Tunisian and subsequent Arab uprisings is the song "Rais Lebled," or Leader/President of the Country, by the then largely unknown rapper El Général (born Hamada ben Amour). Arriving in the mid-1990s to the Arab world, rap music quickly established itself as a major force for aesthetic expression and innovation among Arab youth from Morocco to Iran [21].

With a brooding tempo and hiphop beat and minor piano melody, the grim mood of "Rais Lebled," which follows a long line of "gangsta" style Arabic rap, sets up El Général's at turns plaintive and excoriating missive to then President Ben Ali. Beginning by informing the President that "your people are dying...eating from garbage...We are living like dogs," he goes on to describe the myriad indignities and violence, corruption and oppression suffered by ordinary Tunisians, this despite the seemingly progressive but actually worthless constitution. He focuses then, explaining: "Mr. President, you told me to speak without fear/I spoke here but I knew that my end would be palms [*i.e.*, slaps and beatings]/I see so much injustice. That's why I chose to speak out/even though many people told me that my end will be execution./But how long [must] the Tunisian live in illusions?" [22].

It's hard to overstate the power of "Raid Lebled," not least because such words could in fact get a person killed, or at least imprisoned and tortured for a very long time. But in speaking about overcoming fear, El Général captured the essence of the Arab uprisings—the loss of fear of a generation which, at least for a moment, would rather "die on our feet than live on our knees," as one revolutionary chant borrowed from many another uprising before it intoned. Aesthetically, it was precisely because El Général was not that experienced or innovative a rapper, and thus rhymed slowly in an easy to understand manner, that the song could be learnt and chanted easily, becoming an anthem of the revolution.

Studying these cultural performances is crucial to understanding the transformation from traditional to a more progressive, innovative set of cultural norms [23]. There are dozens of revolutionary hiphop songs in the "Arab Spring canon." Most every country from Morocco to Bahrain produced at least one song that helped united and motivate people, reflecting their pains and dreams, and bringing them out onto the streets. Whether Arabian Knightz's "Rebel" (Egypt), Ibn Thabit's "Ben Ghazi" (Libya), or L'7a9ed's "Klab ad-Dawla" (Dogs of the State), hiphop was truly at the heart of the soundtrack to the protests. In Syria as in Tunisia, hiphop helped announced the revolt. The anonymous song "Bayan raqam wahid" (Statement Number One) exclaims, "Statement number one/The syrian people will not be humiliated/Statement number one/We sure won't stay like this/Statement number one/From the Houran comes good news/Statement number one/The Syrian people are revolting," calling for the revolution that, tragically, led to one of the worst civil wars of the last fifty years [24,25].

This kind of courage and forthrightness owes to the very dawn of Arab hiphop, with the Palestinian-Israeli (*i.e.*, Palestinian citizens of Israel) rap group DAM, whose song "Min irhabi?" (Who's the Terrorist?) was one of the most powerful accusations ever put to music against the Israeli occupation [26]. As with so much in the Arab Spring, everything returns to Palestine (I discuss the role of Jerusalem's El Hakawati Theatre and the Jenin Freedom Theater as among the most important pre-uprisings resistance theaters in the Arab world).

We could easily spend the rest of this article discussing the many contours and contradictions of revolutionary (or not so revolutionary) Arab rap [27,28]. At the same time, a complete discussion would require exploring the many—indeed, majority—of young artists who either stay clear of politics (this is particularly true of the metal scenes around the region now that they are fare freer of direct repression merely because of the music and styles of dress or grooming), and of the instances where regimes have actively sponsored rappers and other artists in the wake of the uprisings as a counter to the revolutionary artists (Morocco and Bahrain are good examples of how government sponsor hiphop artists who otherwise might be dangerous to their power.

In the space available I will focus on one artist: Morocco's El Haqed (a.k.a. L7a9ed; "the Enraged One") [29]. L7a9ed's trajectory began somewhat later than the first group of revolutionary rappers, who were already fairly active, if not well known, before the eruption of the region-wide protests in late 2010. Mouad Belghouat (his legal name) came onto the Moroccan scene in the late summer of 2011, as a February 20 activist after the protests had reached their apex and were already fading in the wake of passage of the referendum put forward by King Muhammad. His stage name can be translated as both the enraged "l'enragé" or the "spiteful," or the indignant. If revolutionary Egyptian singer Essam has brought a kind of Bob Dylan, Ritchie Havens-like hard folk sensibility to Egyptian protest music (not surprisingly, Essam is a metalhead, and counts groups like Rage against the Machine, Korn and Slipknot as major influences), L7a9ed represents the ubiquitous power of hiphop as the world's most politicized musical form today.

Moroccan hiphop has been especially fruitful, producing some of the best examples of the genre anywhere in the twenty years [30]. From the start Moroccan rap was implicitly political, addressing social issues such as poverty, crime and rampant corruption and inequality in the country. But most rappers steered clear of directly challenging the legitimacy of the system, never mind the King.

This began to change around the turn of the present decade, as it did across the region. By 2009 twenty rappers put out a compilation titled "Mamnou3 f'Radio," "Forbidden on the Radio," with the goal of bringing together "the best titles censored on FM radio" [31]. And yet, once the system and the King became targets, rappers like other oppositional voices began to be targeted. Eeven as many rappers were organizing to fight censorship, a clear split opened up between those who would take on core political issues and those, most famously represented by the rapper Bigg (perhaps the most well-known rapper in Morocco), who stood squarely behind the King, becoming in fact court rappers.

Equally an activist and a rapper, L7a9ed came to the authorities' attention by September 2011, when he was first arrested after an altercation with a member of the Royalist youth. It was most likely a set-up, as police and ambulances arrived on the scene almost immediately, and despite no evidence that he'd actually assaulted the person, he was sentenced to four months in prison.

As with most rappers, L7a9ed's prison stint only increased his street credibility, especially among Morocco's poor and disenfranchised young people, from whose midst he'd risen in the slum of Oukacha, in the outskirts of Casablanca. Indeed, as he rose to fame L7a9ed drew his depictions of the worst characteristics of young Moroccans' lives earned him the sobriquet the "Gavroche of the

Moroccoan revolution" ("le Gavroche de la révolution marocaine")—Gavroche was a minor but important character in Victor Hugo's *Les Miserables*, a "street urchin" who joins the revolution and risks his life and in fact dies while collecting ammunition cartridges from dead government soldiers near the barricades during the 1832 popular rebellion in Paris [32].

It is instructive to compare L7a9ed to the "rapper of the Tunisian Revolution, El Général, whose music and career trajectory defined along with Ramy Essam's the politicized youth culture of the Arab Spring. In "Rayes Lebled," the rap song that helped launch the revolution, he pleads and implores the President Zine Abedin Ben Ali that "your people are dying…eating from garbage…We are living like dogs."

L7a9ed's attitude was much more confrontational from the start. Like Essam, L7a9ed's lyrics take on the most taboo subjects in Moroccan politics—corruption, police brutality, poverty and the inherently oppressive nature of the monarchy [33]. Specifically, in "Kleb adDawla," L7a9ed's signature song, the police—as in every Arab country, the most direct and concrete manifestation of state powers—are labeled "dogs of the state" (the translation of the title). There is no pleading for recognition. There is only derision, anger and a direct challenge to the core instrument of state power.

The differing attitudes of the two rappers became apparent in their post-protest trajectories. El Général quickly left political rap after the revolution, becoming more aligned with the growing Islamist movement as the new system emerged. When he did return to politicized lyrics, it was to take on the country's secular and constitutionally weak President, Moncef Marzouki, in the 2014 song, "Rayes Lebled 2." [34] L7a9ed began as a politically engaged rapper, or performance activist, and never backed down. His activities earned him two more stints in jail, for a year in 2013 after a conviction for insulting the police in "Kleb adDawla" and, as of the time of writing, a four-month jail term after again being arrested in a likely frame-up for allegedly selling scalped tickets at a soccer match and resisting arrest (in fact, witnesses confirm that L7a9ed was badly beaten while being taken into custody). He also saw his press conference to mark the release of a new, anti-regime album, attacked in February 2014. Essentially L7a9ed, like Ramy Essam, has become the closest thing to famed Nigerian political artist Fela Kuti in Africa today.

Meeting together in Amman in the winter of 2014, L7a9ed expressed growing concern that he'd soon return to prison, especially after the release of his new mixtape, *Walou* (Nothing). He previewed the album for me and other artists and activists during the Fourth Arab Bloggers' Meeting, a gathering which itself was dominated by the ongoing detention of bloggers, artists and social media figures from Egypt, Syria, and other Arab countries [35]. It was clear upon first listen that fans who worried that L7a9ed might tone it down after his stint in jail (at a press conference upon his release he intimated that he would focus more on his studies and less on politics) could rest easy—or better, again be as "enraged" as L7a9ed—as one song after another excoriated the ongoing corruption, police brutality, inequality, lack of freedom, and particularly hopelessness, that characterizes life in what for most Westerners remains one of the most "modern" and "moderate" Arab monarchy [36]. As L7a9ed raps in the title track, "Walou", mixing defiance and despair:

"Nothing satisfies us...We are so sick. No culture, no art, no creation...No, no way. We won't back down. It's my slogan. Choose my side or theirs...Put this in your head: Never give up your rights...This country is ours, not his [the king's]."

While hiphop gets most of the attention, the roots of the youth music scenes in the Arab and larger Muslim worlds lies as much if not more in heavy metal and rock, with elements of traditional national music (Palestine) and folk rock (Lebanon), among others also playing a role. Indeed, the original musical subcultures-turned-countercultures in the Arab world are the extreme metal scenes of the region, which were already threatening enough to launch many "Satanic metal scares" from Morocco to Iran in the late 1990s and early 2000s, as I documented in my Heavy Metal Islam.

These foreign-born music scenes served as incubators for marginalized youth to express themselves and create relationships and solidarities, and as important, develop the kinds of do-it-yourself skills in spreading their music (in other contexts, message), particularly via the burgeoning internet and social media, that would prove crucial for the revolutions when they erupted. Indeed, it's no surprise that in Egypt and Tunisia, many of the grass roots leaders of the revolutions came directly out of the metal scenes in those two countries [5,37]. And it's not just the male artists. One of the most important revolutionary singers of Tunisia, Emel Mathlouthi, started off her musical life playing covers for melodic death metal bands like In Flames, Dark Tranquility, and The Gathering before electrifying her fellow protesters in front of the Municipal Theatre during the Jasmine Revolution with an acapella folk song.

Ultimately, extreme metal and rap are not that distant in origin even if they tend to sound quite distinct (aside from the hybrid "rap metal" genre), as both have long featured dissonant, even jarring music based on minor scales and themes that are closely related to certain Arab maqamat, or modes (and thus are easily appropriated by local artists). Lyrically, the grittiness, anger and themes such as poverty, unemployment, police brutality, and lack of life opportunities—were at the heart of American hip hop culture before it was taken over by bling. Similarly, extreme metal's focus on war, corruption, and chaos played a major role in the genre's increasing popularity with young people across the Middle East and North Africa in the last twenty years.

One direct musical heir to the Arab metal scenes is none other than Ramy Essam, the "singer of the Egyptian revolution" whose song "Irhal" is considered along with "Rais Lebled" the most important tune in the revolutionary Arab canon and one of the most influential songs of the last century. Like Mathlouthi, Essam started off as a metalhead and fan of such groups as Slipknot, Korn and System of a Down, an edge he clearly brought to the sound of "Irhal."

No artist better symbolizes the changing—and in many ways, waning—fortunes of political music in the Arab world than Ramy Essam. It's difficult to overstate the impact of Essam's presence on the protests in Tahrir Square during the 25 January uprising. Arriving with nothing but an old acoustic guitar and a sleeping bag on 31 January, within twenty-four hours he'd absorbed the words, and as important, the rhythms of the protesters' chants in Tahrir, and composed "Irhal!" (Leave!), the song that quickly became the anthem not just of the Egyptian Revolution, but of the Arab uprisings from Morocco to Bahrain.

"Irhal" and "Rais Lebled" reflect two entirely different ways in which music impacts revolutionary events. El Général never performed his song live during the Revolution (similarly, today in Morocco L7a9ed finds it almost impossible to perform live in his native country). Rather, the song was known primarily through its video, whose dark and foreboding tones matched that of the music perfectly and which was circulated endlessly through social media as well as cell phones. His arrest was in fact that factor that multiplied his renown and made him a revolutionary icon; until then the song was not nearly as popular as it became while he was in jail.

"Irhal" was quite different. While a very dark video of a nighttime crowd in Tahrir singing along with Essam went viral in the first days of February, the song's popularity soared not because of social media, but because Essam played the song dozens of times each day in Tahrir, each time gathering more crowds until its popularity was such that people came to hear it and the majority of the crowd in fact knew the words (since the words comprised the most important slogans of the revolution, it wasn't hard to memorize it).

Indeed, it was Essam's physical presence in Tahrir during the key fighting, his literal embodiment of the struggle that helped make "Irhal" the anthem of the revolution. "If I were just a singer coming to the square and then leaving, it wouldn't have had the same impact," Essam believes. It was his physical presence, his performance of what I have elsewhere described (with Bryan Reynolds) as "theater of immediacy," that overcame any possibility of government control or repression of the music, the message or the messengers [38]. Essam explained to me that "my job is to listen to all the things Egyptians are saying, distill them into their essence, and share it as widely as possible." [39].

The post-revolutionary trajectories of artists like Essam and El Général are quite interesting. Essam's stock rose considerably in the year after the ouster of Mubarak, as he won numerous international accolades and became a frequent presence on Egyptian television, his family's history of political activism serving him well as he quickly became one of the most important fully revolutionary voices in Egypt, as opposed to the rising Muslim Brotherhood as to the military (he remained one of the few public figures who remained opposed to both sides in the fateful summer of 2013). On the other hand, El Général moved towards Ennahda, as did his close friend Psycho-M, another rising revolutionary rapper. Since the revolution he has not written any serious political music. And yet, today he remains free to perform across Tunisia as well as abroad. For his part, Essam was increasingly persecuted both under Morsi's rule and particularly after the military coup of 2013.

His situation became so precarious that he could no longer perform, while his music was banned from the airwaves. In October 2014, he left Egypt for a 2-year musical residency in Sweden. He fears for his safety if he is forced to return home. Essam and his counterparts across the region such as L7a9ed, have functioned as organic intellectuals and sociopolitical conductors for a new generation of revolutionaries, generating enough valence to help shape not merely a counter-cultural but revolutionary cultural counter-hegemonic discourse grounded in the simple but profound task of overcoming generations of fear and reclaiming citizenship [40–42]. But without a constant physical presence in and control over space that valence will diminish over time. L7a9ed and Essam, one in professional exile inside his country and the other physically removed from his homeland, can continue to make videos that are accessible at home and travel abroad spreading the stories of their struggles. But while such activities keep the revolutionary embers glowing, they can't change or even challenge the balance of power on the ground in Morocco or Egypt, and their inability to perform locally is symptomatic of the present weakness of the movements they represent.

It's worth noting that while most of the international attention has gone to youth-oriented music such as hiphop, rock and dance across the region, the protests across the region have from the start feature and especially music from the youth, older popular and traditional/folkloric music was also an important part of the sonic landscape of the protests across the region, particular in Egypt [43]. At the same time, songs like "Irhal!" or Muhammad Mounir's now classic "Ezzay," which dominated Tahrir during the crucial 2011–2012 period of the Revolution, had all but disappeared by mid-2013, replaced by the counter-revolutionary pop hit "Teslam Ayadi" (Bless Your Hands), a hyper-melodramatic, chauvinistic tribute to the military and the Egyptian state sung by 1990s-era star who were close to the Mubarak regime [44]. Similarly, the Moroccan King deftly used patronage and sponsorship of some of his country's most popular pop and rap artists, such as Don Bigg and Fnaire, to serve as key supporters of his supposed "reforms" in the wake of the February 20 protests [45–47].

5. Revolutionary Poetics "Behind the Sun"

It is no surprise that hiphop would prove to be a particularly apt cultural form for young Arabs to adapt to their revolutionary expression, as it is one of the most directly poetic forms of music available today. But poetry more broadly is also at the heart of the revolutions. As the poet Mazen Maarouf points out, "We should not be surprised that in these revolutions ordinary Arabs are capable of such poetry. In schools across the Arab world, poetry precedes other forms of art" [48]. Indeed, everything is poetry; from the rhymes dropped by rappers to the captions written by cartoonists, and thus poetry suffuses most other art forms.

Poetry has always been considered within Arab cultures as a vital "record" of their history and civilization; today it has its own television shows devoted to it—a poet's idol to compete with the *Arab Idol* style shows that regularly captivate tens of millions of viewers. For over a century Arabic poetry has been focused in good measure on nationalism and politics, as much if not more than love and romanticism. At times it could seem "irrelevant, outdated and boring"—precisely why young people would look to other media, like hiphop, to express themselves. Slogans taken from protest would shape poetry, which would then be reinserted into the spaces and voices of protest, creating a virtuous feedback loop of creativity within a renewed and enlarged public sphere stretching across and through the boundaries between public and private, with both protests and poetry increasingly adopting the liberatory voicings and speech of colloquial language [49].

Every culture and generation produces poetry in response to crises. We need look no further than Wordsworth's monumental "The Prelude" in response to the anti-democracy crackdown by the English government in the wake of the French Revolution, or Shelley's "The Masque of Anarchy" written after the Peterloo massacre of 1819, to see how spread this tradition is [50]. Poetry has a unique historical role within Arabo-Islamic culture and Arabic language. Without exaggeration we could state that it remains far deeper embedded in Arabo-Islamic culture than in most other cultures and languages, "a central pillar of our cherished heritage that continues to shape our cultural identity" [51]. This is as true for the modern period as it is for classical Arabic poetry, which was directly tied to the poetic language of the Qur'an.

As with music, so too poetry is understood as "the essence of life," as the poet Shukri Ayyad describes it. Not just the essence, in fact, but an "antibody" against reaction and regression of authoritarian societies, "that is able to take us from life as we know it and then bring us back to it." What is key for poets like Ayyad and Egyptian poet and lyricist Ahmed Fouad Negm (who famously was jailed by Nasser, Sadat and Mubarak for his anti-regime poems, often sung by the great Sheikh Imam), whose song "Thawra" (Revolution) was not surprisingly one of the first songs chanted in the streets during the January 25 protests. Poetry is, at its core, a revolutionary "philosophy...the philosophy of resistance to death and to face and acknowledge death as well."

Moreover, as the Yemeni poet Ibtisam Mutawakkil argues in explaining the strong presence of both colloquial and formal poetry during the Yemeni revolution, "Yemeni society is still an aural society. For this reason, the spirited rhythm and phrases move the people...In the history of the Arab revolutions poets has always been at the forefront of awareness led the revolutionary action, and this action is still present in Yemen to the day since the revolutions of 1962 and 1963 [52]." Indeed, yemen is a good example of how tribal poetry can inflect itself into more urban politics, causing deep aesthetic changes to both precisely because of its traditional role as an aesthetic of mediation between disputing factions in a conflict [53].

There is a strong relationship between what is known as "committed music" (al-ughniya al-multazimah) and protest poetry; and more, between them and fiction, cinema, theatre and art. All have evolved over the half century specifically to articulate a kind of "double discourse" that can speak both within and outside the imposed discursive and political boundaries imposed by the regime. Such a double voicing at all times certainly produced its share of schizophrenic identities and behaviors (never mind art), but it also gave enough flexibility to survive until more direct speech could be uttered [6].

Poetry was in fact central to the revolutions from the start. The most famous slogan of the revolutions, chanted in Tunisia, Egypt, Yemen, Libya, Bahrain, Syria, and beyond, is an adaptation of the poem "Izza ash-sha'b yowman arada al-haya" ("If the People One Day Will to Live"), written in 1933 by the Tunisian poet Abou el-Kasem Chebbi (1909–1934), which after the revolution became incorporated as the closing lines of Tunisia's national anthem. During the Tunisian Revolution, and particularly at its climax on 14 January 2011, people chanted parts of the poem, such as "If one day, a people desire to live/then fate will answer their call/And their night will then begin to fade/and their chains break and fall," but also chanted their adaptation of the poem: "The people want to bring down the regime"—in front of the Ministry of the Interior on Bourguiba Avenue [54]. The speed and flow of a march in Tahrir or down Bourguiba Boulevard, or around The Pearl roundabout in Manama would be determined by the poetry being chanted. Banners featured poetic slogans dozens of meters long at times. Songs, whether "Rais Lebled" or "Irhal" were nothing if not extremely poetic.

As the Moroccan poet Mohammed al-Ash'ari explained of the Arab Spring's poetry, "Poets have the capabilities to enable them to escort civilian movements and educate consciences in the midst of significant changes in today's world." In particular, they help people want life—perhaps the most important function of any artform, "But even the poetry of the revolutions and beyond is weak and modest when compared what happened in the street or in the fields or the actions of the rebels," Egyptian poet Girgis Shukri explains [52]. But something has certainly changed in the last half decade, and numerous articles in Arabic and English have attempted to decipher just what is unique about the present day [55,56].

As Mazen Maarouf explains, "The mission of the poet today, in the midst of mass uprisings and revolution, is different. It is more precise, direct and fateful. The poets must articulate their words clearly and sharply to agitate people while knowing it can be deadly. The agents of the regime may prosecute the poet at any moment, which means that the written poem might be a final word. The poet cannot deny it later [48]." He or she can, however, change recognized poems into something more apropos of the moment, as Tunisian revolutionary youth did with the words of the well known couplet about their country—" The smell of my country Is roses and jasmine It pleases the eye"—to the more immediately relevant and powerful "The smell of my country/Is gas and gun-powder./It burns the eye." [57].

Similar to other art forms deployed during the last half decade, the themes of the poetry of the Arab uprisings is extremely varied, as are the styles, dialects and forms it has taken. Some, following Chebbi, take on dictatorial leaders directly. Others, Hisham aj-Jakh, writing in his poem "Ta'shira" (Visa), rebels equally against the aristocracy of formal Arabic and the attempts by regimes to prevent Arabs from unifying and the damage it does to the possibilities of being poetic as well: "I am Arab and not ashamed/I was born in 'Tunis the Green' of Omani origin/And I grew a thousand-fold/I am Arab in Baghdad [with] the palms/Sudan is my artery/I am Egyptian, Mauritanian, Djibouti and Oman/Christian and Sunni and Shiite and Kurdish and Alawi and Druze [58]."

In this international theme, Palestine stands above most other Arab countries, as the unending symbol of all that has been lost to Arab culture as the result of foreign and internal imbalances and distortions of power, ideology and identity. The one of the "songs of the revolution" (ughniyat al- thawrah), "Raji' libladi" (Returning to my country), is directly influenced by the Palestinian narrative of return. Mahmoud Darwish's poetry was particularly crucial to the broader Arab Spring project—one writer called him "the conscience of the Arab revolutions," just as Palestine itself remained symbolically central [59,60].

A particularly insightful, if not well known poem, by Tari Youssef-Agha, a Syrian expatriate, re-terms "resistance" from the struggles against autocratic regimes to the "regimes of resistance" themselves, who have "turned the rulers into gods/transferred the whole country, horizontally and vertically/With its streets and squares, into shrines to worship the ruler/It made the people knee for him day and night [61]." Here it is the revolutionaries who represent a new state—of being as much as political institutions—and the existing systems which are holding back progress [62]. And this is what make it so different to the aesthetic and poetry of the religious extremists, who valorize only the killing and dying, almost as ends in themselves, rather than the struggle for greater freedom. As the Syrian exile Hala Mohammad writes in a poem dedicated to a martyred activist, Ghiyath Matar, "Heroes die in my life, my son, and rise/Death does not become you [52]."

6. Theaters of Immediacy

Not surprisingly, the historical and political power of Arab(ic) poetry increases as it is incorporated into other art forms, perhaps none more so than theater. Such is the affective power of theater as it's been experienced across the region that one of Egypt's foremost poets, Girgis Shukri, has declared that "the language of drama and of theater is much stronger than that of poetry or written texts" alone [58]. That language is in fact quite ancient—puppetry (*Khayal al-zill*), story-telling (*as-sard*), and for Shi'i Muslims, Ta'ziyah (passion plays involving the martyrdom of Ali's son Hussein at Karbala) are the roots out of which modern theater emerged and matured, spreading across the region thanks both to increased European penetration (and ultimately rule) and, equally important, the movement of Arab writers, dramatists, and theater companies throughout North Africa and the Levant in the Late Ottoman and colonial/Mandate eras, particularly via the phenomenon of "popular dramas" (dramia ash-sha'biyya) [63–66].

In the post-1952 era rising nationalism and competing ideologies dampened the level of contact as countries developed their theatrical traditions based on the governing political ideologies [67]. On the other hand, because the highly ideological environment in which Arab theater evolved in this period (similar to its counterparts in the Soviet world) left little room for the theater to offer the kind of "safe" space for exploring difficult social and political issues that existed in the West. Arab theatre practitioners have rarely "enjoy[ed] the luxury of safety," even as their work has had to preserve the humanity and independence of people in the most troubled of times [68,69].

But lack of safety should not be equated with lack of importance or consequence. In Egypt, for instance, there is a workers' theater at the entrance to the factory complex at Mahallah, the main industrial center of the country that was quite important—as befits its position at the entrance—to the life of the workers during the Nasser and into the Sadat eras, if under a highly ideologized and controlled manner. It fell slowly into disrepair only in the Mubarak era when, as Saadallah Wannous, one of the leading lights of Arab theater, it came "under siege and [was] on the verge of vanishing from our lives" [70,71] because of increased censorship, an unwillingness of dramatists to engage their audiences off the stage in civil society, and the weakening support for the arts as part of the broad contraction of social spending in the wake of the rise of neoliberal governmentality.

Theater was by no means a completely moribund in the neoliberal era of the 1980s through 2000s. Cairo has been home to the International Festival of Experimental Theater since 1988 [72]. Palestine has been home to companies such as the Jenin Freedom Theater and El Hakawati that have been (and remain) at the forefront of cultural resistance against Occupation and oppressive regimes across the region. And countries where one might not expect a strong theatrical tradition, such as Yemen, in fact boast a powerful history going back a century in which foreign influences such as Shakespeare and Shaw have blended with extremely sophisticated and critical poetic traditions among the tribal heartlands to create one of the region's best kept artistic secrets [73,74].

Indeed, the developments in Yemeni theater between 2009 and 2013 "represent the quintessential performances of Yemen's Arab Spring...and an increasing awareness within Yemeni society of the dire necessity of revolution, not merely against a particular political regime but against an entire stagnant and corrosive economic, social, and political status quo [75]." But it was in the wake of the outbreak of the uprisings that theater returned to its own again, regaining the "immediacy, urgency and relevance" theater generally lacks in "safer, more comfortable societies [76]." A number of factors, including the freedom to produce new works dealing with difficult social issues (such as gender) as well as revolutionary themes, as well as to be in closer contact and dialog with the international theater scene, has enabled Arab theater to once again function as a "seismograph of societal conditions [68]."

In Morocco, experimental theater influenced by Theater of the Oppressed or less confrontational styles such as "L'khbar fi masrah" ("the news through theater") has both encouraged and diffused potentially explosive social and political tensions [16]. Dramatists such as Egypt's Sondos Shabayek and Laila Soliman or Tunisian Lofti Achour, have used both classical themes and techniques (such as storytelling) and references and direct engagements with the immediate, pre-revolutionary past, to great affect with local and (increasingly) international audiences [77]. At the same time, some of the most relevant pre-Arab Spring plays, such as Fadhel Jaibi's *Amnesia-Yahia Yaish* (which dealt with the fall of a despotic Tunisian minister of state), have received even more enthusiastic reactions from crowds after the revolutions, when its implications could be appreciated more openly [77,78]. The broader question that remains for theater makers, like other artists across the region, is whether their art can help foster "a radically new mindset and a new thought until all this is reflected on the culture and art in general [79–81]."

Here special mention should be made of Palestinian Theater, especially troupes like El Hakawati Theater (also known as the Palestinian National Theater) in Jerusalem, established in 1984, and The Jenin Freedom Theater in Jenin, established in 2006. These groups operated before the uprisings, and because they were created specifically as means of resistance against a colonial occupation, they were much more directly confrontational against the oppressive government, in this case Israel, than were their counterparts in the Arab world.

Both theater companies have long focused on theater productions that reinforce Palestinian national culture and act as a means of retelling and amplifying stories of resistance. They also have acted as schools for teaching acting and the technical skills necessary to create theater and in so doing have influenced other companies, such as al-Kasaba Theater in Ramallah and Yes Theater in Hebron. These companies have been targets of Israeli harassment and closures, in particular the first two; El Hakawati because of its sensitive Jerusalem location and The Freedom Theater because of its highly charged political profile. The theater was founded by the well-known half-Jewish Israeli, half-Palestinian actor Juliano Mer-Khamis, whose mother Arna was a well-known Jewish communist who started the Stone Theater in Jenin during the first intifada to help heal and train young Palestinians [82–84]. Indeed, since its eruption, it's fair to say that the Freedom Theater remains at the forefront regionally of resistance theater embedded in local cultural contexts, despite the high price paid by the theater for its work—Mer-Khamis was gunned down by still unknown assailants in April, 2011 in front of the Theater; its artistic director Zakaria Zubaidi remains imprisoned, and the theater is routinely raided and its members arrested and attacked because of their work [85–88].

Outside Palestine, from stagings of various Shakespeare plays with postcolonial themes to Iraqi playwright Hassan Abdulrazzak's *The Prophet*, set in Cairo in the midst of the January 25 Revolution, or Sondos Shabayek's *Tahrir Monologues*, Arab theater, both performed in the Arab spring countries and increasingly on tour, has proved a "particularly efficient medium" for enabling the catharsis that must accompany revolutionary outbursts if they are to be sustained. Given the constant interaction of local and international dramaturgy, it's no surprise that theater has enjoyed a period of intense renewed productivity, in particular theater geared towards the stories and narratives of women, as exemplified by the powerful play, *Queens of Syria*, which tells the story of sixty women from Syria via the medium of their performance of Euripedes' tragedy, *The Trojan Woman* (the play is emblematic of the broader more public articulation of women's voices in the wake of the uprisings) [79,89–96].

Red lines continue to exist, even in the most democratic of Arab countries, Tunisia, where actors have been charged with "public indecency" and "indecent acts" and physically attacked by audience members, as happened to members of the Tunisian street theater company, Fanni Raghman Anni (in Tunisian dialect, "My Art In Spite of Myself" or "Artist Against My Will") in response to the perception that actors were wearing too little clothing during a performance [97,98]. As in the pre-revolutionary era, theater retains the power to anger those in political and social—particularly religious—power; but it remains to be seen whether it can regain the broader social valence that made it an incubator of broader social trends and conflicts across the region in previous generations.

7. The Revolutions' "War Paint"

The Arab uprisings were certainly televised (as Gil Scott-Heron predicted they would be), and disseminated via many other communications media. But they were even more so drawn—by cartoonists, caricaturists, everyday people, and particularly graffiti artists. It was impossible to attend a protest anywhere, from Rabat to Manama, without being inundated with the artwork of everyone from small children to major artists of the day. Let us remember, the most far-reaching and bloody revolution of the region, Syria, was sparked by the arrest and torture of fifteen children for painting anti-government slogans on the wall of their school [99].

The Arab world's "history of social upheaval and textual illumination provides fertile soil for innovation" in the graphic arts, especially graffiti, one of the oldest and most politicized genres [100]. It can be divided into several sub-categories, depending on whether it is created by professional artists or ordinary people and/or activists, and whether it features only text (however stylized) or images as well.

In that regard, what separates Arab graffiti—both Arabic-language graffiti and graffiti in Arab countries (which could also be in French, Amazigh, English, Spanish, Italians and other local or international languages depending on the intended audience) are its intimate relationships with and debt to the well-developed and highly skilled Arabic and Qur'anic calligraphic traditions. Indeed, in a very profound sense, Qur'anic calligraphy and the newest street art are "daughters of the same parents [101]."

However deeply rooted, graffiti cannot be appreciated outside of the broader context of cartoons and other forms of graphic images, whether created by professionals and published in newspapers or other media, or drawn by ordinary people and brought to protests. Finally, graffiti is also deeply related to paintings, videos, sculptures and installations that have been exhibited in galleries, museums, and revolutionary spaces. During the uprisings, the verbal messages of the graffiti have been complex and multifarious; from simple repetition of revolutionary slogans—*Dégage!*, *Irhal!*, *Yasqut hukma-l 'askar!*—to the ubiquitous turns at humor ("Game Over!" "Doctor, it's your turn"—*i.e.*, one-time optometrist Bashar al-Assad will see himself out of power soon), and references to facebook, Google and Twitter. Images of all types have "play[ed] a central part in processes of political struggle" by conveying mediated and mediating political messages and ideologies [102]. More than just art, such visual messages were the "war paint" of the revolutions and a weapon in the hands of civil resistance against authoritarian regimes [11,103]. Aesthetic quality alone was not the most important reason for the impact of visual arts in the uprisings and revolutions. Even the simplest drawings—like those of Daraa's school kids—can spark a civil war.

Yet it is also clear that graffiti remains the signal visual icon of the Arab uprisings, distinguished both by its power as well as its vulnerability and ephemerality [104]. Its often overwhelming affective/aesthetic power simultaneously raises a number of crucial issues—the immense violence of state power, collaboration with oppressive regimes, the return of long-suppressed histories and secular-religious conflicts, to name just a few. Its ability to move so many people is precisely why governments across the region—and indeed, globally—consider it vandalism and sabotage [105].

As the Egyptian artist Ganzeer explains, graffiti has the power to "plant a flag" in the public sphere in a manner that directly undermines the state's sense of public security. It does so precisely because its presence (especially when prolonged) clearly marks a location's transformation into a revolutionary space, or at least one outside of real government control [106–109]. Even more, as the artist Mohsen Al-Ateeqi points out, graffiti helps "encircle the hegemony" of regimes that have spent decades "containing" their societies by its offering of highly visible counter-hegemonic mechanisms for producing public opinion—better, of publicness and being public [106,110].

If rap legend chuck D of Public enemy once intoned that "Hiphop is the CNN of the streets" then it's clear that graffiti—not surprisingly, a core original element of hiphop cultural practice—performs a similar function, with the added power that comes from being situated in one place and thereby marking it as, at least momentarily, a revolution place, enabling the public to encounter messages and motivations that have been censored in more "legitimate" media and in so doing becomes "in itself a form of public power to resist the ruling power [106]."

Although not directly related to the "Arab Spring" uprisings, it's impossible to discuss the history of Arab graffiti apart from its role in Palestinian resistance to the Israeli occupation. Indeed, most of the young activists behind the initial waves of protests came of age during the Second Intifada, and saw Palestinian resistance as an inspiration and model for their own organizing and protests. Not surprising, the walls of the West Bank and Gaza have been fertile ground since the First Intifada for expressing anti-occupation, anti-Israel and as important, Palestinian nationalist sentiments and narratives towards independence. The construction of the "separation" or "Apartheid" wall has, quite naturally, offered a huge canvas on which Palestinians and international artists have created elaborate works of art. At the same time, the rubble of Gaza has served as the tableau for some of the most intimately powerful graffiti ever created, both by local artists and artists of the stature of Banski [111–114].

In Tahrir during the 18 days of the January 25 Revolution the most exciting and charged location was the "Revolutionary Artists Union," a fifteen meters square plot located in front of—and more important, on the wall of—the KFC restaurant on the northwest section of the ring, where dozens of cartoonists, caricaturists, painters, poets, rappers, musicians and other artists—young and old, amateur as well as professional—gathered night and day to put up their artwork, and share poetry or songs. The spot, a classic "culture jam" if there ever was one (it took one of the Midan's most well-known symbols of Western capitalism and conquered it, at least temporarily, with revolutionary and broadly anti-capitalist art), was in many ways the cultural engine of Tahrir, providing a constant sense of urgency and creativity which would radiate towards the rest of the Midan and encourage artists of all kinds and skill levels to bring their art to Tahrir.

Whatever the historical importance of written graffiti, images have always played crucial components of Arab graffiti. In the uprisings era, such imagery often has portrayed or represented people or events occurring on the ground, from murals featuring the faces of martyred protesters to, in one well known case, a stencil of nude self-portrait by the young Egyptian photographer Aliaa Magdy Elmahdy (which was overlaid with an elaborate defense of her (in)famous photo contextualizing it vis-a-vis rampant assaults on women by regime forces).

Equally frequent are far more elaborate and symbolized murals or representations of revolutionary heroes, hated regime figures, or various revolutionary scenes. These are composed in a variety of styles, including traditional graffiti or "street art" styles, "social realism," and various engagements with Ancient Egyptian themes and aesthetics, from stenciled images of "anarchist pharaohs" (the image a pharaoh in the guise of Guy Fawkes with an iconic headdress) to mixed-media transdisciplinary works by artists such as Hanaa El Dagham and highly stylized "neo-pharaonic" tableaus—epitomized by the work of the Luxor-based fine artist Alaa Awad, that bring the far past and the immediate present into intense dialog [115–117]. In Tunisia and Egypt cartoon figures also became—and remain—central symbols of political graffiti, as characters like Nadia Khiari's Willis the Cat in Tunis, and Sad Panda in Cairo have rendered some of the most powerful—and in Sad Panda's case, almost always mute—judgements on the oppressiveness and even absurdity of the ancien and post-revolutionary regimes [118–124].

As Don Karl and Pascal Zoghbi argue in their *Arabic Graffiti* (published just as the uprisings were spreading across the region in early 2011), graffiti doesn't merely have aesthetic and political valence in its own right; it constitutes a powerful affirmation of the value of street art across the region [100,125]. When the words "Be with the revolution" began appearing during the initial uprisings, it helped make the spread the revolts all but inevitable [100].

Despite the natural affinity for graffiti within Arab culture, it did not flourish everywhere in the pre-2010 era. While prevalent in Palestine, Lebanon and Iran (where it was used both to mark territory and to publicize powerfully hegemonic—or hegemonizing—official ideologies) it was largely absent from Tunisia before the revolution, practiced mostly "in secret" and comprising largely visual references to football teams placed by their most rabid fans until the "glass dome of dictatorship exploded" with Bouazizi's self-immolation. But within a matter of days of the outbreak of the protests in Tunis, the acronyms for famous soccer teams like EGS Gafsa or CA (for Club Africain, in Tunis) were replaced by the far more dangerous "ACAB"—all cops are bastards, the call letters of resistance against police power world-wide [103,126]. Suddenly, the walls were transformed from football tags to "insane wall books" that fed revolutionary action in the street. In this regard, what has yet to be explored in any detail is the aesthetic dynamics of the transformation of these football fanatics—today known around the world as the Ultras, whose years of experience battling police in the soccer-crazy country's stadiums gave them the skills to fight them successfully on the streets—into the front line soldiers and fiercest defenders of the January 25 Revolution.

As I have already alluded, one reason for graffiti's social power is that it's the most important medium and long-term indicator of who controls physical space—the state or the opposition. Other forms of art and media—music, poetry, film—are not immediately tied to one location and could be circulated endlessly via cell phone, the internet and other means. But as long as it remains, graffiti marks the spot in which it is created as revolutionary. This is why it was so important for the headmaster of the Daraa elementary school where anti-regime graffiti was scrawled by young boys to ensure they were harshly punished, and why we can mark the switch in the balance of power in Egypt back towards the military as soon as it was able to paint over the "martyr's wall" of Muhammad Mahmoud Street next to Tahrir, where much of the most beautiful, iconic and provocative graffiti was done and ultimately prevent it from being repainted.

Each country has had its own specific stylistic innovations and themes, owing to local artistic and poetic traditions, as well as the kinds of structures on which graffiti can be created and their availability to the general public (large and open walls on high traffic streets in a situation of relative political weakness (or at least tolerance) by the state as existed in Cairo will produce very different graffiti than half-rubbled buildings in Aleppo or Sanaa). Countries such as Tunisia, where there was little tolerance for political graffiti and even less support or credibility from the local artistic elite and patrons, naturally saw less graffiti in the pre-uprisings era than Palestine or Egypt, which had stronger traditions. And even graffiti that has a profound political aura—such as Sad Panda, can be imagined by its creator as more only implicitly so (as with most scholarship, assumptions about the intentions, meanings and impact of any specific work of graffiti are very likely to lead to misinterpretations unless thoroughly researched) [122,127].

Aside from Egypt and Palestine, Bahrain has the most developed, organized and belligerent graffiti movement in the region (explicit calls for the overthrow of King Hamad were as ubiquitous as representations of the Pearl roundabout where the early protests were centered) [128,129]. Equally important, Yemen, understood mostly in the West as a bastion of feudalism and extremism, quickly saw the emergence of one of the most sophisticated public graffiti scenes in the region that epitomized the unprecedented and almost entirely non-violent grass-roots protests in the country [130]. The web portal Muftah organized a fascinating review of the most important graffiti across the region which shows just how quickly the walls of affected regions filled with graffiti, and how each has responded to the increasing repression that developed in response. What this review demonstrates is the combination of individual artistic inspiration, local themes, and broader regional and international styles that comprise the broad field of Arab graffit in the Arab uprisings era [131].

Perhaps the most beautiful archive of the Egyptian Revolution, the book *Wall Talk: Graffiti of the Egyptian Revolution*, offers a detailed portrait of the full power and range of the graffiti of the revolution, hundreds of images strong. What is most striking about leafing through its almost 700 pages is the impossibility of summarizing the numerous styles, subjects, themes and aesthetics comprising Egyptian graffiti, from images that require no words—a mouth in the process of being unzipped, Mubarak with Devil horns, to powerful slogans—"A people's assembly of the people's blood" (Maglis sha'b min dama' sha'b), to makeshift cinderblock "security walls" on the border of Tahrir being painted completely over with street scenes from the other side (in the manner of the detailed scenic art on the Separation/Apartheid Wall throughout the West Bank ([104], pp. 28, 89 140, 168, 406, 558–59; [132]).

If Graffiti is the most celebrated form of revolutionary visual art of the uprisings era, its "silent cry" (*cri muet*) more powerful than even the loudest gun or most repressive regime [133], it's by no means the only one or isolated from other forms. Both visually and in terms of the often brutally honest satirical wit, cartoons have played a crucial role, not just in the Arab uprisings, but for a century of Arab journalist and media. It is not an understatement to argue that Arab(ic) graffiti would be as impossible to imagine without the history and presence of Arab cartoons as it would be without Arabic calligraphy. Indeed, the importance of cartoons or cartoon-inspired artwork, such as Willis the Cat and Sad Panda, in the graffiti of the uprisings points to the difficulty of fixing boundaries between these media.

The history of cartoons, and particularly political cartoons in the Arab world, is an immense subject that cannot be adequately addressed in this setting. Whether in Revolutionary France or contemporary Egypt or Morocco, cartoons are "vivid primary sources" for understanding larger events and the broader public mood [134]. As cartoons have migrated from newspapers and books to social media and the internet their subjects have increasingly focused on regional and international subjects, while leaving aside domestic issues that could lead to censorship or worse (exceptions to this rule include Palestine and Lebanon, both of which retained relatively more freedom of expression for artists compared with other Arab countries (although Palestinians have been jailed and even killed by Israel for their art) [135]. But while the majority of cartoonists were staying clear of local politics in the years leading up to 2010, pre-Revolutionary era, some, like Egyptian cartoonist Andeel, have been consistently political since the early 2000s, attacking Mubarak then and Sisi now with the same lack of concern for the consequences [136].

A final and perhaps least discussed form of visual and plastic arts associated with the uprisings is installation art. In some ways revolutionary spaces like Tahrir, the Pearl, Change Square, and other long-term protest locations were themselves large-scale installations, theater of immediacy where emurgent forms of highly aesthetized and affective cultural production motivated people to take unprecedented risks to change their lives and the political life of their countries. Such processes always leave behind their detritus—the hulks and scraps of fights between forces of order and repression and those of (at least temporary) anarchy and change.

In Tahrir, for example, the pitched battles of the first year and a half left many a burn out military or police vehicle abandoned around the environs of the Midan. Street artist Amor Eletrebi took full advantage of these remnants of a seemingly weakened state power to create evocative and inviting works of art, engaging local residents and street kids to help him paint the carcass vibrant colors with images of hearts, zebras and other positive imagery. He also created ad hoc exhibition spaces in the burned out or abandoned buildings in the immediate vicinity of Tahrir [137]. This kind of street art was rare in its scope and duration (the vehicles Eletreby painted remained in their spots for many months before finally being cleared away). Equally important were the larger installations developed by Egyptian and Tunisian artists such as the collaborative Association L'Art Rue in Tunis, and Huda Lutfi and Hani Rashed in Cairo, through which a new kind of art, "concept pop," has emerged that moves beyond the rather meaningless appropriation of everyday objects that had often characterized pre-revolutionary contemporary art in the Arab world, pointing viewers to the revolutionary implications of the events they represent [138,139].

The internet and social media have today become perhaps the most important vector for the dissemination of artistic content. Every country in which significant protests have occurred can boast highly developed internet cultures on the user and particularly developer ends. But while organizations like the Tunisian Nawaat or Morocco's *Mamfakinche* served as indispensable portals for the dissemination of subversive and even revolutionary knowledges, it is Egypt that has been home to the groups that have most boldly and effectively blended visual art and activism. Two media collectives in particular have played an important role in this process since 2011, the Moisireen collective and Kazeboon (liars). Together they epitomize how the internet as a medium for dissemination and circulation has influenced the production of art.

Mosireen (a combination of the words "Egypt" and "determined" in Arabic) is a Cairo-based media collective created during the 18 days of the January 25 revolution. Its goal has been to use citizen-produced art—in particular short films based on documentary footage of events that contradict government claims about who was responsible for acts of violence against citizens, which could be easily circulated on the internet and/or shown publicly in open-air gatherings. When effective these films constitute politically inspired art possessing the power to "wrong-foot censorship and empower the voice of a street-level perspective." Mosireen's focus has been attuned particularly to archiving the visual record of the revolution and showing revolutionary inspired films to the public, often on the street in order to reach the most people [140,141].

The Kazeboon, or "liars" campaign, was founded by some of the same people as Mosireen in December 2011 when military police attacked protesters at a sit-in at the Cabinet headquarters. The name pertains to the penchant for the military (at that time, SCAF, the Supreme Council of the Armed Forces) to lie when accused of using violence against protesters. This time, protesters had recorded video of the attack, which activists used to produce a video, uploaded onto YouTube, that directly challenged the lie. So successful was this campaign, and so ubiquitous was the violence and the lies about it by the military and then the Morsi government, that the group's modus operandi became using video to confront the lies of the regime (the Muslim Brotherhood would adopt a similar strategy during the Raba al-'Adawiyya sit-in, but with far less success). Like Mosireen, Kazeboon would sometimes hold events in public at revolutionary-friendly locations (such as the Sawi Culture Wheel in Zamalek, which had long sponsored edgey and even subversive cultural events and political meetings). But it's primary means of communication has been the internet.

8. Conclusions: Art and/as Religion in the Arab Spring

Paul Tillich, one of the greatest theologians of the twentieth century, provided one of the most useful definitions of religion for the twenty-first: Religion, he argued, is whatever is of "ultimate concern" to an individual. Sacred or secular, moral or immoral, overtly spiritual or seemingly mundane, that which we hold in the highest and most intense position in our hearts "can destroy us as it can heal us [142]." The relationship between art and religion—specifically, the use of most every artistic medium to represent and express religious belief, faith, and doubt—is too well-documented to require discussion here. Of course, art and religion do not just act in synergy, with art a tool for the expression of religious sentiments. They can also be in competition, as the same intensity and quality of emotions, actions and experiences that define religious experience also define artistic experience at its most intense—that is, for those for whom art is of "ultimate concern." In this context, it's no surprise that Ayatollah Khomeini dismissed—and prohibited most forms of—music as no better than "opium" and other drugs; just like Marx termed religion over a century before [143].

At their best, both encourage liminal, transformative experiences, but their similarities put them in competition—usually from the point of view of many religious people, including Muslims, who see artistic expression as a distraction from the focus on God [144]. It's thus not surprising, then, that many of the threats to artists in the wake of the uprisings have involved conservative religious forces, sometimes acting in concert with counter-revolutionary regimes (or elements within regimes in the midst of transformation). In the wake of the eruption of the protests and uprisings, and in the midst of seeming transformations towards democracy, Egyptian artists have been sued, Moroccan and even Tunisian musicians, graffiti artists and actors have faced harassment and arrest, for "moral" as well as political "crimes." In Syria throats have been slit, tongues cut out and hands cut off (depending on the offending artist's specific mode of work). Perhaps Tunisian artist Jalila Baccar best captured the dynamic at work when she explained a year after Ben Ali's ouster: "During Bourguiba and Ben Ali's regimes, political content was censored from any artworks. During the current regime, political content is still forbidden, only under the guise of ethics and religion [145]."

At the same time, however, religious forces in the Arab world are not uniformly or even mostly against artistic expression. Extremist groups like ISIL might destroy works of art and threaten or even harm artists, yet at the same time, such movements are suffused in their own aesthetic sensibilities and even artistic production—in the case of ISIL, prominently featured in their glossy, high quality magazine, *Dabiq* [146,147]. But religiously grounded aesthetic/artistic production and expressions are not just or even mostly negative in intent or content, as the centuries-long histories of Sufi-inspired art and the beauty of "Islamic" art, architecture, poetry and music reminds us. Nor is it always accurate to create make a separation between "religious" or "secular" forms of art.

Of course, every religious movement has its own aesthetic component, even those against art produce reams of artistic content, as Dabiq so well demonstrates. Indeed, jihadis even have their own music and, even more powerful, poetry [148]. The Brotherhood has long dabbled in art; Hassan al-Banna's Brother himself was a playwright, and the Brotherhood's magazine has long featured very interesting artwork on its covers and in its pages, as a recent analysis in the journal *Kalamat* makes clear [149].

While the "religious" *vs.* "secular" division is often abused, in the context of the Arab uprisings such a distinction often remains relevant, as the religiously grounded movements and parties that emerged in their wake, particularly the Muslim Brotherhood, but also Tunisian Ennahdah, have articulated very particular views towards art. Moreover, they have engaged in significant artistic creation based on these principles. They thus warrant separate consideration from other forms of engaged art.

Beginning with the Brotherhood, it's clear that elements within the movement had begun to liberalize their attitudes towards culture by the early to mid-2000s. Forms of "secular" cultural production, such as rock and heavy metal, which were excoriated by the movement and other religious leaders until then (during the 1997s "Satanic metal affair" fans were threatened with execution for apostasy by religious leaders if they didn't "repent" of their sinful musical habits) [150], suddenly adopted a far more laissez faire attitude towards seemingly amoral or even "un-Islamic" art. This was in line with their broader criticism of the harsh cultural positions of key figures like founder Hassan al-Banna and Sayyid Qutb [151,152]. As the Freedom and Justice Party developed its party platform, it turned its attention directly to art, declaring that "art is a significant form of expression which sends an influential message to its audience. Following the January revolution it is imperative we embrace the changes and blend with it," the group stated [153].

The party attempted to quell fears by more secular-minded artists that it would "turn theaters into mosques" or encourage a broader "Brotherhoodization of art" by declaring that it would crack down on what it viewed to be un- or sacrilegious art by declaring its opposition to prior censorship as a core element of its political platform [151,154,155]. During the period of its political ascendancy it held several meetings and symposia with filmmakers, actors, and other artists (featuring Brotherhood-aligned cultural figures such as Sayed Darwish) as part of its efforts to articulate a seemingly moderate yet religiously-grounded position towards art [155].

Most important, however, the Brotherhood supported its own often intensive artistic activity, including theater, music and art. In the wake of its first electoral victory, the Freedom and Justice Party sponsored the production of at least a dozen songs and several theater shows ostensibly "in support of the revolution," and declared that "anyone who has any kind of creative artistic act can participate with us and help shape the conscience of the nation." These productions included Drama Teatro's play "Wassa'a Tareeq" (Clear the Way), the group "Faces" production of "Atwa President of the Republic" and other plays, not only in Cairo and Alexandria, but in cities such as Fayoum, Damanhur Bilbeis, Beheira, Badrasheen, Giza and Sharqiya. It even had its own theater troupe in Cairo, featuring trained actors and focusing on issues such as Sunni-Shi'i unity and the role of women in society [154].

The Brotherhood also sponsored theatrical and musical competitions. The goal, as epitomized by the musical production of Brotherhood-affiliated artists, was to straddle the line between the "clean" art (in music, known as *anashid*) and more secular (and potentially more problematic) "secular" genres (in music, known as *aghani*, or songs).

The Muslim Brotherhood's changing view of the relationship between religion and art was mirrored in many ways by that of Ennahda in Tunisia. While the movement did not devote the resources to produce its own art, theater, film, poetry or music to any significant degree, its leaders, and particularly Rachid Ghannouchi, went out of their way to declare their support for the arts and opposition to the harsh orthodox view of non-religiously focused art. Its political literature focused a lot of attention to issues of "culture" and particular as it referred to the "culture of human rights" (thaqafa huquq al-insan) [156]. When scores of actors and artists were arrested for allegedly indecent or anti-government art, Ghannouchi himself came out against prosecution, and condemned attacks by Salafis on artists or patrons of theaters and other artistic events [157,158]. Even El Général and Psycho MC, two of the Tunisian revolution's musical icons, took what many other rappers and commentators believe was noticeably "Islamist" turns with their music and their public persona after the revolution, as Ennahda quickly rose to prominence [159].

However, what the Muslim Brotherhood-inspired art or its and Ennahda's policies have not been, in any meaningful sense, is revolutionary, particularly when compared to the vast majority of artistic production described in this article. Culturally, The Brotherhood was motivated by different concerns than the revolutionary artistic production described in this article. As Sayed Darwish argued, "We are seeking to adapt all the tools of art, and to use all available talents to produce serious works that respect the intelligence of the audience and improve the fabric of the community—art that builds and promotes society, not works that destroy its morals and values [155,160]."

For the Brotherhood, this lack of revolutionary themes or motivations is in keeping with the overall outlook and strategies of the movement in the last twenty years, at least until the overthrow of President Muhammad Morsi. The movement was already being slowly incorporated into the existing power structure in the 2000s and rose quickly to the top of the post-Mubarak political order despite—in fact, because of—its distance from the revolutionary currents that animated it. Politically, economically and especially culturally, the Brotherhood had little interest in inspiring, never mind instigating, any large-scale changes in society, and in fact time and time again sided with the military and deep state (to which it was being integrated until its utter mismanagement of the government led the military to turn on it) against revolutionary forces.

Similarly, Ennahda quickly became one of the most powerful parties in Tunisia, and in fact governed the country for several years. Thus it too had little reason to sponsor art that continued to advocate a revolutionary view when the main goals of the revolution from its perspective had already been accomplished. And like the Brotherhood, Ghannouchi articulated a view of art and artistic freedom that declared it to be "not absolute, but should be restricted by customs and values prevailing in each society [157,158]."

Unlike the Brotherhood and its political party, the FJP, Ennahda had a powerful motivation to remain moderate in its cultural views. Not only was pre-revolutionary Tunisia the most secular country in the Arab world, but Ennahda had to contend with a growing extremist Salafi movement in Tunisia on the one hand, and the consequences of the Brotherhood's lack of compromise while in office in Egypt. Moderation and a lack of compulsion have been central components of Ennahda's political strategies, whatever the personal views of members towards art (in interviews with members, they have rarely expressed interest in engaging in debates of what kind if any art is religiously permissible or prohibited), and has been key to its successful navigation of the treacherous post-revolutionary political landscape in Tunisia.

Ultimately, while it is not difficult to spot "religious" versus "secular" art in the post-uprisings Arab world, the main distinction between various forms of artistic production is not centered on religion, ethics or morality. It is centered around the contentious question of whether the region and individual countries are still living in revolutionary or normal time, whether artists should and can continue to motivate citizens into the streets to fight for a wholesale change in their societies, or should either support the status quo or ignore politics all together. It is undeniable that the Arab uprisings and revolutions of the last five years has produced some of the most politically as well as aesthetically powerful and innovative art the world has seen in generations. The question that remains is whether today the aura of revolution can continue to inspire artists and ordinary people to continue the struggle for "bread, freedom, and social justice" that half a decade ago helped launch the Arab Spring.

Conflicts of Interest

The author declares no conflict of interest.

References and Notes

1. Fela Kuti. *Coffin for Head of State*. Lagos: Universal Records, 1980.
2. Fela Kuti. *Music is the Weapon of the Future*. Lagos: Exworks Records, 1998.
3. I develop this theory of culture fulling in *Why They Don't Hate Us: Lifting the Veil on the Axis of Evil*. Oxford: Oneworld Publications, 2005, pp. 17–191.
4. John Tomlinson. *Globalization and Culture*. Chicago: University of Chicago Press, 1999.
5. Mark LeVine. *Heavy Metal Islam: Rock, Resistance and the Struggle for the Soul of Islam*. New York: Random House, 2008, pp. 31–32.
6. Mohamed-Salah Omri. "A Revolution of Dignity and Poetry." *Boundary* 2 (2012): 138–65.
7. Reda Allali, and Hassan Hamdani. "Société. Blad Schizo." *TelQuel Online #243*. Available online: http://m.telquel-online.com/archives/243/couverture_243_1.shtml (accessed on 23 July 2015).
8. Dalai Lama. Speaking at UC Irvine Global Compassion Summit, 5 July 2015.
9. Theodor Adorno, quoted in Mark LeVine. "New Hybridities of Arab Musical Intifadas." *Jadaliyya*, 29 October 2011. Available online: http://www.jadaliyya.com/pages/index/3008/the-new (accessed on 20 September 2015).
10. Mark LeVine, and Bryan Reynolds. "Theater of Immediacy: Performance Activism and Art in the Arab Uprisings." In *Islam and Popular Culture*. Edited by Karin van Nieuwekerk, Mark LeVine and Martin Stokes. Austin: University of Texas Press, in press.
11. Cf. Waleed Rashed. "Egypt's Murals Are More than Just Art, They Are a Form of Revolution." *Smithsonian Magazine*, 2013. Available online: http://www.smithsonianmag.com/arts-culture/egypts-murals-are-more-than-just-art-they-are-a-form-of-revolution-36377865/#Dvuz GHgjTZ5455bv.99 (accessed on 10 July 2015).
12. Diana al-Rifai. "Anatomy of a Revolution through Art." *al-Jazeera English*, 2015. Available online: http://www.aljazeera.com/news/middleeast/2015/03/anatomy-revolution-art-150311065922830.html (accessed on 30 September 2015).
13. Fanun ath-thawra as-suriyya (Syrian Revolution Art facebook page). Available online: https://www.facebook.com/Syrian.Revolution.Arts (accessed on 10 July 2015).
14. For a good compendium of much of the artistic production by Syria, see Cathrin Schaer. "Syrian Refugees: Making Sense of War through Art." *Der Spiegel*, 2013. Available online: http://www.spiegel.de/international/world/syrian-refugees-process-war-through-art-in-lebanon-a-905490.html (accessed on 20 July 2015).

15. Miriam Cooke. "It's a revolution: the cultural outpouring fueled by Syrian war." *PS21*, 2015. Available online: http://projects21.com/2015/03/08/its-a-revolution-the-cultural-outpouring-fueled-by-syrian-war/ (accessed on 21 July 2015).
16. Kamran Rosen. "5 Incredible Art Movements that Exploded After the Arab Spring." *World.mic*, 29 December 2013. Available online: http://mic.com/articles/77497/5-incredible-art-movements-that-exploded-after-the-arab-spring (accessed on 2 August 2015).
17. Rosen. "5 Incredible Art Movements..."
18. Sherifa Zuhur. *Colors of Enchantment: Theater, Music and the Visual Arts of the Middle East.* Cairo: American University of Cairo, 2001, p. 7.
19. Mark LeVine. "Theorizing Revolutionary Practice: Agendas for Research on the Arab Uprisings." *Middle East Critique* 22 (2013): 191–212.
20. A good discussion of the photograph and the events surrounding the scene it depicts, is provided by "The Story behind the Libyan Guitar Hero Photo." *Channel Four Television Corporation*, 13 October 2011. Available online: http://www.channel4.com/news/the-story-behind-the-libyan-guitar-hero-photo (accessed on 4 August 2015).
21. Mark LeVine. "Morocco: When the Music is banned, the Real Satanism Will Begin." In *Heavy Metal Islam: Rock Resistance and the Struggle for the Soul of Islam.* New York: random House, 2008.
22. Full Arabic and English lyrics for Raid Lebled. Available online: http://revolutionaryarabraptheindex.blogspot.se/2011/08/el-general-rais-lebled.html (accessed on 21 July 2015).
23. Hawas Mahmoud. "al-Rabi'a al-arabiya wa al-thaqafa al-taqlidiya (The Arab Spring and Traditional Culture)." *Minhbar al-Huriya*, 2012. Available online: http://minbaralhurriyya.org/index.php/archives/6938 (accessed on 20 September 2015).
24. "Babylon and Beyond." *Los Angeles Times Blog*, 5 April 2011. Available online: http://latimesblogs.latimes.com/babylonbeyond/2011/04/syria-rap-music-revolution-freedom-deraa.html (accessed on 10 July 2015).
25. A good compendium of Syrian revolutionary music is "La mémoire créative de la Révolution Syrienne." *Creativememory*. Available online: http://www.creativememory.org/?cat=17 (accessed on 21 July 2015).
26. The song was released in 2001 and was, reportedly, the first Arabic language hiphop song to garner 1 million youtube views. DAM, "Min Irhabi." Available online: https://www.youtube.com/watch?v=duwsH-gAmuM (accessed on 20 July 2015).
27. For a good compendium of the first "generation" of revolutionary hiphop, see Ted Swedenburg. "Hip-Hop of the Revolution (The Sharif don't like it)." *Middle East Report Online*, 2012. Available online: http://www.merip.org/hip-hop-revolution-sharif-dont-it (accessed on 12 July 2015).
28. Freemuse. "Hiphop is a soundtrack to the North African revolt." *FREEMUSE*, 2011. Available online: http://freemuse.org/archives/4999 (accessed on 21 July 2015).
29. The 7 and 9 in L7a9ed are Arabic chat characters representing the letters "ḥā" (ح) and "qaf" (ق).
30. For a summary of the history of Moroccan rap. See [21].
31. "Le rap marocain censuré?" *Selwane.com*, 2009. Available online: http://www.selwane.com/index.php?option=com_content&task=view&id=2658&Itemid=358 (accessed on 31 August 2014).

32. The comparison with Gavroche was made on several websites, including Solidarité Maroc. "Un pouvoir marocain inquiet mais qui ne lâche rien." 2012. Available online: http://solidmar.blogspot.com/2012/08/un-pouvoir-marocain-inquiet-mais-qui-ne.html (accessed on 1 September 2014).
33. One of the only other popular figures to speak so honestly in the past has been Nadia Yassine, the leader of the Adl Wa-Ihsane movement, the country's most important Sufi order and opposition movement, and she has millions of followers to protect her from retribution. L7a9ed has no one but his fans, who are as powerless as he is.
34. "Rayes Lebled 2" was uploaded officially 14 January 2014, on the 3rd anniversary of Ben Ali's ouster. El General. "El General - Rayes Lebled 2 (Clip Officiel)." *YouTube*, 2014. Available online: https://www.youtube.com/watch?v=5H0QIM_blZg (accessed on 1 September 2014).
35. Amman. Available online: http://ab14.globalvoicesonline.org/english (accessed on 3 November 2015).
36. Paul Schemm. "Morocco's Rebel Rapper Released from Prison." *AP News*, 29 March 2013. Available online: http://bigstory.ap.org/article/moroccos-rebel-rapper-released-prison (accessed on 3 November 2015).
37. Interviews with Tunisian and Egyptian revolutionary leaders. February 2011–June 2012, Tunis and Cairo.
38. We describe theater of immediacy as cultural (often, but not necessarily artistic) creation and performance for an intended audience that is not merely emergent—that is, in the process of formation—but "emergent" (emergent + urgent): Developing rapidly and in the context of intense sociopolitical struggle that destabilizes and even reconfigures previously dominant, congealed structures and networks of power and identity. It is, to borrow a concept from Benjamin that will be considered more fully below, a space and experience in which performance becomes auratic, and thus transformative [10].
39. Interview with Mark LeVine, April 2012, Cairo.
40. Mark LeVine. "Morocco." In *Heavy Metal Islam. Rock, Resistance and the Struggle for the Soul of Islam.* New York: Random House, 2008.
41. Kendra Salois. "Jihad against Jihad against Jihad." *New Inquiry*, undated. Available online: http://thenewinquiry.com/essays/jihad-against-jihad-against-jihad/ (accessed on 2 September 2014).
42. Houda Abadi. "Celebrating El Haqed's Freedom." *jadaliyya.com*, 2 August 2013. Available online:http://www.jadaliyya.com/pages/index/10988/celebrating-el-haqed's-freedom_soundtracking-resis (accessed on 2 September 2014).
43. Specifically, in Egypt artists like Sheikh Imam and Ahmed Fouad Negm, folkloric groups like Tanboura and pop bands from Iskinderilla and Muhammad Mounir, all had a role to play in the play list of the revolution. See Mark LeVine. "New Hybridities of Arab Musical Intifadas." *Jadaliyya*, 29 October 2011. Available online: http://www.jadaliyya.com/pages/index/3008/the-new-hybridities-of-arab-musical-intifadas (accessed on 30 June 2015).
44. The Clip Can Be Viewed on Youtube. Ninette. "Teslam el Ayadi with English Caption." *Youtube*, 2013. Available online: https://www.youtube.com/watch?v=jDgyzOTmeiY (accessed on 21 July 2015).

45. Interview with Reda Allali, leader of Hoba Hoba Spirit, July 2008, Casablanca. Their music is Available online: http://www.hobahobaspirit.com (accessed on 17 August 2015).
46. Mohammad al-Khudairi. "Halal Rap: Morocco's MCs preach politics and conservatism." *al-Bawaba*, 11 November 2012. Available online: http://www.albawaba.com/entertainment/morocco-rap-450324 (accessed on 25 July 2015). Don Bigg has numerous youtube videos and facebook pages.
47. Amanda Rogers. "Warding off terrorism and revolution: Moroccan religious pluralism, national identity and the politics of visual culture." *Journal of North African Studies* 17 (2012): 1–20. Available online: http://www.tandfonline.com/doi/abs/10.1080/13629387.2012.657882 (accessed on 19 July 2015). She provides several sources for the accusations against Don Bigg, which are generally accepted among the activist and hiphop community in Morocco, though the artist has denied it publicly.
48. Mazen Maarouf. "The Poetry of Revolution." *al-Jazeera English*, 2 September 2012. Available online: http://www.aljazeera.com/indepth/opinion/2012/08/201283014193414611.html (accessed on 12 July 2015).
49. Rachael Allen. "Early 20th century Arabic poetry." *Granta*, undated. Available online: https://granta.com/Poetry-and-the-Arab-Spring/ (accessed on 21 July 2015).
50. Alex Miller, Jr. "How Wordsworth informed the poetry of the Arab Spring." *The Conversation*, 9 January 2015. Available online: http://theconversation.com/how-wordsworth-informed-the-poetry-of-the-arab-spring-35412 (accessed on 22 July 2015).
51. Muhammad Ayish, quoted in John Lundberg. "Poetry is Thriving in the Arab World." *Huffington Post*, 15 April 2009. Available online: http://www.huffingtonpost.com/john-lundberg/poetry-is-thriving-in-the_b_174746.html (accessed on 10 July 2015).
52. Reem Najami. "Ma huwwa dawr ash-shi'r fi-th-thawrat al-'arabiyya? (What is the role of poetry in the Arab revolutions?)" *Qantara.de*, 2012. Available online: https://ar.qantara.de/content/lshr-wlthwrt-lrby-m-hw-dwr-lshr-fy-lthwrt-lrby (accessed on 3 July 2015).
53. Steven C. Caton, Hazim al-Eryani, and Rayman Aryani. "Poetry of Protest: Tribes in Yemen's 'Change Revolution'." In *The Political Aesthetics of Global Protest: The Arab Spring and Beyond.* Edited by Pnina Werbner, Martin Webb and Kathryn Spellman-Poots. Edinburgh: Edinburgh University Press, 2014, pp. 121–46.
54. Cf. John Lundberg. "The Poetry of the Revolution." *Huffington Post*, 27 February 2011. Available online: http://www.huffingtonpost.com/john-lundberg/the-poetry-of-revolution_b_828282.html (accessed on 23 July 2015).
55. See for example George A Simon. "Poetry and the Arab Spring." MA thesis, University of New York, Graduate Center, 1 February 2015. Available online: http://academicworks.cuny.edu/cgi/viewcontent.cgi?article=1623&context=gc_etds (accessed on 30 June 2015).
56. "Tawfiq Abed-Aqan, ar-Rabi' al-'arabi shi'ran." *aljazeera.net*, n.d. Available online: http://www.aljazeera.net/news/cultureandart/2012/9/11/الربيع-العربي-شعرا (accessed on 30 June 2015).

57. Mohamed-Salah Omri. "Tunisia: A revolution for dignity and freedom that cannot be colour-coded." *tni.org*, 29 January 2011. Available online: https://www.tni.org/en/article/tunisia-revolution-dignity-and-freedom-can-not-be-colour-coded (accessed on 24 July 2015).
58. Muhamad ad-Dihaji. "Fi-l-hajat ila shi'r: aq-qasida ar-risaliyya wa-l-rabi' al-'arabi (The need for Poetry: The Messianic Poem and the Arab Spring)." *al-Quds*, 19 March 2014. Available online: http://www.alquds.co.uk/?p=145499 (accessed on 5 July 2015).
59. Amr Sa'd Eddin. "Shi'r Mahmoud Darwish fi wajdan ath-thawrat al-'arabiyya (The Poetry of Mahmoud Darwish in the Conscience of the Arab Revolutions)." *Majalat al-dirasat al-falastiniyya* 92 (2012): 52–68. Available online: http://www.palestine-studies.org/sites/default/files/mdf-articles/11476.pdf (accessed on 21 July 2015).
60. Reem Abou-El-Fadl. "The Road to Jerusalem through Tahrir Square: Anti-Zionism and Palestine in the 2011 Egyptian Revolution." *Journal of Palestine Studies* 41 (2011/12): 6. Available online: http://www.palestine-studies.org/jps/fulltext/42573 (accessed on 21 July 2015).
61. The Poem Can Be Found at His Website. Available online: https://sites.google.com/site/tarifspoetry/tarifspoetry-11 (accessed on 10 July 2015).
62. Cf. Tawfiq Abed-Akan. "al-Rabi' al-'arabi shi'ran. (Arab spring poetry)" *al-Jazeera*, 11 September 2012. Available online: http://www.aljazeera.net/news/cultureandart/2012/9/11/%D8%A7%D9%84%D8%B1%D8%A8%D9%8A%D8%B9-%D8%A7%D9%84%D8%B9%D8%B1%D8%A8%D9%8A-%D8%B4%D8%B9%D8%B1%D8%A7 (accessed on 20 September 2015).
63. Ali al-Ra'i. *al-Masrah fi-l-watan al-'arabi* (*Theater in the Arab World*). Kuwait: Majlis al-watani li-l-thaqafa wa-l-fanun wa-l-'adab, 1978.
64. Riad Kamil. "Nasha' al-masrah al-arabi al-hadith. (The Emergence of Modern Arab Theater)." *Diwan al-Arab*, 14 February 2015, Available online: http://www.diwanalarab.com/spip.php?page=article&id_article=41035 (accessed on 2 August 2015).
65. Fadil Khalil. "Ta'rikh al-masrah al-'arabi (History of Arab Theater)." *al-Hewar al-mutamaddun*, 20 January 2007. Available online: http://www.ahewar.org/debat/show.art.asp?aid=86424 (accessed on 20 September 2015).
66. Fadil Khalil. "an-Nasha' wa-l-tatawwur fi-l-masrah al-'arabi (The Emergence and Development in Arabi Theater)." *al-Hewar al-mutamaddun*, 16 February 2007. Available online: http://www.ahewar.org/debat/show.art.asp? aid=88836 (accessed on 2 August 2015).
67. One of the best historical exploration of the history of theater, and drama and literature more broadly, across the region, is Roger Allen. *An Introduction to Arabic Literature*. Cambridge: Cambridge University Press, 2000.
68. Charlotte Collins. "Playing Brecht in the Damascus: A Book on Post-Revolutionary Arab Theater." *Goethe Institute*. Available online: http://www.goethe.de/ges/phi/prj/ffs/the/a101/en13048444.htm (accessed on 2 August 2015).
69. Tunisian playwright Noureddine El Ata, quoted in Carlotta Gallaug. "A Cafe Where the Spirit of the Arab Spring Lives On." *New York Times*, 7 August 2013. Available online: http://www.nytimes.com/2013/08/08/world/africa/a-cafe-where-the-spirit-of-the-arab-spring-lives-on.html?_r=0 (accessed on 20 June 2015).

70. Eyad Houssam. "Introduction." In *Doomed by Hope: Essays on Arab Theatre.* Edited by Eyad Houssami. London: Pluto Press, 2012, pp. 3–4.
71. For a similar view see Dina Ami. "Egyptian Playwright Alfred Farag Analyzes Decline of Arab Theater." *Al Jadid Magazine*, 1999. Available online: http://www.aljadid.com/content/egyptian-playwright-alfred-farag-analyzes-decline-arab-theater (accessed on 21 July 2015).
72. For information about the festival. "The Honor of the 18th of the Cairo International Festival for Experimental Theater." *Cultural Development Fund.* Available online: http://www.cdf-eg.org/English/exp_theater/old/honor_e2006.htm (accessed on 21 August 2015).
73. Sa'id Aulaqi. *Saba'un 'Aaman Min al-Masrah fi al-Yaman (Seventy Years of Theatre in Yemen).* Aden: Warizat ath-thaqafa wa-l siyaha, 1983.
74. For a good English summary of Yemen's theatrical history, see Katherine Hennessey. "The rich history of theater in Yemen." *La voix du Yémen*, 22 October 2013. Available online: http://www.lavoixduyemen.com/en/2013/10/22/the-rich-history-of-theater-in-yemen/5157/ (accessed on 3 August 2015).
75. Katherine Hennessy. "Mettre en scène la révolution: le théâtre du 'Printemps arabe' yéménite." *Arabian Humanities*, 2015. Available online: https://cy.revues.org/2848 (accessed on 26 June 2015).
76. Rolf C. Hemke. *Theater im arabischen Sprachraum (Theater in the Arab World).* Berlin: Verlag Theater der Zeit, 2013.
77. Cleo Jay. "Staging the Transition in North Africa: Theatre as a Tool of Empowerment." *Ibraaz* 004/2 November 2012. Available online: http://www.ibraaz.org/essays/44 (accessed on 21 July 2015).
78. For *Amnesia* see: "Yahia Yaïch Amnesia de Fadhel Jaïbi et Jalila Baccar/ teaser." *YouTube*, 2010. https://www.youtube.com/watch?v=4Z9A7fmsM6E (accessed on 3 November 2015).
79. Moncef Karimi. "al-Mahrajan ad-dawli lil-masrah an-nisa'i (The International Festival of Women's Theater)." *lemaghreb.tn*, undated. Available online: http://www.startimes.com/f.aspx?t=35144621 (accessed on 10 July 2015).
80. See Professor Mohammed Abazh of the University of Tunis, quoted in "ar-Rabi' al-'arabi mada aj-jadl fi mahrajan al-masrah bil-maghreb (The 'Arab Spring' of a controversial theater festival in Morocco)." *El-fagr*, 16 January 2015. Available online: http://www.elfagr.org/1627339 (accessed on 21 July 2015).
81. "Tabayan al-'ara' bi-sha'an 'ar-rabi' al-'arabi' fi mahrajan al-masrah al-'arabi bil-maghreb. (Divergence of views on the 'Arab Spring' in the Arab theater festival in Morocco)." *Reuters Arabic*, 15 January 2015. Available online: http://ara.reuters.com/article/entertainmentNews/idARAKBN0KO0WK20150115 (accessed on 21 July 2015).

82. Palestinian theater companies have from the start been expert at blending traditional forms of artistic expression—puppet theater, dancing—and avant-garde dramaturgy, to produce the widest and most affective forms of content as part of the broader cultural resistance struggles. As such they represent the power of Palestinian cultural organizations to act like "iceberg[s] of Palestinian resistance that remain underwater;" harder to repress than more direct forms of resistance, they clearly served as a model, if not direct inspiration, for theater elsewhere in the Arab world in the era before the Arab spring (Amitai Ben-Abba. "El-Hakawati Theater—The complementary nature of stones and puppets." *+972 Magazine*, 1 July 2013. Available online: http://972mag.com/el-hakawati-theater-the-complementary-nature-of-stones-and-puppets/74837/ (accessed on 20 June 2015).
83. For a good early history of El Hakawati, see Reuven Snir. "The Palestinian al-Hakawati Theater: A Brief History." The *Arab Studies Journal* 6/7 (Fall 1998/Spring 1999): 57–71.
84. The best summary of Mer-Khamis's life and death is Adam Shatz. "The Life and Death of Juliano Mer-Khamis." *London Review of Books* 35 (2013): 3–11.
85. I have written about the struggles of the Freedom Theater in several articles: "At Midnight in Jenin, The Smell of Resistance." *al-Jazeera America*, 21 March 2015. Available online: http://america.aljazeera.com/opinions/2015/3/at-midnight-in-jenin-the-smell-of-resistance.html (accessed on 3 November 2015).
86. "Freedom Riders on the Move in Palestine." *al-Jazeera English*, 9 April 2014. Available online: http://www.aljazeera.com/indepth/opinion/2012/04/20124483146411159.html (accessed on 3 November 2015).
87. "A Year after Juliano Mer-Khamis's Murder, It's Time to Board the Freedom Bus." *al-Jazeera English*, 4 April 2012. Available online: http://www.aljazeera.com/indepth/opinion/2012/04/20124483146411159.html (accessed on 20 July 2015).
88. Jullian Kestler D'Amours. "West Bank Theater Pays Price for Freedom." *al-Jazeera English*, 11 June 2012. Available online: http://www.aljazeera.com/indepth/features/2012/06/201261165349126599.html (accessed on 25 July 2015).
89. Cleo Jay. "Staging the North African Transition: Theatrical Productions since the Arab Spring." *Panorama: Strategic Sectors|Culture Society*, undated. Available online: http://www.iemed.org/observatori-es/arees-danalisi/arxius-adjunts/anuari/iemed-2013/Jay%20Arab%20Spring%20Theatrical%20Production%20EN.pdf (accessed on 23 September 2015).
90. Tanjil Rashid. "Theatre's Arab Turn." *The White Review*, 2012. Available online: http://www.thewhitereview.org/features/theatres-arab-turn/ (accessed on 10 July 2015).
91. For descriptions of the various forms in practice today see, inter alia, "Egyptian Theatre of the Oppressed: Nora Ameen at TEDxShibinelKom." *TedX*, 18 September 2012. Available online: http://tedx.ushahidi.com/reports/view/8890 (accessed on 3 November 2015).
92. "Forum Theatre workshops & launching the Arab network for Theatre of the Oppressed." *AFAC*, 2012. Available online: http://www.arabculturefund.org/grantees/grantee.php?id=115 (accessed on 23 September 2015).

93. "B7al B7al" (all equal) is a street theatre show created by Mix City in Casablanca, a "Diversity, Drama and Development" project co-funded by the European Union within the framework of the regional programme Med Culture. Available online: http://www.medculture.eu/information/videos/b7al-b7al-street-art-theater-challenging-stereotypes#sthash.tLo9IUbW.dpuf (accessed on 23 September 2015).
94. Laith Nakli. *Shesh Yak.* Directed by Bruce McCarty. DVD. Available online: http://www.rattlestick.org/shesh-yak/ (accessed on 23 September 2015).
95. Clair Beaugrand, and Najla Nakhlé-Cerruti. "D(rôles) de printemps arabes au théâtre." Available online: http://orientxxi.info/lu-vu-entendu/d-roles-de-printemps-arabes-au,0853 (accessed on 23 September 2015).
96. For Queens of Syria, see Available online: http://www.shubbak.co.uk/queens-of-syria/ (accessed on 23 September 2015).
97. "Despite Attacks, Performance Artists Bring Activism to Tunisia's Streets," *Voice Project*, 30 January 2015. Available online: http://voiceproject.org/post_news/performance-artists-bring-activism-tunisian-streets/ (accessed on 23 September 2015).
98. Nissaf Slama. "Fifteen Actors on Trial for 'Public Indecency'." *Tunisia Live*, 2013. Available online: http://www.tunisia-live.net/2013/07/08/fifteen-actors-on-trial-in-el-kef-for-public-indecency/#sthash.ZBznPSzX.dpuf (accessed on 23 September 2015).
99. A good summary of the events surrounding the boys' arrest is Joe Sterling, "Daraa: The Spark that Lit the Syrian Flame." *CNN*, 1 March 2012. Available online: http://edition.cnn.com/2012/03/01/world/meast/syria-crisis-beginnings/ (accessed on 26 July 2015).
100. David Stelfox. "Arabic Graffiti: Dances with Walls." *The National*, 15 July 2011. Available online: http://www.thenational.ae/news/world/middle-east/arabic-graffiti-dances-with-walls#full (accessed on 23 July 2015).
101. As the renowned Iraqi artist Hassan Massoudy described it in [100].
102. Lina Khatib. *Image Politics in the Middle East: The Role of the Visual in Political Struggle.* London: IB Tauris, 2012.
103. Thamer Mekki. "Fann graffiti fi Tunis (Graffiti Art in Tunis)." *Qantara.de*, 2 September 2012. Available online: https://ar.qantara.de/content/fnw-ljrfyty-fy-twns-ljrfyty-fy-twnsslh-fy-yd-lmqwm-lmdny (accessed on 10 July 2015).
104. Sherif Boraie. *Wall Talk: Graffiti of the Egyptian Revolution*. Cairo: Zeituna Press, 2012.
105. Noor Ahmed Said. "al-Graffiti al-'Arabi (Arab Graffiti)." *Watny News*, 5 January 2015. Available online: http://watny-news.com/new_top/12759 (accessed on 2 August 2015).
106. Nicola Tama. "Ar-rassam 'ala-l-judran: risa'il ash-shabab bi-lubnan (Drawings on Walls: Messages of the Youth in Lebanon)." *al-Jazeera*, 17 May 2012. Available online: http://www.aljazeera.net/news/cultureandart/2012/5/17/الرسم-على-الجدران-رسائل-الشباب- بلبنان (accessed on 29 July 2015).
107. Cinnamon Nippard. "al-Ghrafiti fi-l-'alam al-'arabi (Graffiti in the Arab World)." *Qantara.de*, 17 June 2011. Available online: https://ar.qantara.de/content/lgrfyty-fy-llm-lrby-lgrfyty-lrby-khtwt-rby-bhbr-lmtlb-lsysy (accessed on 30 June 2015).

108. Tristan Bazot, J.-F. Thierry, Charles Allainmat, and Geoffroy Lomet. "Le graffiti comme moyen d'expression." *socioarchi*, 5 January 2014. Available online: https://socioarchi.wordpress.com/2014/01/05/le-graffiti-comme-moyen-dexpression/ (accessed on 2 August 2015).
109. Yve Gonzalez-Quijano. "La révolution graphique égyptienne." *OWNI*, 2011. Available online: http://owni.fr/2011/12/22/la-revolution-graphique-egyptienne/ (accessed on 2 August 2015). Here we should recalls that graffiti was not originally meant to be tied to one place. In its original contemporary form, in New York City, it was either done on trains precisely so that they'd be, literally, moving murals taking the messages from the poorest neighborhoods to the richest that young African American and Latino taggers rarely could access, or painted alongside train routes to travelers would be forced to confront it while they moved.
110. Mohsen al-'Atiqi. "Rasa'il aj-judran (Messages on the Walls)." *al-Doha Magazine* #57, July 2012. Available online: http://www.aldohamagazine.com/article.aspx?n=fb91b73d-5db9-415c-b5c9-f7ce9e4bf651&d=20120701#.VbfuzmCiKBI (accessed on 2 August 2015).
111. For the role of graffiti in Palestine see inter alia Hugh Lovatt. "From national resistance to global movement-An intro to Palestinian graffiti." *Your Middle East*, 3 March 2015. Available online: http://www.yourmiddleeast.com/culture/from-national-resistance-to-global-movement-an-intro-to-palestinian-graffiti-photos_30295 (accessed on 1 August 2015).
112. Ashley Toenjes. "This Wall Speaks: Graffiti and Transnational Networks in Palestine." *Jerusalem Quarterly* 61 (2015): 55–68. Available online: http://www.palestine-studies.org/sites/default/files/jq-articles/This%20Wall%20Speaks_JQ%2061.pdf (accessed on 3 August 2015).
113. "Bansky and the History of Palestinian Graffiti." *For MENA*, 20 March 2015. Available online: http://formena.org/en/articles/banksy-and-the-history-of-palestinian-graffiti-208038 (accessed on 1 August 2015).
114. A good gallery of Palestinian graffiti can be found at N.A. "al-Fann 'al-ghrafiti' fi falastin. wa li-l-judran 'ayanu (Graffiti Art in Palestine... and the Walls [have] Eyes)." *al-Bawaba*, 5 September 2012. Available online: http://www.albawaba.com/ar/slideshow/-جرافيتي-فلسطين440938 (accessed on 2 August 2012).
115. A nice collection of Hannah El Degham's Murals. Available online: https://suzeeinthecity.wordpress.com/2012/03/25/street-art-on-mohamed-mahmoud-photos/ (accessed on 2 August 2015).
116. Some of Alaa Awad's most important work. "Alaa Awad." *ArtTalks*, 2012. Available online: http://www.arttalks.org/artist.php?id=769113012 (accessed on 23 September 2015).
117. Jonathan Rashad. "Alaa Awad: The Artist from Luxor." *Flickr*. Available online: https://www.flickr.com/photos/drumzo/6979350709 (accessed on 2 August 2015).
118. Nadia Khiari's "Willis in Tunis" is now available in many formats, but on the web is most easily viewed." Available online: http://www.cartoonmovement.com/p/6844 (accessed on 2 August 2015).
119. "Willis from Tunis: 'Christmas time in Tunisia'." *The Arab World in Revolution(s)*. Available online: http://monde-arabe.arte.tv/en/willis-from-tunis-christmas-time-in-tunisia/ (accessed on 2 August 2015).

120. "Willis from Tunis." *Cartooning for Peace*. Available online: http://www.cartooningforpeace.org/en/dessinateurs/willis-from-tunis/ (accessed on 2 August 2015).
121. "Nadia Khiari's 'Willis in Tunis'." *Citizen Reporter*, 2012. Available online: http://citizenreporter.org/2012/11/nadia-khiari-willis-in-tunis/ (accessed on 2 August 2015).
122. Sad Panda see "An Afternoon with Sad Panda." *The Twenty Fourteen Theme*, 2011. Available online: https://suzeeinthecity.wordpress.com/2011/07/11/an-afternoon-with-sad-panda/ (accessed on 11 July 2011).
123. "Sad Panda on graffiti in post-revolution Egypt." *Place of War*, 2012. Video interview with artist, at Sad Panda on graffiti in post-revolution Egypt, 23 September 2015. Available online: http://www.inplaceofwar.net/sad-panda-on-graffiti-in-post-revolution-egypt (accessed on 2 August 2015).
124. Fatma Ibrahim, and Thoraia Abou Bakr. "The melancholy of Sad Panda." *Daily News Egypt*, 2 July 2013. Available online: http://www.dailynewsegypt.com/2013/07/02/the-melancholy-of-sad-panda/ (accessed on 2 August 2015).
125. Don Karl, and Pascal Zoghbi. *Arabic Graffiti*. Berlin: From Here to Flame Publishing, 2011.
126. For examples of Ultras graffiti, see ([115], pp. 478–524).
127. Interestingly, these words were uttered in July 2011, when there still seemed to be much hope for the future. But only four months later, at the start of the Muhammad Mahmoud riots, he became much more explicit, painting an image of a soldier tossing the baby into a fire to symbolize the demise of the next generation of Egyptians at the hands of the violence of the interim government [123].
128. For a good description of the place of Bahrain in the larger tapestry of Arab graffiti in the uprisings era, see Charlotte Schriwer. "Graffiti Arts and the Arab Spring." In *Routledge Handbook of the Arab Spring*. Edited by Larbi Sadiki. London: Routledge, 2014, pp. 376–91.
129. *Judran 14 Fibriar: Ghrafiti Thawrat Al-Bahrain* (*The Walls of 14 February: Revolutionary Graffiti in Bahrain*). Dhaka: Awal Centre, 2013.
130. A good summary of the evolution of Yemen's graffiti scene is Mohammad al-Absi, "Graffiti gets political in Yemen." "al-Yemen: mu'alajat tashrawahat as-siyasa 'an tariq ar-rasm. (Yemen: Addressing Political Shortcomings through Drawing)." *Al-Monitor*, 12 September 2014. Available online: http://www.al-monitor.com/pulse/ar/originals/2014/09/youth-yemen-graffiti-art-campaigns-criticize-politics.html# (accessed on 1 August 2015). (An English version).
131. Gisele El Khoury. "Telling the Story of the Arab Spring: An interactive graffiti map." *Muftah*, 16 October 2014. Available online: http://muftah.org/telling-story-arab-spring-interactive-graffiti-map/#.VcELT2CiKBI (accessed on 28 July 2015).
132. Mia Gröndahl. *Revolution Graffiti: Street Art of the New Egypt*. Cairo: American University of Cairo\Press, 2013.
133. Omar Fathi. graffeur, alias Picasso, "Graffiti-Baladi—Un hommage aux graffeurs de la Révolution égyptienne." part of Graffiti baladi: Street Art et révolution en Égypte. Available online: http://www.graffiti-baladi.com/ (accessed on 29 July 2015).

134. Gisele El Khoury. "Understanding Politics in the Arab World through Naji al-Ali's Cartoons." *Muftah*, 16 October 2003. Available online: http://muftah.org/understanding-politics-in-the-arab-world-through-naji-al-alis-cartoons/#.VcEZ42CiKBI (accessed on 1 August 2015).
135. Andreas Qassim. "Arab Political Cartoons: The 2006 Lebanon War." MA Thesis, Lund University, 2007. Available online: http://andreasqassim.com/download/MA_thesis.pdf (accessed on 25 July 2015).
136. Barney Thompson. "Why cartoons and comics are flourishing in the Middle East." *Financial Times*, 25 July 2015. Available online: http://www.ft.com/cms/s/0/26a80334-31fa-11e5-91ac-a5e17d9b4cff.html (accessed on 2 August 2015).
137. While these spaces and art works have long since disappeared—as has almost all the graffiti—at the time they were among the most directly engaging visual works, bringing people directly into the artistic process in a manner that only singing along with artists in the Midan could rival Images of Eletrebi's work are available at his blog "From Beautiful Cairo." *The McKinley Theme*. Available online: https://amoreletrebi.wordpress.com/street-art/ (accessed on 23 September 2015).
138. Among the more prominent exhibits in Tunis after the revolution were the Laaroussa Collaborative Art Project and the Dream City Arts Festival (a compendium of articles on these exhibits can be found at the Jadaliyya portal. Available online: http://www.jadaliyya.com/pages/contributors/154017/page6 (accessed on 23 September 2015).
139. Ganzeer. "Concept Pop." *The Cairo Review of Global Affairs*, 6 July 2014. Available online: http://www.aucegypt.edu/GAPP/CairoReview/Pages/articleDetails.aspx?aid=618 (accessed on 4 August 2015).
140. Mosireen's work is available on its website. "قضية الشوري: سنة وشهرين من العبث." *WordPress*, 2015. Available online: http://mosireen.org (accessed on 23 September 2015).
141. The group has produced upwards of 250 videos and short films, many of which can be accessed at their YouTube page, "A Brief History of the Shura Council Trial so far." *YouTube*. Available online: https://www.youtube.com/user/Mosireen (accessed on 23 September 2015).
142. Paul Tillich. *Dynamics of Faith*. New York: Harper & Row, 1957, p. 18.
143. For a discussion of various Muslim views on the permissibility of art, and particularly music see Mark LeVine. "Like a Flower Growing in the Middle of the Desert."." In *Heavy Metal Islam: Rock, Resistance and the Struggle for the Soul of Islam*. New York: Random House, 2008.
144. Ayatollah Khomeini. "Obituary." *New York Times*, 4 June 1989.
145. "Tunisia: Artists under attack." *Arts Freedom*, 22 June 2012. Available online; http://artsfreedom.org/?p=1439 (accessed on 23 September 2015).
146. For an example of how the extremists were underestimated, see Seyla Benhabibi. "The Arab Spring: Religion, Revolution and the Public Sphere." *Social Science Research Council*. Available online: http://publicsphere.ssrc.org/benhabib-the-arab-spring-religion-revolution-and-the-public-square/ (accessed on 14 July 2015).
147. Copies of the ISIL magazine *Dabiq* are. Available online: http://www.clarionproject.org/news/islamic-state-isis-isil-propaganda-magazine-dabiq (accessed on 23 September 2015).

148. For a description of jihadi poetry and its importance, see Robyn Creswell, and Bernard Haykel. "Battle Lines: Want to Understand the Jihadis? Read their Poetry." *The New Yorker*, 8 June 2015. Available online: http://www.newyorker.com/magazine/2015/06/08/battle-lines-jihad-creswell-and-haykel (accessed on 23 July 2015).
149. "Muslim Brotherhood Pop Art." *Kalimat Magazine*, 2015. Available online: http://www.kalimatmagazine.com/muslim-brotherhood-pop-art (accessed on 10 July 2015).
150. Mark LeVine. "Egypt—Enemies of the State: Bloggers, Brothers and the General's Son." In *Heavy Metal Islam: Rock Resistance and the Struggle for the Soul of Islam*. New York: random House, 2008.
151. One mid-level Muslim Brotherhood leaders explicitly blamed Qutb and his extremism in an interview with me for most of the ills that befell the group. See "Muslim Brotherhood Rejects Censorship on Creativity, Has Clear Vision on Art and Politics." *The Muslim Brotherhood*, 28 August 2012. Available online: http://www.ikhwanweb.com/article.php?id=30265 (accessed on 2 August 2015).
152. "Dr. Khattab: Brotherhood's Badie Art Statements Bode Well." *The Muslim Brotherhood*, 22 February 2012. Available online: http://www.ikhwanweb.com/article.php?id=29702 (accessed on 23 September 2015).
153. Ikhwanweb. "MB and FJP Delegation to Visit Actors' Syndicate." *The Muslim Brotherhood*, 20 December 2011. Available online: http://www.ikhwanweb.com/article.php?id=29439 (accessed on 26 July 2015).
154. Paul Cuno-Booth. "Band of Brothers: The Muslim Brotherhood's Artistic Side." *Muftah*, 20 August 2013. Available online: http://muftah.org/band-of-brothers-the-muslim-brotherhoods-artistic-side/ (accessed on 2 August 2015).
155. As Sayed Darish declared, "Those who claim that the art of the Muslim Brotherhood is purely preaching are simply following the falsehoods of the former regime that painted the Brotherhood as the frightening scarecrow to scare the whole public." "Sayed Darwish: Muslim Brotherhood Encourages Art and Creativity." *The Muslim Brotherhood*, 25 October 2011. Available online: http://www.ikhwanweb.com/article.php?id=29228 (accessed on 31 July 2015).
156. Biram Naji. "Harika Ennahda al-Islamiyya at-tunsiyya: dirasa naqdiyya (The Tunisian Islamic Renaissance Movement: A Critical Study)." *al-Hewar al-mutamaddun* #3824, 19 August 2012. Available online: http://www.ahewar.org/debat/show.art.asp?aid=320544 (accessed on 20 July 2015).
157. Yasmine Ryan. "Ghannouchi says political Islam on track." *Al Jazeera Media Network*, 13 September 2012. Available online: http://www.aljazeera.com/indepth/features/2012/09/20129 13653599865.html (accessed on 23 September 2015).
158. "Scores arrested after Tunis art riots." *al-Jazeera English*, 12 June 2012. Available online: http://www.aljazeera.com/news/africa/2012/06/2012612101946542727.html (accessed on 2 August 2015).
159. Interview by Mark LeVine with several revolutionary hiphop artists in Tunis, September 2011, July 2013, August 2014.

160. "Badie: Meaningful Art is Important to Restore Egypt's Leading Role." *The Muslim Brotherhood*, 5 January 2012. Available online: http://www.ikhwanweb.com/article.php?id=29511 (accessed on 2 August 2015).

Violent Jihad and Beheadings in the Land of Al Fatoni Darussalam

Virginie Andre

Abstract: The early 2000s has seen a revival of the Patani resistance manifesting in a violent jihad and new forms of extreme violence never witnessed before in the century-long Southern Thailand conflict. Transported by neojihadism, this new energised generation of fighters is injecting new meaning to their struggle, re-identifying friends and foes, spreading terror in hearts and minds to control mental and physical spaces through the slashing of the body, all in the hope of establishing Al Fatoni Darussalam. This article examines the reflexive repositioning of the Patani struggle through the process of transference of neojihadism and its transformation into a glocalised violent jihad.

Reprinted from *Religions*. Cite as: Andre, V. Violent Jihad and Beheadings in the Land of Al Fatoni Darussalam. *Religions* **2015**, *6*, 1203–1216.

1. Introduction

The long-standing Muslim separatist conflict of Southern Thailand is a one of those forgotten wars that rarely attracts any attention from the media or the international community. This can be partially explained by the discrete nature of the Muslim extremist separatist movement and its domestic focus. Unlike other Islamic extremist movements in the region, it has not pledged any allegiance to Al Qaeda. Yet, the revival of the resistance in the early 2000 under the banner of a localised neojihadism transported by a new energised generation of fighters is particularly informative of the process of neojihadism transference in the region, and how it could potentially serve as a blueprint to other Muslim minority conflicts in the Southeast Asian region, and other parts of the world.

The Patani[1] movement of resistance finds its roots in the period that follows the signature of the Anglo-Siamese Treaty (1909) by which the Sultanate of Patani was officially annexed to the Kingdom of Siam, now known as Thailand, formalising the subjugation of a distinct people to a foreign entity [1–3]. Following the signature of the Treaty, the Siamese government was confronted by different waves of organised Muslim political resistance, ranging from civic activism to armed resistance. More recently (late 2001 and increasing in 2004), after an almost 20 year period of apparent peace, the Patani struggle has taken on a new turn with the resurgence of violence expanding against civilians (including the beheadings of monks and attacks on Buddhist temples), reflecting a level of brutality never before witnessed in the century long conflict. The brutal killing of both Buddhists and Muslims, arson attacks against schools and systematic violence

---

[1] Please note the author's usage of different spelling of "Patani" when referring to the people of Patani or the former Sultanate of Patani, which derives from the Malay language and of "Pattani" when relating to the Thai administrative territorial division.

against teachers, coupled with the emergence of an exclusivist Islamic discourse and the refusal of all parties to engage in meaningful peace negotiations suggest the conflict is passing through a transformational stage and that over time it could depart from traditional patterns of violence characteristic of ethno-nationalist struggles in Southeast Asia in the post-colonial period and evolve into a more broad-based violent campaign with a greater blurring of the distinction between civilian and combatant. Today, the region is home to 1.5 million Melayu[2] Muslims who live in the three southernmost border provinces of Pattani, Yala and Narathiwat of Buddhist Thailand.

The failure in late 2001 of the Thai state to anticipate the resurgence of violence in the three southern provinces, and its parallel failure to develop a sustainable peace process, stems from two principle sources; its poor understanding of Southern Muslims as a distinctive people with their own sense of a separate identity and culture, and secondly a failure to grasp the capacity of external forces to re-energise and rejuvenate secessionist sentiment that is based on these distinctive patterns of culture and identity. To this end, the growing sense of global Islamic consciousness has given new meaning to the struggle that many Thai Muslims believe confronts them. This sense of supraterritoriality is increasingly encroaching into the political discourse of the new insurgent groups as they strive to differentiate themselves and their communities from wider Thai society.

In the 1970s secessionists in Southern Thailand described the Thai state as "colonialist" constituted by "Siamese fascist officials" who had "illegally colonised Patani" [4–6]. The flavour of this discourse shows the importance of historical context in shaping the way resistance movements interpret their own struggles. In the case of the resistance groups in Southern Thailand, it reflects the influence of the wider international anti-colonial movement and its embrace of nationalism and socialism. Translating these concepts into a political agenda was complicated by the centrality of Islam as an identity marker in defining the grievances of the Patani Muslims. Islam was the reason they were considered marginal by wider Buddhist society and hence it was Islam that become a core identity marker and the fulcrum upon which the resistance movement grew [6]. Merging the predominately secular themes of anti-colonialism with Islam was complex, and as a result for much of its existence the insurgency failed to define clearly an ideology beyond the general maxim of "liberating the homeland" to create the Republic of Patani. By the onset of the twenty-first century the situation had changed and although the goal remained the same for many Thai Muslims it was based on firmer ontological ground. By defining itself in Islamist terms, the separatist movement managed to distance itself from the secular concepts that defined the Thai state ("nationalism") and which precluded support for its struggle from other states ("sovereignty"). The objective now is the creation of Al Fatoni Darussalam (Islamic Land of Patani) by "purging all Siamese infidels out of our territory to purify our religion and culture" [7]. In short, the shift in terminology indicates an ideological shift in the way the insurgents frame the conflict but also, more importantly, in their identification of the "enemy" [6]. The "liberation of the Republic" has now evolved into a "struggle to liberate an Islamic Land" [6]. From being a "colonialist" and "fascist" state, the Thai state has assumed the status of "infidel" [6]. The insurgents' embrace of

---

[2] Melayu in English means Malay. In Thailand, the people of the former Patani Sultanate are referred to as Melayu in opposition to the more general labelling of Thai Muslim. Hence, here the term Melayu is used when referring to the Patani Malay Muslims or the Patani Malay community.

Islamism as the organising principle of their resistance is progressively transforming the conflict into what Juergensmeyer has called a "Cosmic War" [8].

The reflexive repositioning of the struggle by a new generation of militants within a larger transnational Islamic context has not only raised their own international profile in global Islamist circles but it has helped revitalize the struggle for a new and more internationally savvy generation of Patani Muslims, allowing them to feel as though they are part of a larger global movement. The intertwining of the global and the local is driving political violence to unprecedented extremism in Southern Thailand. From a traditional ethno-nationalist struggle the insurgency in Southern Thailand has now morphed into a glocalised jihad that is inspired by global forces but which is focused on local injustices [5,6].

2. Patani's Neojihadist Sphere

The Patani insurgency's adoption of Islamic radicalism and its extreme manifestation has progressively moved the struggle away from ethno-nationalism and classical jihadism propelling them into the neojihadist sphere of influence. Neojihadism distinguishes itself from jihadism in that it advocates terrorism to effect political change, draws on global processes and operates within the context of a global rather than local consciousness ([9], pp. 15–16). Because jihadism was mainly concerned with the establishment of sharia within Muslim-majority states where Muslims were being oppressed, it involved combat with state agents, not civilians or non-combatants ([9], p. 16). Furthermore, neojihadism uses selective literal interpretations of the Qur'an and the traditions of the Prophet Muhammad to sanction terrorist violence ([9], p. 16); a characteristic shared by the Patani insurgency. Neojihadism in southern Thailand is in fact a localised form of neojihadism, which shares some elements with its global form but not all, as its goal remains the restoration of its sacred ancestral homeland (not the formation a pan-Islamic state) which has brought some neojihadists to question the nature of the southern struggle. In Patani localised neojihadism new global forms are hybridized with old local forms of the struggle, tactics are knocked off and localised, all giving birth to a glocalised jihad and new forms of violence in the view of establishing Al Fatoni Darussalam. At the same time, because of the similarities it shares with the global form of neojihadism, it places the insurgency within the content of global Islamic struggle resulting in an increased interest within the global neojihadist community.

By injecting new meaning to their struggle through the localisation of the locus of neojihadism, the Patani insurgents have transformed their struggle into a religious obligation for all Melayu Muslims and created a motivational appeal for its core group, the Patani youth; an appeal that nationalism alone could no longer generate in a new globalised era [6,7]. Globality has facilitated the ideological transference processes by which the insurgency has localised elements of neojihadism within its renewed ideological discourse. In this new global context, Islam acts as globalising agent, shaping, on one hand, the inward and outward worldview of the movement while on the other hand providing it with a vision from which models can be derived. Moreover, Islam also acts as a filtering framework in the hybridisation of this global form or elements of global forms. Neojihadism is such a model from which the separatist terrorist insurgency has drawn ideological and tactical elements. What makes neojihadist transference possible and its subsequent hybridisation into Patani instrumentalisation of Islam successful is the affinities they share, *i.e.*, a common Islamic and Muslim culture.

The tenets of Patani radical Islam revolve around the central themes of defensive jihad, kafir (infidel), munafiq (traitor), Al Fatoni Darussalam and shahid (martyr). The insurgency is leading a defensive jihad, which they believe finds its justification in the forced annexation of the Sultanate, the oppression endured by its people and the enslavement of Islam under Siamese rule. Additionally, emphasis is made on the transcending irreversible and binding nature of the conversion of the land to Islam (dar al-Islam) which must be dutifully restored (dar al-harb); an emphasis which differs from the Melayu nationalist rhetoric of an earlier generation of insurgents.

Within this defensive jihad, fellow Muslims who collaborate with the state or criticise publicly the insurgency are identified as munafiq who will be punished for their treachery against "their nation, religion and selves". Fellow Muslims, however, are forewarned and hypocrites are given the opportunity to repent. An emphasis is made on the religio-ethnicity proscribing them from joining or allying with other groups than theirs, especially the kafir Siam and failure to do is punishable by death resulting in the killing of innocent Muslim civilians. This is another element closely related to neojihadist movements where the takfiri practice by which a Muslim is declared an unbeliever justifies the shedding of Muslim blood. The munafiq and the kafir are declared enemies of Islam and the movement.

According to the Al Qur'an (4:140; 9:68), "God will gather all the hypocrites and disbelievers together into Hell" and "promises the Fire of Hell as a permanent home for the hypocrites, both men and women, and the disbelievers: this is enough for them. God rejects them and a lasting punishment awaits". In these verses, both the *munafiq* and the *kafir*, indistinctly are declared enemies of the faith and share a common destiny that is of rejection and punishment by death. The same logic of association is found within the insurgency's process of identification of friends and enemies where Muslim collaborators (or *munafiq*s) are associated with the enemy (*kafir* Siam). The insurgents claim:

> "The enemy is only the kafir siam, [but] whoever follows them or offer their services to them, we will consider these individuals to be the same kind as them [kafir]. If you or your relatives offer their services [to the kafir], we will not guarantee your own safety";
> "Do not believe the kafir siam under any circumstances because the kafir people are Shaytan [satan] in human's clothing. Both kafir and Shaytan are the enemies of Allah. The enemies of Allah are our enemies and anyone who follows the way of Shaytan and the kafir will be called 'munafiq', is it not? All, shaytan, kafirs and munafiqs as a rule live in everlasting hell".[3]

This religious dichotomy of friends and enemies is particularly significant as it allows a better understanding of the logic and mechanisms that legitimise the expansion of insurgent violence to the civilian Buddhist and Muslim communities, another trait of neojihadism. Furthermore, it appears that Al Fatoni Darussalam cannot be established as long as it remains under kafir rule. Its establishment requires a liberation and a freedom from any form of Thai encroachment calling for a

---

[3] Separatist leaflet, the Fighters of the state of Fatoni Darussalam, undated.

tabula rasa. However, the insurgency has yet to expand on its definition of an Islamic state that would transcend their utopian description of an Islamic state where justice and righteousness would rule under the love of God until Judgement Day.

The southern separatist insurgency's instrumentalisation of Islam should not be reduced to a fashionable trend characteristic of post 9/11 Islamic resistance movements from which it has drawn its rhetorical inspiration. Rather, it should be envisaged as a necessity to the movement's survival. By localising the struggle in the locus of neojihadism, not only has the separatist insurgency successfully injected new meaning to its fight but also is successfully elevating the conflict to unprecedented levels of legitimacy and authority, *i.e.*, of a Holy war.

By leading a defensive jihad that aims to restore the Islamic Patani state by waging a vengeful violent war against the Infidel Siamese oppressor, the southern separatist insurgency appears to fall within the sphere of influence of "neojihadism". Neojihadism is an ideology that can be adopted and localised within the context of the struggle in Southern Thailand to achieve its own end. In truth, although the nature and the ideology may have changed, the struggle's ultimate goal remains the same; it is after all about the creation of an independent nation-state, surely Islamic in essence but of which the contours remain to be defined. In fact, the insurgency's re-interpretation of the scriptures serves the sole purpose of establishing this independent nation-state.

By re-defining the Thai state as kufir, the insurgents have proclaimed violent jihad not only against the Thai state but also on its ontological essence, its "Thai-ness", including chart (nation), satsana (religion), and phramahakasat (the monarchy). Through this insurgent process of re-identification of the enemy, the Thai Buddhist is dehumanised, demonised and eventually killed; the kafir harbi siam becomes the "cosmic foe" or "shaytan in human's clothing". This process of satanization of the enemy, explains Juergensmeyer ([8], p. 175), is part of the construction of an image of cosmic war, which becomes particularly operational when people, like the Patani Melayu Muslims, feel oppressed or have suffered injuries at the hands of the dominant.

The new generation of insurgent stated goals to purify their religion and culture requires a purge of "Siamese infidels" and is the raison d'être behind the movement's recent expansion of its targets to include civilians, including children, women and elders. Now that Thailand and the Thai Buddhists have become the "infidel enemy", transforming everything that incarnates "Thainess" into a worthless "Other", stripped of any personhood, acts of terrorism against the "enemy" have become acceptable in the eyes of the insurgents, and the use of beheading in Southern Thailand is an outgrowth of this re-identification process.

In its re-interpretation of the scriptures and mobilisation of religious symbolism, the insurgency has paid particular attention to religious concepts instrumental in the legitimisation and waging of a jihad and its enactive violent form.

3. The Sacralisation of a Conflict and Its Praxis

By casting the Patani struggle within the locus of neojihadism under the impulse of globalisation, it has transformed the movement's ideological nature and scope resulting in new forms and patterns of violence characteristic of new wars, significantly transforming battlefield violence and its effect on local communities. It has given birth to a new praxis with distinct features symptomatic of new wars, and departs significantly from the classical models of revolutionary struggle. The insurgency's justification and strategy for the Patani armed struggle in its early days spoke the language of Melayu nationalism and drew less on Islamic traditions than on models of revolutionary struggle or "people's war" developed by the Vietnamese and Algerians in their struggle against colonialism. In fact, anti-colonial struggles springing across the Southeast Asian region in the post World War II heavily influenced the movement in its claim for a separate and independent state while the communist insurrections influenced the insurgency in its strategy for armed struggle.

Where an older generation of insurgents—communists and separatists—relied on the people's support for their survival, the new generation seeks political mobilisation through terror and elimination of the kafir siam and the munafiq, giving birth to a hybridized notion of people's war. The new generation of insurgents draws more heavily on the Islamic traditions of war and the narratives of neojihadism in its justification and strategy for its armed struggle giving birth to a hybridized insurrectional model where political violence predominantly affects civilians. The re-definition of the enemy along religious and ethnic fault lines has translated into an expansion of violence to civilian citizens and an increase in victimisation of Thai Buddhists. In this new cosmological ideology, civilian citizens are no longer protected by conventional rules of war, creating and blurring at the same time the line between civilians and combatants, and a previous notion of a people's war which in the past depended on the people's willing support and not fear. Today, this new warfare features a tendency to avoid battle and to direct most violence against civilians, which is evidenced by the dramatic increase in the ratio of civilian to military casualty. Government and village officials, politicians, civil and municipality servants, teachers, students, doctors and nurses, businessmen, merchants, religious leaders and villagers have now come under insurgent fire [10].

To sustain a climate of fear, the use of indiscriminate means of violence, mainly of bombs or IEDs in open spaces, has drastically increased. Roadside bombs, motorcycle and car bombs exploding in public spaces have become part of the daily violence landscape. The insurgency increasingly uses extreme violence, nonexistent in an earlier era, against civilians with the aim to force people "to take sides" in its "people's war", thus, widening communal tensions between Buddhist and Muslim communities and forcing each community to entrench itself behind the security of their respective identities. The daily violence and its more extreme strand have eroded Southern Thailand's social fabric by generating fear, mistrust and division among Thai Buddhists and Melayu Muslims.

The new praxis of Patani terrorism derives both from the transformation of the struggle into a cosmic war and the centrality of a religious identity which are shaped by a mixture of global and local forces further transforming the movement. As a result of the convergence of these forces, Patani separatist terrorism is taking on a dangerous and extreme trajectory.

The use of extreme violence is a distinctive feature of this new type of warfare, which takes new meaning within the Patani struggle and the extent to which these practices, in particular beheadings, are manifestations of the glocalisation of neojihadism in the region.

4. Extreme Violence and Transference of Neojihadism

In its localisation of neojihadism, the insurgency not only has expanded its violence to civilians who now embody the enemy kafir or munafiq, but also adopted extreme forms of violence that follow ethnic fault-lines—a pattern departing significantly from a previous campaign of violence. Particular forms of extreme violence have been adopted as fear strategies in order to exert and preserve political control over the population. The human body has, in fact, become a political symbol, where the barbaric desecration of flesh and bones cuts across the interfaith and intercultural relationships between the communities.

In Patani, the extreme violence takes on the forms of machete hacking, torching of victims (sometimes alive), beheadings and isolated cases of crucifixion and genital mutilation while violence is characterised by drive by shootings, roadside bombs, motorcycle and car bombs. Between 2004 and 2009, over one hundred fifty cases of extreme violence have been recorded: fifty-nine machete hackings, forty-seven killing and burning incidents, fifty-two decapitations, one crucifixion and two cases of genital mutilation [10].

The broadcasting of insurgent atrocities over the Internet on platforms such as YouTube increases the spectacle effect of extreme violence by ensuring it reaches wider audiences [11,12]. Additionally, it enables the lifting of any notion of temporality on these exactions, as the act is continuously played and replayed and the body of the victims repeatedly desecrated. It becomes an indefinite political spectacle of human body desecration.

A significant extreme form of violence, which further indicates a shift from a previous campaign of violence, is the Patani insurgents' use of beheadings. As noted above, a total of fifty-two cases of decapitations were recorded. The practice of beheading is of particular interest, as unlike other types of extreme violence, it results both from the ideological transformation of the movement, and, the "knock off"[4] ([13], p. 184) and glocalisation of a neojihadist practice. The adoption of the neojihadist beheading strategy by Patani insurgents is particularly useful in understanding the mechanism of transference and glocalisation of neojihadist ideas and tactics at play within the region, which in turn further informs us on the transformative process of the insurgency.

The contemporary use of beheadings in the Patani insurgent terror campaign has prompted many local and international observers to link the practice to the Middle Eastern trend. Certainly, the increasing access to the Internet, the circulation in southern Thailand of video recordings showing beheadings from Iraq or Chechnya [5] and the recovery of such material by security personnel in 2007 suggest that the southern insurgency has not only knocked off its contemporary theological-ideological inspiration from neojihadism but also its extreme violent strand.

These types of recordings allow the insurgency to enter the discourse of neojihadism and to draw from this rhetoric to imbue their own struggle with a renewed contemporary significance, but also more specifically it enables them to penetrate the violent praxis of this particular sphere of influence. Although the insurgent groups are not the primary target audience of these videos, the relative "success" of the methods utilised in the conduct of political violence shown in these have

---

[4] According to Lentini, knock-off terrorism "implies that potential terrorists have observed a model of conducting political violence that has worked and they attempt to knock off the procedure for their own purposes" [8].

become a source of symbolic and technical know-how easily adaptable and readily available for acquisition by groups such as the Patani insurgency. However, as Lisa Campbell ([14], p. 609) notes, while "global access of video-taped beheadings may be inspiring more worldwide beheadings, (…) in many locations beheadings are not new and have historical cultural precedent".

Henceforth, beheadings in southern Thailand should not be perceived as copycat. Here, the concept of "knock off terrorism" [8] is particularly useful to understand the underlying rationale of the Patani insurgency for adopting the practice of beheading in their struggle. More than what is perceived by Thai authorities to be a mere reproduction or copycat of the Iraqi beheadings, it can be argued that Patani insurgents recently adopted decapitation as a strategy for its (believed) propensity to generate political change by instilling fear; a characteristic intrinsic to knock off terrorism ([8], p. 184). Patani beheadings can be considered a form of terrorism innovation in the sense that the movement has adopted a tactic, which is new to the organisation but "has already been used by other organisations in the past" [15].

Although the appearance of beheadings in Southern Thailand may have found its inspiration from the contemporary Middle Eastern trend, particularly from the Iraqi insurgency, the practice of beheading is not new to Thailand. Significant differences in practices emerge suggesting that the southern trend departs from its Middle Eastern counterpart, unveiling a locally rooted tradition and the significance of cultural memory in the perpetuation of extreme violence.

Former insurgents have denounced these brutalities, in particular the use of beheadings, as it is probably the form of extreme violence that strikes people's imagination the most (which in turn provides further information on the spectacle value of such practice and the emotional fear it inspires).

The bodies of kafirs and munafiqs have become a "theatre for social performances and productions" [16]. The body is in fact used "to establish the parameters of this otherness, taking the body apart, so to speak, to divine the enemy within" [16]. These extreme forms of violence aim to show that the perpetrator does not "recognize the identity of the others as legitimate" and implies it a negative ascription or labelling ([17], p. 419).

The dismemberment and burning of human bodies, mainly of Thai Buddhists, reflects an attitude, which perceives the identity of the enemy as illegitimate, undeserving of any respect. And when such violence is directed towards Melayu Muslims, the insurgents reflect the labelling of all these individuals as the enemy, for not taking sides, or for not fighting alongside the insurgents. The dismemberment, burning or mutilation of the body, therefore, can be seen as a symbolic gesture at the rest of the community, the communities of the area that witness the aftermath or hear of the head or corpse found down the street. These acts indicate cultural design and violent predictability ([16], p. 235).

These exactions are not only about destruction but also reflect "bloodshed executed in a deliberately intense and vivid way", which seeks to "maximize the savage nature of their violence" and "purposely to elicit anger" ([8], p. 121). These acts of terrorism are "deliberately exaggerated violence" ([8], p. 122) as it is about creating a spectacle of violence, a symbolic and theatrical act. Juergensmeyer ([8], p. 125) discusses this in detail, with specific attention to religious terrorism more generally, which he states is heavily symbolic because incidents are "intended to illustrate or refer to something beyond their immediate target".

Incidents take place in public places usually when villagers are often on their way to work, school or home. By executing such violent acts on the streets or in places such as rubber plantation sites, the insurgents are attempting to control central spaces, "by damaging, terrorizing and assaulting them" ([8], p. 134).

These acts of exaggerated cruelty seek not only to kill the opponent, but to humiliate, to undermine and crucially, to generate immense fear among the population. The body of the victim is portrayed and perceived as a symbol in the theatre of this violence. The attacks generate major rifts and anger among the Thai Buddhist community—precisely the intention of the act itself. The stabbing or slashing of a Buddhist monk does not only cause harm or leave wounds on his body, but also cuts across the interfaith and intercultural relationships between the people. Where a Muslim man is attacked on his way home from a mosque, it can be interpreted as a criticism for not taking sides and joining the fight. This violence has intimidated the vast bulk of "the Muslim population into acquiescence or at least into silence" ([18], p. 92). Attacking individuals who are in places of worship, or attacking weak targets such as the elderly, are very much considered as violations of taboo and social norms [19]—generating the hysteria and rifts the insurgency strives for.

The beheadings, attacks with machetes, the shooting and burning of Buddhist and Muslim victims forces everyone to engage with the conflict, take over public spaces and make them threatening or dangerous, and also, crucially, use the human body as a means to challenge the sovereignty of the Thai state.

While the significance and purpose of the use of extreme violence by the Patani insurgency lies in the spectacle and political value it carries, which was enabled by the instrumentalisation of an Islamic identity as a motivational factor and ideological rhetoric, it does not allow to explain why particular forms of extreme of violence are chosen over others. In this instance, the examination of the Patani beheading praxis helps unfolding the processes at play in adopting particular forms of violence.

In their transformation from an ethno-nationalist conflict into a cosmic war, the Patani insurgents had to draw from several sources to revive and imbue their own struggle with a renewed contemporary significance and legitimacy. In this respect, the decision and justification to use beheadings by southern insurgents in their fight to liberate the homeland can be regarded as an outgrowth of their transformative process into a cosmic war.

In Southern Thailand, history and their narratives are instrumental in the Muslim community's formation of collective memory and identity. As such, the insurgent movement draws its inspiration from these different competing historical narratives—Thai and Muslim—in the articulation of its ideology and its extreme violent manifestation, such as the use of beheading. On one hand, the historical continuity of decapitation in Thailand constitutes for the insurgents a source into which they can tap, which in turn enables them to signify their resistance to the state but also to make a blatant declaration of power by exercising a practice that was originally the state's exclusive prerogative.

On the other hand, Muslim history and scriptures provide the insurgents with an almost inexhaustible source from which they can draw upon without any consideration for the context in which these historical precedents took place. In fact, the fluidity of Islamic concepts and their interpretations is an intrinsic characteristic of Islam. For instance, as British Muslim academic Mona Siddiqi points out, "fiqh, [Islamic jurisprudence] though a pious endeavour was still a human attempt to elaborate what might be God's will and though it may have outlined ethical norms using the various tools at hand including the scripture, it never ceased to be a fluid expression of the Divine will". Because the Qur'an is open to interpretation, this means that Muslim communities can either use or abuse the Scriptures [20]. Religious concepts are not syncretised to one place or one era, they become fluid and traverse different boundaries [20]. If the notion of decapitation becomes a fluid concept (as it has) that Muslims across the world can fill with other sorts of grievances that legitimise their action, it is not difficult to understand how southern insurgents have adopted the practice of beheading.

Thus, not only do the Patani insurgents draw their inspiration from the historical continuities of the practice of beheading within Thai and Muslim histories but they also tap into neo/jihadist symbolic and semantic rhetoric.

The separatist insurgency's use of extreme violence and more particularly the practice of beheading appears to be effective as Thai Buddhists choose to desert their villages rather than having to face separatist violence, allowing the insurgency to reclaim control over sacred ancestral geographical spaces. Nonetheless, although, a majority of Thai Buddhists has fled the region, the insurgents' terror campaign has also sparked strong feelings of nationalism among those Buddhists who have chosen to stay and protect their homeland, generating a significant increase in small arms proliferation in the region under the benevolent eye of the Thai state [21]. Where recapture of the land for some equates with independence, it is a synonym for the loss of territory and ultimately of sovereignty for others. In fact, the southern politics of fear is a process largely bounded by a conventional notion of territory in which terror reigns, transforming and reconfiguring the geosocial spaces of southern Thailand and subsequently enforcing political change.

While Thai Buddhists describe decapitations as "hotrai" or atrocious, beheadings are used above all for their high emotional intensity impact on its audiences. In the context of southern Thailand, decapitation and other forms of extreme violence are used primarily to frighten the Thai Buddhist community, ultimately seeking to push them to leave the region while at the same time inspiring the Melayu Muslims either to join the struggle or stop collaborating with the enemy.

In failing to do so, Melayu Muslims are likely to be branded munafiq and in most cases will be punished, often by death. In some cases, the insurgents have threatened to cut off the ears of fellow Muslims who would disregard their warnings [22]. Threats of mutilation or beheading illustrate the way the insurgency uses fear of imminent physical harm or death to keep the Melayu community in line and their religious counterparts in disarray. In 2006, after 19-year-old Salahudin Toja was shot dead, his face was hacked beyond recognition [23]. The following year, in 2007, a 58-year-old Muslim assistant headman was killed, then after his attackers failed to decapitate him, he was crucified on two crossed planks and left to be found on a side road ([24,25]). In 2009, a young Melayu Muslim was found with his head and arms severed.

When observing the casualty data on Southern Thailand, the transformative process of the struggle into a cosmic war becomes particularly evident. Statistics reveal that insurgent violence (and beheadings) target mainly the civilian population followed by civil servants and security personnel. The primary victims of insurgent beheadings are Thai Buddhist civilians.

When examining more closely the professional activities of beheading and general separatist violence victims in southern Thailand, a similar pattern can be found between the base and extreme types of violence. The victims' professions are particularly informative on the insurgency's re-identification process of the enemy. The insurgents not only have identified the state representatives and the Thai Buddhist civilian population as the kafir enemy that has to be crushed, but also any Melayu Muslim who would be in a line of work that can be affiliated with the state.

Ultimately, the insurgent use of beheadings and other types of extreme violence in Southern Thailand, although an outgrowth of the movement's transformation of the struggle into a cosmic war, can be interpreted as psychological operations in guerrilla warfare. The Patani practice of decapitation falls within a psychological strategy of "terrorism spectacle" which targets "the population, all population, one's troops, the enemy troops and the civilian population" [26] in order to win its audience's minds and hearts.

In Iraq, the beheadings of westerners are spectacle images destined to punish, humiliate and terrify a Western audience ([27], p. 30; [28]). In Southern Thailand, although the beheadings of kafir and munafiq present similar cognitive functions, they are, unlike the Iraqi experience, specifically targeted towards a much smaller immediate localised collective audience—*i.e.*, the Thai Buddhists and Melayu Muslim communities inhabiting the three southern border provinces of Thailand. Because their target audience is not the international community but a smaller pool of witnesses, Patani insurgents have not or rarely advertised their acts of beheading in the media. When these have eventually found their way onto the Internet, it was aimed at enhancing the Patani insurgents' profile amongst (neo)jihadist circles and legitimising their claims to a defensive jihad. A possible explanation for the different situations in the two countries may lay in the divergence of registry within each insurgency's neojihadist discourse. Despite the glocalisation of neojihadism in Southern Thailand, the Patani struggle remains a localised conflict and the direct target audience of insurgent violence is the local community. The movement's ultimate preoccupation remains the creation of an independent Patani Darussalam rather than the re-establishment of a caliphate. Unlike in Iraq, the anti-western dimension is absent from the Patani neojihadist locus. However, although anti-western sentiments are not explicitly apparent they are not rejected either, they simply are not instrumentalised within the Patani rhetoric. Iraqi beheadings and Patani decapitations respectively target different audiences, diffuse different messages and seek a different type of publicity. Patani decapitations seek a more immediate impact on the ground. On this, the insurgents are clear: "Our fighters behead these victims because they want to spread fear and reach independence [of the Patani state] quickly" [29].

Therefore, it can be reasonably argued that the movement adopted the practice of beheading in their leading of a new campaign of terror for strategic purposes. In fact, it has been "knocked off" from the neojihadist arsenal of fear and terror tactics for its (perceived) propensity to trigger political change but also revived both a local historical tradition, which distinctively differentiates it from the Middle Eastern experiences. Hence, as the southern separatist insurgency progressively positions itself within the periphery of neojihadism, it is therefore not surprising that the insurgents have also adopted the use of extreme violence in addition to the jihadist rhetoric in the conduct of its struggle.

Finally, while insurgent beheadings are at the same time strategically causing the Thai Buddhists to flee their homes and hardening their attitudes towards the Melayu Muslims, it is also alienating the Patani community and its religious leaders who cannot condone the use of decapitation in the three southern border provinces. This begs the question of whether the separatist insurgency's use of beheading as a method of execution, although relatively "successful" so far, will not become in the long term counter-productive, as it was for Al Qaeda in Iraq which perceived the Iraqi beheadings as potentially damaging the organisation's cause by alienating Muslims ([14], p. 607; [30], p. 317). The absence of reported beheadings after June 2009 suggests that the community's disapproval of the practice may have gained the upper hand pushing the militants to abandon their use of this type of extreme violence in the conduct of their struggle.

5. Conclusions

In their transformation of an almost century old struggle into a cosmic war against the Thai state, the separatist terrorist insurgent movement in Southern Thailand adopted and glocalised a new locus of resistance located within the neojihadist sphere, propelling the struggle to unprecedented levels of violence. Not only have the insurgents knocked off some of their ideological ground from neojihadist radicalism but also some of its most extreme violent praxis, morphing in effect the southern conflict into a glocalised jihad.

In a sense, neojihadism has become the culture of reference from which violent Muslim radical groups can pick and choose elements that will be transferred and adapted to their needs. However, the process of praxio–theolo–ideological transference is not a straightforward one and is heavily influenced if not conditioned by the host culture, particularly in the different forms these consecutive specific violent manifestations will take. Therefore, to understand the specific forms in which transferred violence(s) will manifest itself in a particular culture, it is necessary to consider not only the global culture of reference but also the subculture(s) of reference within the host culture. As such, the specific form of manifestation of contemporary Patani beheadings can be better understood within the cultures of reference of the host culture.

The insurgency's adoption of extreme violence, in particular beheadings, results from the process of praxio–theolo–ideological transference of neojihadism and these new forms of violence are radically transforming the nature of Patani terrorism. While the perception that neojihadism and its violent praxis may be an adaptable blueprint to any Muslim identity conflict, the shapes, forms and significance that a violent glocalised jihad may take will depend on the local cultures of reference and the insurgent movement's ultimate pursued goal itself, *i.e.*, an independent Patani Darussalam, which demonstrates how the current movement is shaped by a convergence of global and local forces under the impulse of globality. While global neojihadism impacts on the movement's mechanism of transference, the local Patani culture of reference continues to shape the struggle, while at the same time giving birth to a mediated glocalised jihad.

Conflicts of Interest

The author declares no conflict of interest.

References and Notes

1. Andries Teeuw, and David Wyatt. *Hikayat Patani. The Story of Patani*. The Hague: Martinus Nijhoff, 1970.
2. Sukree Ibrahim. *History of the Malay Kingdom of Patani*. Athens: Ohio University, Center for International Studies, 1985.
3. Daniel Perret, Srisuchat Ammara, and Thanasuk Sombun. *Études sur l'Histoire du Sultanat de Patani*. Paris: École française d'Extrême-Orient, 2004.
4. Virginie Andre. "Southern Thailand: A Cosmic War?" In *Radicalisation Crossing Borders: New Directions in Islamist and Jihadist Political, Intellectual and Theological Thought and Practice*. Edited by Sayed Khatab, Muhammad Bakashmar and Ela Ogru. Melbourne: Global Terrorism Research Centre, Monash University, 2009, pp. 169–89.
5. Virginie Andre. "Globalization: A New Driving Force in Southern Thailand". In *Terrorism and Social Exclusion: Misplaced Risk—Common Security*. Edited by David Wright-Neville and Anna Halafoff. Cheltenham: Edward Elgar Publishing, 2010, pp. 116–35.
6. Virginie Andre. "From Colonialist to Infidel: Framing the Enemy in Southern Thailand's 'Cosmic War.'" In *Culture, Religion and Conflict in Muslim Southeast Asia: Negotiation Tense Pluralisms*. Edited by Joseph Camilleri and Sven Schottmann. Oxon: Routledge, 2012, pp. 109–25.
7. Human Rights Watch. *No One is Safe. Insurgent Attacks on Civilians in Thailand's Southern Border Provinces*. Bangkok: Human Rights Watch, 2007.
8. Mark Juergensmeyer. *Terror in the Mind of God: The Global Rise of Religious Violence*. Berkeley: University of California Press, 2003.
9. Pete Lentini. "The Transference of Neojihadism: Towards a Process Theory of Transnational Radicalisation." In *Radicalisation Crossing Borders: New Directions in Islamist and Jihadist Political, Intellectual and Theological Thought and Practice*. Edited by Sayed Khatab, Muhammad Bakashmar and Ela Ogru. Melbourne: Global Terrorism Research Centre, Monash University, 2009, pp. 1–32.
10. Virginie Andre, and Ela Orgu. *Mapping Violence in Southern Thailand*. Melbourne: Global Terrorism Research Centre, Monash University, 2011.
11. Virginie Andre. "Neojihadism and YouTube: Patani Militant Propaganda Dissemination and Radicalization." *Asian Security* 8 (2012): 27–53.
12. Virginie Andre. "The Janus Face of New Media Propaganda: The Case of Patani Neojihadist YouTube Warfare and Its Islamophobic Effect on Cyber-Actors." *Islam and Christian-Muslim Relations* 25 (2014): 335–56.
13. Pete Lentini. "Antipodal Terrorists? Accounting for Differences in Australian and Global Neojihadists." In *The Globalization and Political Violence: Globalization's Shadow*. Edited by Richard Devetak and Christopher Hugues. London: Routledge, 2008, pp. 181–202.

14. Lisa Campbell. "The Use of Beheadings by Fundamentalist Islam." *Global Crime* 7 (2006): 583–614.
15. Interview by Virginie Andre with former military general, Bangkok 2008.
16. Arjun Appadurai. "Dead Certainty: Ethnic Violence in the Era of Globalization." *Public Culture* 10 (1998): 225–47.
17. Heinrich Schäfer. "The Janus Face of Religion: On the Religions Factor in 'New Wars.'" *Numen* 51 (2004): 407–37.
18. David Camroux, and Don Pathan. "Borders of/on the Mind, Borders in the Jungle: Islamic Insurgency and Ethno-Religious Irredentism in Southern Thailand". In *Promoting Conflict or Peace through Identity*. Edited by Nikki Slocum-Bradley. Aldershot: Ashgate Publishing, 2008, pp. 82–102.
19. Consuelo Corradi. "Identity and Extreme Violence—Some Elements for a Definition of Violence in Modernity." In *Issues and Trends in Italian Sociology*. Edited by Alessandro Cavalli. Naples: Scriptaweb, 2007, pp. 85–110.
20. BBC RADIO 4. "Islam and the Sword." BBC Podcast, 2 October 2006.
21. On arms proliferation in Southern Thailand, please kindly refer to Diana Sarosi, and Janjira Sombutpoonsiri. *Rule by the Gun: Armed Civilians and Firearms Proliferation in Southern Thailand*. Bangkok: Nonviolence International Southeast, 2009.
22. Separatist leaflet. "From violent incidents occurring presently which build confusion and unrest from the news received." Undated.
23. "Four More Killed in Shootings in South." *The Nation*, 17 October 2006.
24. "Muslim Crucified, Two Buddhists Beheaded in Thailand: Police." *Agence France Press*, 28 November 2007.
25. "The Necessity of Moderation." *Bangkok Post*, 4 December 2007.
26. Tayacan. *Psychological Operations in Guerrilla Warfare*. Washington: Congressional Research Service, Library of Congress, 1984.
27. Jean-Claude Burger. "Journalisme Télévisuel." In *La Révolution Internet*. Edited by Antoine Char and Roch Côté. Quebec: Presses Universitaires du Quebec, 2009, pp. 21–32.
28. Victoria Fontan. *Voices from Post-Saddam Iraq: Living With Terrorism, Insurgency, and New Forms of Tyranny*. Westport: Praeger Security International, 2008.
29. Marc Askew. "A Tale of Two Insurgents." *Bangkok Post*, 19 July 2009.
30. Pete Lentini, and Muhammad Bakashmar. "Jihadist Beheading: A Convergence of Technology, Theology, and Teleology?" *Studies in Conflict and Terrorism* 30 (2007): 303–25.

Boko Haram: Religion and Violence in the 21st Century

John O. Voll

Abstract: Boko Haram in Nigeria provides an important example of the combination of religion and violence in the conditions of the twenty-first century. It is both a movement in the pattern of religiously-justified violence and a significant representative of the emergence of new types of modern terrorism in recent years. This article examines both of these aspects of Boko Haram as an example of religious violence. In the general development of religiously justified violence, Boko Haram is the heir to a long jihad tradition in West Africa. Its emergence follows well-established patterns of older militant Muslim groups, but it also departs significantly from those patterns as it shapes itself as a movement in the patterns of contemporary, twenty-first century modes of religious violence. Boko Haram is also identified, in twenty-first century terms, as a religious terrorist organization. As a religious terrorist group, it fits the pattern of what David Rapoport calls the fourth wave—the religious wave—of modern terrorism. However, in the second decade of the twenty-first century, Boko Haram exhibits characteristics of a new style of religious terrorism that is more like the so-called Islamic State than the older type of terrorist organization of al-Qa'idah.

Reprinted from *Religions*. Cite as: Voll, J.O. Boko Haram: Religion and Violence in the 21st Century. *Religions* **2015**, *6*, 1182–1202.

1. Introduction

"Boko Haram is an Islamic Revolution." [1]. This statement by Mallam Sanni Umaru, the acting leader of Boko Haram in 2009 affirmed the religious identity and mission of the organization after the killing of its founder, Muhammad Yusuf. Beginning as a small group of young Islamist activists in northeast Nigeria around 2002, Boko Haram, within a decade, became internationally identified with groups like the so-called Islamic State (IS) as "the poster boys of extremism and radicalisation" ([2], p. 5). Its importance was recognized by both its allies and its enemies. IS accepted Boko Haram as its province in West Africa in 2014 and the United States Department of State designated it as a Foreign Terrorist Organization. This rapid development and global visibility make Boko Haram an important example of the combination of religion and violence in the 21st century.

Violence by religiously-identified groups is an increasingly important element of global affairs and local social hostilities around the world. In the words of a major study of global religious conflict in the twenty-first century, "religiously motivated violence has become a pervasive element of modern conflicts."([3], p. 1). Religious violence has a long history in most of the world's major religious traditions, but in recent modern history its nature changed significantly. "Religion," as defined by many social scientists, was not seen as a major element in modern-style socio-political violence during much of the twentieth century. Scholars note that in 1968, for example, none of the groups identifiable as international terrorist organizations in a major databank "could be classified as 'religious'" ([4], p. 42). However, by 1995, 25 out of the 58 international terrorist organizations identified in the database could be classified as "religious" ([4], p. 42). Increasingly, "religious" terrorism dominates discussions of terrorism although terrorism takes many different forms. Similarly, the broader phenomena of religious violence involve more than terrorism, and what a Pew study identifies as "social hostilities involving religion" also increased dramatically in the first decade of the twenty-first century ([5], p. 7). This development was unexpected in the world of secular scholarship. As Mark Juergensmeyer notes, "No one in the secular world could have predicted that the first confrontations of the twenty-first century would involve, of all things, religion." ([6], p. 130).

With its self-identification as a religious revolution, Boko Haram is an important example of how religious violence is justified by extremist militants and how traditions of legitimized religious violence evolve in the contexts of globalization and new technologies in the twenty-first century. In addition, since Boko Haram is described as a terrorist organization by many people, it also provides an important example of the changing nature of terrorist organizations. Its experience and history suggest that an important new wave of terrorism is visible in the contemporary world. So Boko Haram needs to be viewed both within the traditions of religiously justified violence, especially in West Africa, and as a representative of a new kind of terrorist phenomenon.

Many descriptions of Boko Haram have been written in recent years [7–10]. Briefly, Boko Haram arose out of a complex cluster of Islamic reformist teachers and groups in northern Nigeria in the 1990s. By 2002, one of the groups, under the leadership of a religious scholar and student leader, Muhammad Yusuf, gained visibility as an activist Salafi organization, that is, an organization characterized "by being literalist and puritanical in its interpretation of the Qur'an and *hadiths*." ([7], p. 47). After some clashes with police and armed attacks on some villages by the group, the organization entered a teaching and organizing period in which it became the Society of the People of the Sunnah for Propagation and Jihad (*Jamā'ah ahl al-sunnah lil-da'wah wa al-jihad*). As Mallam Sanni Umaru, the interim leader of Boko Haram in 2009 explained, "Boko Haram" is a description of its position that "Western Civilization" (Boko) is forbidden (haram) [1], rather than the formal name of the group. The organization changed course in 2009 when Muhammad Yusuf was killed by the police, and moved steadily in the direction of militantly violent campaigns to gain control of the region. Although there was some splintering of the group, Muhammad Yusuf's successor, Abubakar Shekau, led the group into more international networking in an effort to establish an extremist Salafi-style state in Nigeria with ties to a global jihad and caliphate.

The goal of this essay is not to present another account of the history of the group but, rather, to examine the movement as an example of two intertwined types of religious violence: the general religiously-legitimized violence that in the Islamic tradition is associated with jihad, and the more specific modern and contemporary manifestation of religious violence as religious terrorism.

Religious Violence and Terrorism

In examining the relationships between religion and violence in the contemporary world, it is important to distinguish between the more general evolution of forms of religious violence and the specific development of modern and contemporary religious terrorism. In recent years, some people have argued that religion itself, especially monotheism, legitimizes violence [11] or, in the words of the polemical critic of religion, Christopher Hitchens, "religion poisons everything" ([12], p. 13). However, although most people do not advocate violence in general terms, there is broad acceptance of the idea that some violence is legitimate, as in self-defense or in the historical concepts of just war.

Major religious traditions have concepts of religiously justified violence and world history presents narratives of "holy wars" from ancient times to the present. In the modern era, the legitimizing of state violence was often expressed in more secular terms, but the major twentieth century conflicts like the two World Wars and the Cold War were viewed within the framework of a secular morality that justified violence. At the beginning of the twenty-first century, these forms of what Mark Juergensmeyer calls "cosmic war" became more explicitly justified within the framework of the major historic religions. In his broad comparative study of violent religious movements, Juergensmeyer concludes, "It is not so much that religion has become politicized, but that politics have become religionized. Worldly struggles have been lifted into the high proscenium of sacred battle." ([6], p. 131).

Debates among religious leaders and policy makers about the religious and moral justifications for violence and war are important parts of political life in the twenty-first century. Long established criteria for just war "suggesting that war is justified only when certain conditions are met" are being questioned as the technologies of warfare change ([13], p. 337). These issues of moral justification for violence are not just related to the actions of extremist non-state organizations and terrorists, but they also involve state policies as well. The use of drones by states in fighting terrorist groups, for example, "potentially alters the parameters of *ad bellum* ['how one determines the justice of *going* to war'] and *in bello* ['how one determines what one can do *in* war'] just war principles" ([13], p. 338). Similarly, discussions about emergence of new military power related to waging "cyberwar" sometimes involve traditional issues of defining the nature of just war [14].

It is, however, the violent actions of non-state organizations claiming religious justification for that violence that represent the most visible assertions of religious violence in the contemporary world. In what Juergensmeyer calls the "global rebellion" involving "religious challenges to the secular state," most major historic religious traditions—Christian, Muslim, Jewish, Hindu, Sikh, and Buddhist—have been used to give legitimacy to religious violence [15]. Some analysts argue that many of these groups are not "fundamentally religious" and that issues of "national, cultural, and linguistic identity" are also significant elements in their violent extremism ([16], pp. 18–19). Few groups can be easily identified as purely religious, and religion is an element in ethnic and national identities, as well as often being a part of secular radical ideologies. However, in the late twentieth and early twenty-first centuries, for an increasing proportion of violent revolutionary movements, it is religious tradition that provides the legitimizing identity of the movements.

Although these groups utilize the vocabulary and symbolic repertoire of the historic religions, they are creating "new forms of religiosity" ([6], p. 137) that reflect the realities of the globalized world of the twenty-first century. Jeurgensmeyer concludes that these militant opposition groups "have done far more than resuscitate archaic ideas of religious rule. They have created something new: a synthesis of religion and modern politics" ([15], p. 263). Michael Walzer, in his study of the emergence of "religious counterrevolutions" in India, Israel, and Algeria, comes to a similar conclusion. In the religious counterrevolutions responding to the secular movements of liberation, religion is not old-style, conservative traditionalism; it appears "in militant, ideological, and politicized forms—modern even in its anti-modernism" ([17], p. 28).

Boko Haram provides an important example of this development with its claims to be engaging in a true jihad to establish a new caliphate. In the framework of West African history, Boko Haram can be seen as part of a centuries-old tradition of jihad—of militant opposition to rulers viewed as non-Islamic and rejection of social practices judged not to be in accord with Islam. However, Boko Haram's militant Islamism is not just a continuation of older religious militancy, it also is a product of contemporary Muslim radical beliefs identified as Salafism. In this way, in teaching and practice, Boko Haram shows significant departures from the historic Muslim understandings of both jihad and caliphate. Its relationship to contemporary Salafism and historic jihadism is part of the ideological and political conflicts in contemporary Nigeria [18]. Its distinctiveness, reflecting the new global modes of religious violence, is that "it is the first Islamic group in Nigeria to carry out an ideological hybridization and synthesis of the theologico-juridico resources of the global *jihadi-Salafism* coupled with the cultural framing of the historical tradition of *tajdid* [religious renewal] in northern Nigeria, specifically the *jihadi* legacy of Uthman Dan Fodio" [19].

In West Africa, a long tradition of militant Muslim revivalism involving jihads exists, and Boko Haram provides an important case study in how a longstanding historic framework of religious violence is reshaped and rearticulated in the conditions of the twenty-first century. While Boko Haram exhibits continuities with past movements of Muslim activism, it also is an example of the new-style movements of religious violence that have emerged in recent years. To support this conclusion, this essay compares Boko Haram with pre-modern jihad movements like that of Uthman dan Fodio, twentieth century movements like Maitatsine in Nigeria, and contemporary movements like the Islamic State and al-Qa'idah. This analysis concludes that Boko Haram is a major example of the new styles of religious social movement organizations emerging in the age of what Sidney Tarrow calls "the new transnational activism" [20].

Boko Haram is also seen as a terrorist organization, and represents an important example of new types of terrorism that have emerged in the twenty-first century. Not all violent religious organizations are terrorist. Religious militias may be violent in their methods but they are not necessarily terrorist, although analysts tend to use a variety of definitions of terrorism. There was a general consensus that al-Qa'idah, as led by Osama bin Laden, was a terrorist organization. However, especially in the years following his death, new violent religiously-identified groups have emerged and represent new organizations of religiously-identified violence. The most prominent of these is the so-called Islamic State or ISIS, and reflecting the changing nature of these militant organizations, Audrey Kurth Cronin argues that although ISIS "uses terrorism as a tactic, it is not really a terrorist organization at all" ([21], p. 88). In contrast to al-Qa'idah, ISIS has a large military force and controls and administers territory. In Cronin's words, ISIS is "a pseudo-state led by a conventional army" ([21], p. 88). Boko Haram is similar to ISIS in these terms.

ISIS and Boko Haram provide important examples of how religious terrorism is evolving. In an influential conceptualization, David Rapoport describes the evolution of modern terrorism in terms of four waves, with beginnings in the late nineteenth century. The fourth wave, beginning late in the twentieth century, is the wave of religious terrorism, and in Rapoport's analysis, "Islam is at the heart of the wave." ([22], p. 61). The Iranian Islamic Revolution in 1978–1979 and the jihad opposing the Soviet invasion and occupation of Afghanistan in the 1980s are seen as important in the launching of this fourth wave. ([22], p. 61). As an organization engaged in religious terrorism, Boko Haram can be viewed as a part of this fourth wave. However, the changing nature of religious violence and the emergence of new types of militant organizations suggest that Boko Haram might also be part of a new, "fifth wave" of terrorism.

2. Boko Haram and Religiously-Legitimated Violence

Religious violence in the form of militant Muslim movements of reform is an important part of West African history. Beginning in the late seventeenth century, a series of activist teachers criticized the pluralist mixture of Islamic and indigenous cultures that characterized states and societies in the region. They sought to create institutions and practices in accord with Islam as understood in the more exclusivist terms of conservative scholars. Some of the resulting groups clashed with the political rulers in a series of jihads, creating a jihad tradition of militant Muslim revivalism extending from the seventeenth century to the end of the nineteenth century (and beyond). While the jihad movements were distinctive in their local manifestations, they were historically connected and shared many characteristics [23,24]. This jihad tradition provides an historic foundation for popular acceptance of religious violence in the cause of religious renewal. Boko Haram, in the twenty-first century, is heir to this jihad legacy and the similarities and differences between the contemporary movement and the earlier tradition help to show both the continuities and changes in the nature of religious violence in the twenty-first century.

2.1. Pre-Modern Religiously-Legitimized Violence in West Africa

The jihad tradition was part of the long historic process of Islamization in West African societies. Islam was brought to the region by merchants and itinerant religious teachers in the period after the original Muslim conquests in the Middle East. These early migrant Muslims became part of the local societies and the result was a blending of Islamic and indigenous local elements in social and political institutions. However, this development also meant that the people became aware of and respected Muslim concepts and teachings, so general opposition to oppressive rulers eventually could be expressed in Islamic terms. Muslim scholars who were critical of the synthesis of Islamic and indigenous elements became both reformers of religious life and leaders of political opposition with the goal of establishing Islamic states. In this framework, violence against the political authorities was legitimated in Islamic terms as jihad in the path of God. Religion defined an identity that opposed pluralist syncretism in favor of a clearly defined, exclusivist community.

Already in medieval times, Muslim scholars in West Africa discussed when religious violence in the form of jihad was appropriate and their works, especially the writings of Muhammad ibn Abd al-Karim al-Maghili (d. c. 1505), remained influential in the following centuries. Al-Maghili wrote a major study in the late fifteenth century in response to questions posed by the ruler of the Songhay Empire, the most powerful state in West Africa at the time. Al-Maghili explicitly approved jihad against those who professed Islam but continued indigenous local religious practices. These were people who "have idols…[and] venerate certain trees and make sacrifices to them," among other practices ([25], pp. 76–77). He stated that they are "polytheists without doubt" and said that there "is no doubt that *jihad* against them is more fitting and worthy than *jihad* against [born] unbelievers who do not say: 'There is no god save God'" ([25], p. 78). In this framework, jihad against corrupt self-identified Muslims took priority over jihad against non-believers. Jihad was a movement of purification more than a movement of conversion.

Al-Maghili also viewed jihad as the means for opposing unjust rulers, even if the violence resulted in killing Muslims. In his instructions, for example, in dealing with a "land having an *amīr* from among those chiefs whom you described as levying [unlawful] taxes and being oppressive and evildoing and failing to set matters right," he says, "If you can bring to an end his oppression of the Muslims without harm to them so that you set up among them a just *amīr*, then do so, even if that leads to killing and the killing of many of the oppressors and their supporters and the killing of many of your supporters, for whoever is killed from among them is the worst of slain men and whoever is killed from among your people is the best of martyrs." ([25], p. 81).

These themes of opposition to mixing indigenous and Islamic practices and to oppressive rulers who did not follow Muslim teachings are central to the West African jihad tradition. Beginning in the later seventeenth century with a movement led by Imam Nasir al-Din (d. 1674) in what is modern-day Southern Mauritania, a chain of interconnected purificationist movements developed. Jihads in Futo Toro and Foto Jalon in the Senegambia established this chain. "At the fundamental levels of Islamization—spreading literacy and building a consciousness of a dar al-Islam—it would be hard to overestimate the importance of the two Futas and of their influence over the vast region stretching from southern Mauritania to Sierra Leone. By their 'success' in at least establishing regimes that could lay claim to an Islamic identity, they 'solved' the great problem of legitimation." ([23], p. 137).

Throughout the savannah region of West Africa in the following centuries, a number of reformist teachers led movements and jihads which resulted in the creation of Islamically-legitimated states. They were often directly connected by networks of students and teachers who were inspired by previous jihads. At the beginning of the nineteenth century in what is modern Northern Nigeria, Uthman dan Fodio, a scholar and member of the Qadiriyya Sufi brotherhood, preached a message of reform that led to conflict with local rulers and the declaration of a jihad in 1805. His victory resulted in the creation of the Sokoto Caliphate, which became a center in the networks of scholars leading later jihads. Al-Hajj Umar al-Tall (d. 1864), for example, who led a major nineteenth century jihad in West Africa, spent a number of years in Sokoto and married a granddaughter of Uthman dan Fodio. The jihad led by Uthman dan Fodio and the state that he established are the quintessential examples of the West African jihad tradition.

2.2. Pattern of the Development of Pre-Modern Jihad Movements

In the histories of the pre-modern militant groups, four stages are usual. The first is the gathering of a group of dedicated students around a particular teacher, who is distinguished from the other teachers at the time by an emphasis on the need for reform. Such teacher-student circles were (and are) common throughout Muslim West Africa and most do not become movements or organized groups. However, some of these circles attract larger numbers of followers, and the second stage is one in which the followers of the teacher become a more consciously organized group, while the teacher continues to develop a distinctive message. If the emerging organization experiences resistance from the local population or the ruler, the group tends to withdraw from direct involvement in society. Sometimes the leader and his followers may move to a more isolated area, often citing the example of the Prophet Muhammad who undertook the migration (*hijra*) from Mecca to what became Medina in Arabia. In this stage, the movement becomes a more formally organized association with an emerging ideological identification of Muslim renewal and reform. Again, such self-contained groups are part of Muslim life in West Africa and many do not move to the next stage, open conflict with religious and political establishments.

It is in the third stage—of open conflict—that the mission of the group becomes a jihad and the movement becomes one of legitimized religious violence. Large organizations of opposition become a threat to rulers and attempts at suppressing the groups can lead to warfare. The leader declares a jihad and the movement becomes an army as well as a movement of religious reform and purification. As an organization of opposition to the ruler, the group becomes an alternative state. The fourth stage of development depends upon the results of the jihad. When the group wins the jihad, a new state is established; when they lose, the organization disappears but usually the memory and teaching survive to inspire later movements.

In the case of dan Fodio, he was a popular religious scholar and teacher who gained a large following in Gobir. When he was opposed by the local religious establishment and attacked by the armed forces of the Sultan of Gobir, he and his followers withdrew to a safer place, from which they declared jihad against Gobir. "This was a new beginning, a new 'Muslim space.' Now the past of Hausaland was classified as Jahiliyya [pre-Islamic paganism]; the true Muslim community had performed *hijra*, sworn allegiance to Uthman, formed the Islamic community, and declared the '*jihad* of the sword'." ([26], p. 144). The result was the establishment of the Sokoto Caliphate, which ruled a significant territory in northern Nigeria and surrounding areas. This political institution has continued in existence in various forms into the twenty-first century. Although it is no longer an independent state, in the twenty-first century, the descendant of Uthman dan Fodio who is the twentieth Sultan of Sokoto is considered to be the leader of the Muslims of Nigeria.

2.3. Boko Haram and the Historic Jihad Movement Pattern

The development of Boko Haram in the twenty-first century follows this pattern of growth to a remarkable degree. Even though its violence is extreme and most Nigerians view its claims as radical and outside of acceptable Islamic traditions, it is recognizably within the long traditions of militant jihad in West and Central Africa.

Many reform-minded Muslim teachers and students were active in the second half of the twentieth century. John Paden described the great diversity of these groups and organizations in Nigeria that were active at the time of the beginning of Boko Haram and many are still active today. Few actually became militant in their actions ([27], pp. 27–38). Teacher-student networks resulted in a number of groupings around locally prominent teachers. One such teacher was the founder of Boko Haram, Muhammad Yusuf. Muhammad Yusuf was associated with important teachers, and was a leader in reformist student groups in Maiduguri, where he became a preacher in a major mosque. When local religious leaders opposed his teachings, he established his own school and then built a mosque which became a center for radicals holding Salafi views with literalist interpretations of the Qur'an and advocates of activist purification of state and society. He named the mosque after Ahmad Ibn Taymiyya, a thirteenth century Muslim thinker whose strict interpretations influenced later activist reformers from Muhammad ibn Abd al-Wahhab to twentieth century and twenty-first century jihadists.

During this second phase of Boko Haram development, Muhammad Yusuf developed a religious ideology of opposition to Western cultural dominance, building on the intellectual traditions of historic and contemporary militant Salafism. His followers clashed with police from time to time, but they tended to withdraw from society, sometimes moving into relatively remote areas. However, as security forces increased pressure on the movement, it "morphed into more of an urban phenomenon" taking actions against "consumption of alcohol and other non-Islamic practices" with a methodology "very much according to the example of Dan Fodio" ([28], p. 4). In 2009 the Nigerian police undertook a major suppression operation in the course of which Muhammad Yusuf was killed. Under the leadership of his successor, Abubakar Shekau, the group declared a jihad in 2010 and carried out its first coordinated attacks in that year ([29], p. 18).

2.4. Boko Haram and Historic Movements Compared

As a movement of activist (and sometimes belligerent) religious reform, the early history of Boko Haram fits well into the pattern of the early stages of the historic West African jihad movements. In examining the nature of religious violence in the twenty-first century, comparing the nature of Boko Haram as a jihad movement with the jihad (third) stage of the historic jihad movements may be useful. Two themes of reform, already defined by al-Maghili in the fifteenth century, provide important areas for comparison: opposition to popular religious syncretism and opposition to unjust rulers who may profess Islam but do not rule in accord with the Qur'an and Traditions of the Prophet.

Opposition to blending together Islamic and indigenous local practices and symbols was an important part of the historic jihad movements. The respect given to particular natural elements, as in regarding trees or springs as sacred, is an example of the continuation of non-Islamic practices that came to be regarded as part of popular Muslim life. Reformers like al-Maghili advocated destroying such symbols and fighting their guardians if necessary (leading to jihads). This opposition to popular religious customs, regarded as idolatrous superstitions, is a significant element in the teachings of Muslim renewalists throughout the Muslim world. It was an important part of the message of reform of Ibn Taymiyya and was a core part of the Wahhabi tradition begun by Muhammad ibn Abd al-Wahhab in eighteenth century Arabia [30,31].

The goal of the reformers was to bring local practice into accord with the historically-evolving cosmopolitan standard Islam. Just as a standardized version of "classical" Arabic became a *lingua franca* for travelers and scholars throughout the Muslim world, a standardized form of Sunni Islam provided guidelines for reformers who could then advocate the socio-moral reconstruction of their own societies. Although local religious and political establishments could dispute details of interpretation, they could not reject the general model, based as it was on a strict and quite literal understanding of the Qur'an and Traditions of the Prophet. In this way, the understanding of Islam presented by the militant reformer was reinforced by the definitions of "pure" Islam as understood by many scholars in the broader global Muslim community (the "ummah").

Boko Haram and other movements of militant Salafism in the twenty-first century are also strongly opposed to what they view as the pollution of "pure" Islam by mixing Muslim ideas and practices with non-Islamic and anti-Islamic elements. The informal name of the group—Boko Haram—emphasizes this aspect of the group's message: "Western Civilization is forbidden." The statement by the acting leader in 2009 emphasizes the cultural dimension of this position: "We are talking of Western Ways of life which include: constitutional provisions as it relates to, for instance the rights and privileges of Women, the idea of homosexualism, lesbianism, sanctions in cases of terrible crimes…blue films, prostitution, drinking beer and alcohol and many others that are opposed to Islamic civilization." [1]; ([10], p. 14). Muhammad Yusuf argued that "present Western-style education is mixed with issues that run contrary to our beliefs in Islam." ([7], p. 48). While Muhammad Yusuf accepted the "purely technological things" of modernity, he rejected "Westernization." ([7], pp. 56–57). The syncretism opposed by Boko Haram was the mixture of local Islamic and modern Western culture visible at all levels of Nigeria society.

The cultural synthesis opposed by Boko Haram is different from that opposed by the earlier jihads and its religious violence played and plays a different role. The early jihads rejected longstanding local religious practices in the name of a more cosmopolitan and transcultural worldview. They were part of the long historical processes of the Islamization of society. Religious violence was justified as contributing to the transformation of society and strengthened important aspects of that historic evolution of society. The jihads were moving with the broader historical trends of the time.

Boko Haram, in contrast, opposes the long term societal transformations of the modern era. The processes of cosmopolitan globalization are reshaping human life around the world. Boko Haram itself is, in many ways, a product of and participant in those processes. However, its goal is to bring an end to the culture(s) created by those developments. In an era of increasingly pluralist societies, Boko Haram seeks to reverse historic trends and establish a culturally exclusivist version of contemporary society based on a narrow, literalist interpretation of Islam. Although both Boko Haram and the early jihad movements were exclusivist, the early jihadists were working within the framework of historical developments in the region, while Boko Haram are working to change the mainstreams of history.

This difference points to an important dimension of religious violence in the twenty-first century. Religious violence takes many forms and Boko Haram is an example of a distinctive mode of religious violence. Although it is opposed to important historic changes that are taking place, it is not presenting a conservative defense of existing society. In its critique of contemporary society it was initially reformist in nature. While there were occasional violent clashes between the followers of Muhammad Yusuf and the police or conflicts with other groups, the effort was aimed at changing existing society. In Islamic terms, it was a *tajdid* ("renewal") movement. However, as Boko Haram became involved in its major jihad, the goal became more explicitly to replace the old socio-political order with a new one. In the early teachings there was little mention of creating a true caliphate. By the second decade of the twenty-first century, Boko Haram joined a number of militant groups in the Muslim world in proclaiming a caliphate as the goal. With the proclamations of caliphates, the most visible religious violence in the Muslim world has tended to shift from militant tajdid movements to militant millenarianism, the type of "religious movements that expect imminent total, ultimate, this-worldly collective salvation" ([32], p. 159). Boko Haram's history reflects this development.

In opposition to unjust rulers, Boko Haram's jihad also is both similar to, and different from, the earlier jihad tradition. The major differences are in the nature of the involvements in the broader global ummah (community of believers). Both appeal to what is frequently identified as the Salafi tradition in Islamic history and both seek to legitimize their violence by showing how it is mandated or at least allowed by Islamic teachings.

Both Boko Haram and the earlier movements involve networks of teachers, students, and militants that were and are transnational. In the seventeenth and eighteenth centuries, jihads and militant movements of tajdid occurred from West Africa to Southeast Asia. To a remarkable degree, student-teacher networks including people who would be involved in these jihads brought people from these diverse areas together, especially as they went on Hajj (pilgrimage) [33,34]. These networks involved significant exchanges of ideas and facilitated developments in scholarship like the development of new approaches to the study of Traditions of the Prophet. The leaders of jihads were part of the broader cosmopolitan intellectual community of Muslim scholarship of the time. Major teachers from Mecca and Medina and in the major educational centers of the Muslim world recognized the legitimacy of the militant tajdid movements.

Although concepts of tajdid and jihad were important parts of the content of the studies in these networks, there were no direct efforts to train people how to fight jihads. The core followers in the movements were students studying the religious sciences and had little training or experience in combat. Training for jihad generally involved study of the rules regulating what was permissible and what was forbidden in fighting jihads. Uthman dan Fodio, for example, wrote a major study on the rules defining what could and could not be done in a jihad [35]. It was accepted by the participants that there were limits to the violence of jihad.

Boko Haram presents a very different picture. It is part of trans-regional networks of activists but these networks differ significantly from the earlier ones. Teachers and students interact but the theological and conceptual contents of the discourses are extremist and marginal in relationship to the broader cosmopolitan intellectual community of contemporary Islam. As a result, the majority of Muslims around the world do not view Boko Haram, and other similar movements, as legitimately engaged in jihad. This negative assessment is strengthened by the view that the contemporary militants do not act in accord with the traditionally understood rules for engaging in jihad. Longstanding rules and precedents about the treatment of women and children, for example, are ignored in the violent campaigns of Boko Haram. This difference emphasizes the dramatically uncompromising positions of Boko Haram and the resulting difficulty of negotiating with the group. Instead, it creates a significant characteristic of the new style of religious violence: violence without limitation or rules like those that shaped the concepts of just war and jihad.

Networks in which Boko Haram participates are also dramatically different in that a significant portion of network activity involves training to engage in violent conflict and terrorism. Such training efforts were absent in the earlier networks involving jihadists. The contemporary networks often become more vehicles for recruiting and training fighters than ways of presenting and advocating Islamic teachings. There is no indication that in the early jihads, recruits received training in the eighteenth century equivalents of "improvised explosive devices" (IEDs).

One significant difference between the networks of the two eras of jihad is in the technology of communication. Many analysts have noted the importance of the new electronic media in the activities of religious (and other) activist organizations [36]. Already in the 1990s, conflicts utilizing electronic resources were recognized as a new form of warfare—netwars [37]. The networks supporting religious violence in the Muslim world make very effective use of this new technology. However, networks of believing scholars and activists perform basically the same functions as they have in the past as vehicles for the exchange of ideas, with contemporary electronic exchanges of ideas being virtually instantaneous, while such exchanges in the eighteenth century often took months or years.

One of the major differences created by the new media for exchanging information is the sudden visibility that they can provide for small isolated groups. Oppositional groups in out-of-the-way places in the past frequently gained little attention outside of their own area. However, contemporary electronic media provide global audiences for even small rural movements. One of the early examples of this change is in the success of the Zapatista movement in Mexico. A local rural insurgency, opposing a repressive government, gained the attention of a network of global non-governmental humanitarian organizations. "Within days, a traditional guerrilla insurgency changed into an information-age social netwar." ([38], p. 187). The various networks of religious militants, drug and arms traders, and pop culture provide similar visibility for many different local groups.

In terms of movements engaged in religious violence in the Muslim world, the old networks of scholars and teachers provided a supportive interregional framework, but were usually not directly involved in the local organizations. During the twentieth century (in the pre-electronic media era), there were many movements of religious violence in the Muslim world, but they received minimal attention. In the 1920s, for example, a Sufi leader in Turkey, Shaykh Sa'id, led a major revolt against the Westernizing reform program of Mustafa Kemal (later Atatürk), which received little world attention, especially when compared with the attention given to the anti-Western jihad of Boko Haram. A similar contrast is between an earlier militant group in Maiduguri in the 1970s and

1980s, Maitatsine. This group had a profile very similar to the early stages of Boko Haram, with a central reformist teacher and a large number of followers who crystalized into an activist community. It represented "a classic example of millenarianism occasioned by the destruction of traditional socio-economic networks on which the wandering *mallams* [teachers] and their students...depended for their survival."([39], p. 525). However, in the days before Internet, Maitatsine received little attention outside of Nigeria. Much of the Nigerian public information about the group was the product of popular rumors [40], the geographically limited equivalent of Facebook and Twitter. When the founder of Maitatsine was killed, the movement ceased to be a significant element in religious violence. In contrast, the successor to Muhammad Yusuf in Boko Haram was able to transform the local group, which many thought would cease to exist after the killing of Muhammad Yusuf, into a globally visible jihad group. An important element in this was the increasingly effective use of the global social media by Boko Haram in the second decade of the twenty-first century.

2.5. The Evolution of Religious Violence in Contemporary History

In many areas of life, the twenty-first century is a time of major transformations. Religious violence is part of these changes, and Boko Haram is an example of the developing modes of religious violence in the contemporary world. As has been discussed, networks are important in both the old jihad traditions in West Africa and in contemporary Muslim militancy. However, the instantaneous nature of electronic media, with its immediate global visibility, changes the role of the networks. Rather than simply being the means for communication of ideas among jihadists, the networks have become part of the militant operations themselves, transforming at least part of the jihad efforts into new style "netwar jihads." Boko Haram joins IS, al-Qa'ida, and other similar groups in this new mode of religious violence.

In broader historical terms, Boko Haram can also be viewed as a renewal of an old style of opposition to unjust rule. In the West African jihads of the eighteenth century, once the initial tajdid (reform) efforts were frustrated, the jihadists strove for the creation of a new political system, not just the replacement of an unjust ruler. This transition from renewalist-reform to a millenarian vision is also part of the development of Boko Haram. However, in the twenty-first century, it represents a new form of militant opposition to the existing state system.

In the modern politics of opposition to imperialism and then to the rulers in post-colonial states, the primary vision was "revolution," either in nationalist or Marxist forms, within the system of polities conceived as "nation-states." The system of interacting sovereign states, identified with the arrangements created by the Treaties of Westphalia in 1648, became the core of European international politics and then spread to the rest of the world during the era of European imperialism. Even religious movements of opposition tended to operate within the framework of the established nation-states—the major Islamic revolution in Iran in 1979, for example, was primarily an effort to take control of the existing modern state structure in Iran. In this way, even religious oppositional violence was less oriented toward the millenarian ideal of total replacement of the political system, and more seeking to control the existing political system and Islamizing it.

By the twenty-first century, post-Westphalian polities like the European Union became important parts of the global structures for political life. In the broader context of the history of modernity, scholars like S. N. Eisenstadt and Robert Hefner note the emergence of "multiple modernities" in which modernity takes many different social, cultural, and political—and religious—forms [41,42]. These new developments not only created new establishments of political and social power, they also involved the rise of new forms of opposition.

Even before the terrorist destruction of the World Trade Center in 2001, scholars noted that global developments changed the role of religious movements. In 2000, Eisenstadt wrote, "The pivotal new development amounts to the transposition of the religious dimension, which was delegated or confined to private or secondary spheres in the classical model of the nation-state, into the central political and cultural arenas, and its significance in the constitution of novel collective identities. But…, the resurgence of religion did not entail a simple return to some traditional forms of religion, but rather a far-reaching reconstitution of this religious component." ([41], p. 600). Hefner noted three types of responses to this new global situation: pluralist acceptance of religious diversity in a competitive religious marketplace, separatist sectarianism (in Islamic terms, the hijra option), and a militant absolutist response (the jihad option). The militant alternative, an "organic and aggressive response," is "to strap on the body armor, ready one's weapons, and launch a holy war for society as a whole." ([42], p. 98). Militant religious millenarianism became a significant mode of religious opposition in twenty-first century societies, and Boko Haram is an important manifestation of this new religious violence.

Boko Haram's millenarian alternative to existing Nigerian state and society is proclaimed as a caliphate. This identification was affirmed early in 2015 when Abubakar Shekau took an oath of loyalty (*bay'a*) to the leader of IS and received recognition as the province of IS in West Africa. This development represents a "re-branding" of Boko Haram, and a shift from networking with the old-style militant terrorist organization of al-Qa'ida: "Boko Haram's merger with the Islamic State was consistent with a broader transnational trend whereby militants formerly loyal to al-Qa'ida have switched sides in favor of the more youthful, social media-savvy, and territorial-focused Islamic State." ([29], pp. 17, 21).

The alliance with IS emphasizes the new forms of religious violence in the early twenty-first century and the contrasts with the extremist groups established in the late twentieth century. These new forms involve increasingly effective use of contemporary social media to recruit and train followers and then to provide the framework for violent operations in new-style netwar jihads. While many of the older groups proclaimed their long term goal as being the establishment of an Islamic polity, often labeled a "caliphate," they usually made little effort to maintain control over significant amounts of territory. IS and Boko Haram consciously view themselves as establishing and maintaining a new territorial entity which is different from the old post-colonial nation-states. They reflect the religious violence of the twenty-first century in its millenarian form.

3. Boko Haram and Twenty-First Century Religious Terrorism

Religious terrorism is a significant aspect of religious violence in the twenty-first century and is an important dimension in the evolution of terrorism in general. The development of Boko Haram reflects key elements in the emerging nature of contemporary religious terrorism, just as it experiences some of the changes in the more general phenomena of religious violence. Specifically, Boko Haram can be viewed as a changing participant in what some scholars identify as the fourth wave of modern terrorism, possibly highlighting the emergence of a fifth wave. In these aspects of its experience, it reflects the growing importance of territoriality in religious terrorism and the emerging neo-medieval style of warfare in religious militancy.

Many analysts identify modern terrorism as a distinctive form, while recognizing that terrorism has a long history and has taken many forms. Some of the distinguishing characteristics of modern terrorism are products of modernity itself. Martha Crenshaw notes that "modernization produces an interrelated set of factors that is a significant permissive cause of terrorism, as increased complexity on all levels of society and economy create opportunities and vulnerabilities. Sophisticated networks of transportation and communication offer mobility and the means of publicity for terrorists." ([43], p. 36). Modern terrorism utilizes the resources of modern globalizing society and has evolved as modern global society itself has evolved.

3.1. The Waves of Modern Terrorism

In analyzing the evolution of modern terrorism, David Rapoport argues that there have been four waves of modern terrorism since the late nineteenth century ([22], pp. 46–73). Rapoport's framework is influential and provides a helpful foundation for examining Boko Haram as a religious terrorist organization. Rapoport's framework starts with late nineteenth century anarchists in Russia: "Modern terror began in Russia in the 1880s." ([22], p. 47). Anarchist terrorism was primarily a Western phenomenon but the second wave became global as a part of anti-colonial movements, beginning in the 1920s. The third wave, called the "New Left Wave" in this schema, was associated with the rise of radical, basically secular, ideological movements advocating revolutionary reform in the new post-colonial societies. This wave began to ebb in the 1980s, as the fourth wave—the "religious wave"—gained momentum.

The waves are not sharply separated; instead there are many continuities with different emphases. "Religious elements have always been important in modern terror because religious and ethnic identities often overlap." ([22], p. 61). However, the nationalist movements of the second and third waves primarily worked to create secular nation-states, while the new religious movements advocate new political models for state and society, within the framework of a religious tradition.

In many discussions of twentieth century religious terrorism, including Rapoport's, al-Qa'ida led by Osama bin Laden is seen as one of the prime examples of the new religious terrorism. Created within the jihad against Soviet occupation of Afghanistan, al-Qa'ida "developed over a 20-year period into the world's first truly global terrorist movement." ([44], p. 2). As a global movement, it went beyond the nationalism of the second and third waves. Each wave of terrorism has many dimensions and the identifying name is not the only feature of the wave. Nationalism is a part of all of the waves, but "each wave shaped its national elements differently." ([22], p. 47). In religious terrorism, as shown in the case of al-Qa'ida, national and ethnic identities are subordinated to the transnational message and followers are recruited globally, with the help of new social media.

Although al-Qa'ida began in a religio-national jihad to gain control of the Afghan state, it soon became a transnational network of activists. Its long term goal was the establishment of a global Islamic caliphate, but it was established as a non-state organization to organize and coordinate terrorist attacks. It advocated a strict adherence to a rigid interpretation of Islam but its basic strategic goal was the destruction the United States and its "apostate" allies in the Muslim world. In its structure—and in its mode of operation—it was not an alternative to the state nor was it prepared to manage and control significant territory. In its proclaimed vision, it was millenarian, looking forward to a time of an Islamically-pure human society, but in practice it was pragmatically operational as a terrorist organization which did not attempt to establish its own exemplary society. In contrast to the pre-modern jihad movements in West Africa and to the experience of Boko Haram in its early days, hijra in al-Qa'ida practice was to training camps in order to participate in terrorist jihad, not to establish a settled community of believers.

If al-Qa'ida is the major example of the wave of religious terrorism, then Boko Haram is both a part of that fourth wave and an emerging example of a possible new mode of terrorism. The continuity is that the basic ideology and framework are religious. Both movements are opposed to secular ideologies and are neither old-style nationalists nor heirs to the leftist radical terrorism of the third wave. Both appeal to the faith and identity of a global community of believers and can appeal to the historic legitimation of religious violence as jihad. After Muhammad Yusuf's death, Boko Haram leaders had many contacts with the broader al-Qa'ida network, especially in dealings with AQIM (al-Qa'ida in the Maghrib). The impact of these contacts could be seen in the improved explosive devices used by Boko Haram, in the adoption of the tactic of suicide bombing, and in increasingly effective use of social media ([7], pp. 85–107).

With these connections with al-Qa'ida, Boko Haram is a part of the fourth wave. However, when Boko Haram became more formally a part of global jihad, it did not do so as a franchise of al-Qa'ida. It did so by recognizing the authority of the Caliphate declared by the IS in 2014. For Boko Haram and IS, the Caliphate is the concrete expression in real time of the millenarian vision of the goal of the global jihad. It is the negation of the nation-state as a legitimate political authority and affirms the identity of the movement as an alternative state system. This characteristic shows that Boko Haram is part of a post-al-Qa'ida formation. The contrast is emphasized by the non-state nature of al-Qa'ida, with neither Bin Ladin nor his successor, Ayman al-Zawahiri, declaring himself to be Caliph.

Although the early Boko Haram did not make claims to control territory, when the organization under the leadership Abubakar Shekau conquered areas, he organized control of territory as a political entity. When Boko Haram took control of Gwoza in 2014, Shekau proclaimed that the region was now part of the Caliphate. The creation of state-like structures and the control of territory distinguish Boko Haram and IS from most of the fourth wave terrorist movements. By the second decade of the twenty-first century, even some franchises of al-Qa'ida adopted this new style of jihadism. Al-Qaida in the Arabian Peninsula (AQAP), for example, following its conquest of Al Mukalla in Yemen in April 2015 established "a civilian council and gave it a budget to pay salaries, import fuel and hire teams to clean up garbage," establishing a political administration [45]. Similarly, in Syria, although Jabhah al-Nasrah broke away from IS and maintained an affiliation with al-Qa'ida, it also created state-like administrations in territories under its control.

Audrey Kurth Cronin argues that ISIS is not simply an outgrowth from or a part of al-Qa'idah. Instead, "ISIS represents the post-al Qaeda jihadist threat." ([21], p. 87). Boko Haram is a part of this emerging "post-al Qaeda jihadist" style organization and along with ISIS possibly represents the emergence of a new—fifth—wave of modern terrorism. This fifth wave is still predominantly a form of religious violence but is a new style of organization and movement.

3.2. Neomedieval Military and New Forms of Religious Violence

A new style of military organization is associated with the statal nature of this Caliphate system. In most of the religious terrorist organizations of the fourth wave, acts of violence were targeted on particular individuals or sites. They were symbolic acts undertaken to create alarm among a target audience and to create instability. They were not undertaken to gain control of territory or to establish a concrete long term presence. Hijackings and hostage takings were developed as terrorist methods already in the third wave of terrorism, and the suicide bomber became a major tactic by the beginning of the twenty-first century. The suicide mission was used widely by al-Qa'ida and its affiliates and became "a hallmark of the organization." ([43], p. 7).

Boko Haram utilized these methods as they developed their jihad under Shekau. A suicide bombing by Boko Haram of the United Nations compound in Abuja in 2011 "was a boundary-creating attack, designed to expel foreigners and the foreign influence epitomized by the UN in Nigeria. It was also clearly designed to demonstrate to Nigeria and the world that Boko Haram's goals were no longer local in nature." ([10], pp. 19–20). However, by the second decade of the twenty-first century, the major force used by Boko Haram was its well-armed militia, which took control of territories, rather than the old-style individual terrorist attack. In this, it went beyond the usual style of fourth wave religious terrorism into an implementation of the religious terrorism in a new, millenarian wave working to establish post-Westphalian political systems in the framework of religious rather than secular polities.

The creation of a military force capable of conquering, and then maintaining control over, a territory is a feature of the emerging new style of terrorist organizations. Boko Haram emerged as a "grass roots rebellion" ([46], p. 135) by the second decade of the twenty-first century with its own military arm. A rebellion with a militia may utilize terrorism as a tactic but it is not simply a terrorist organization. Anticolonial terrorism was part of the broader movements of national grass roots rebellions against foreign imperialist control. Similarly, the revolutionary movements of the "New Left" wave, like Castro's Cuban Communist movement or radical Palestinian nationalist organizations, utilized terror as a part of their campaigns. The emergence of IS as an extremist millenarian organization different from al-Qa'ida—being an organization with its own military capacity to conquer and control territory—is in this broader pattern of terrorist activism. By 2014, Boko Haram's association with IS confirms it as another movement in this next wave of terrorism and political violence.

This new wave brings together two trends of the late twentieth century. One is the wave of developing religious terrorism in which violence is justified by a particular interpretation of a major world religious tradition. Rapoport's fourth wave includes Jewish, Hindu, Sikh, Christian, and Japanese religious terrorism, as well as Muslim ([22], p. 61). The second trend is the increasing importance of non-state military forces, ranging from private contract mercenary groups to militias and militant bands organized around ethnic, regional, or religious identities. Armed conflicts in the twenty-first century are more frequently fought between a variety of state and non-state forces than as inter-state wars. Sean McFate posits that this development involves the rise of "neomedieval" warfare as a part of the broader "reorganization and redistribution of power" in the global (and post-Westphalian) system of state and non-state actors ([47], p. 74).

Organizations of religious terror like Boko Haram and IS combine these two trends in millenarian religious organizations that have non-state armies. "Terrorism today [the second decade of the twenty-first century] embraces a neomedieval agenda. In the twentieth century when the Westphalian system was at its zenith, revolutionaries such as Mao Zedong in China, Ho Chi Minh in Vietnam, Fidel Castro in Cuba, and Che Guevara in Bolivia fought to take over states. In the post-Cold War era, groups such as al-Shabaab in the Horn of Africa, Boko Haram in West Africa, and al-Qaida worldwide fight to leave the state system altogether, abandoning the Westphalian order." ([47], p. 82).

Non-state military forces are an important part of the organizations of religious violence in the twenty-first century. They make it possible for activists to believe in the possibility of establishing the desired state and society in the present. The debates about methods and goals are not primarily the debates of the fourth wave terrorists about whether to concentrate the jihad against the "far enemy" or the "near enemy." [48]. Fourth wave terrorists understood the establishment of the Caliphate to be a long struggle. For the advocates of jihad against the near enemy, "[E]ven the establishment of the caliphate...had to await the destruction of 'apostate' local rulers," while for those advocating the battle against the far enemy, the caliphate would only be possible following the defeat of the United States, at least in the Muslim world ([48], pp. 30, 267).

Twenty-first century jihad organizations with effective military forces are willing to declare the Caliphate as existing in territories under their control. IS and Boko Haram view the Caliphate as a part of the jihad, not the jihad's distant goal. As a part of the jihad itself, their Caliphate becomes militarized, and engages in a brutality that is in contrast to the traditional jihads which recognized limitations on violence. Boko Haram's practices in controlling territories, for example, are in sharp contrast to the policies of Uthman dan Fodio in the Sokoto Caliphate. The treatment of women is an important example of the contrasts. "The tradition of educating women, and women themselves writing tracts as practical guides to both rudimentary life skills and pious behavior, was an integral part of the Sokoto Caliphate community." ([49], p. 76). In Boko Haram, women are subjugated and have little role in the organization other than as servants and slaves.

As a terrorist organization, Boko Haram is evolving away from the type of organization characteristic of Rapoport's fourth wave, like al-Qa'ida, which is networks of activists engaged in acts of terror, who justify their violence by their self-identification as warriors engaged in jihad. Fourth wave Muslim terrorists have a global Caliphate as their goal, but believe that the achievement of that goal is in the distant future. Few, if any, of the leaders, claimed to be the caliph. The new religious terrorism might be thought of as operational millenarianism, in which the goal is proclaimed as achieved, and extreme measures of repressive control are utilized in creating and maintaining a religiously-identified, post-Westphalian political order.

4. Conclusions: Boko Haram as Militant Operational Millenarianism

Movements and organizations utilizing religiously justified violence are an important part of world history. In the modern era, militant religious social movements have taken many forms and in the twenty-first century, distinctive new types have developed, reflecting both continuities with past movements of religious violence and new characteristics shaped by contemporary globalizing developments and new technologies.

Boko Haram provides an important example of these trends. By the second decade of the twenty-first century, it became a part of a proclaimed Caliphate with a non-state military force working to establish a new, post-Westphalian polity. Like IS and other new groups, its religious violence is a part of its operational millenarianism which is a jihad that attempts to convert globalization into a process of global Islamization, imposing an extremist interpretation of Islam.

The non-state military dimension of this jihad has been identified as a neomedievalism which is post-Westphalian in its nature. In broader terms, the millenarian impulse of the new religious violence shows a broader neomedievalism, with a profound continuity of millennial human hopes. In the middle of the twentieth century, Norman Cohn studied historic millenarianisms in Europe and saw in those movements a parallel to the modern secular millenarianisms of fascism and communism. His conclusion has relevance for the vicious millenarian utopianism of twenty-first century violent religious movements like IS and Boko Haram:

> "A boundless, millennial promise made with boundless prophet-like conviction to a number of rootless and desperate men in the midst of a society where traditional norms and relationships are disintegrating—here, it would seem, lay the source of that peculiar subterranean fanaticism which subsisted as a perpetual menace to the structure of medieval society. It may be suggested that here, too, lies the source of the giant fanaticisms which in our day have convulsed the world." ([50], p. 319).

Acknowledgements

The author is grateful for the insights gained from many conversations about Islam in West Africa with colleagues and friends, especially John Campbell, James Saunders, Asch Harwood, and Alex Thurston. They are, of course, not responsible for any errors in this essay.

Conflicts of Interest

The author declares no conflicts of interest.

References

1. Mallam Sanni Umaru, Acting Leader Boko Haram, statement in "Boko Haram ressurrects [sic], declares total Jihad." *Vanguard*, 14 August 2009. Available online: http://www.vanguardngr.com/2009/08/boko-haram-ressurects-declares-total-jihad/ (accessed on 3 May 2015).
2. Thomas Daniel. "Radicalism, Extremism and Militancy." *ISIS [Institute of Strategic and International Studies Malaysia] Focus*, March 2015. Available online: www.isis.org.my/files/IF_2015/IF3/ISIS_Focus_3_-_2015_2.pdf (accessed on 29 September 2015).
3. Gregory F. Trevorton, Heather S. Gregg, Daniel Gibran, and Charles W. Yost. *Exploring Religious Conflict*. Santa Monica: RAND Corporation, 2005.
4. Audrey Kurth Cronin. "Behind the Curve: Globalization and International Terrorism." *International Security* 27 (2002–2003): 30–58.
5. Pew Research Center. "Religious Hostilities Reach Six-Year High." January 2014. Available online: www.pewforum.org/2014/01/14/religious-hostilities-reach-six-year-high (accessed on 29 September 2015).
6. Mark Juergensmeyer. "Religious terror and global war." In *Religion, Terror and Violence: Religious Studies Perspectives*. Edited by Brynan Rennie and Philip L. Tite. New York: Routledge, 2008, pp. 129–43.
7. Virginia Comolli. *Boko Haram: Nigeria's Islamist Insurgency*. London: Hurst & Company, 2015.
8. Mike Smith. *Boko Haram: Inside Nigeria's Unholy War*. London: I. B. Tauris, 2015.
9. John Campbell. *U. S. Policy to Counter Nigeria's Boko Haram. (Council Special Report No. 70)*. New York: Council on Foreign Relations, 2014.
10. David Cook. *Boko Haram: A Prognosis*. Houston: James A. Baker III Institute for Public Policy, Rice University, 2011.
11. Rodney Stark. *One True God: Historical Consequences of Monotheism*. Princeton: Princeton University Press, 2001.
12. Christopher Hitchens. *God is not Great: How Religion Poisons Everything*. New York: Twelve, 2007.
13. Daniel Brunstetter, and Megan Braun. "The Implications of Drones on the Just War Tradition." *Ethics and International Affairs* 25 (2011): 337–58.
14. Edward T. Barrett. "Reliable Old Wineskins: The Applicability of the Just War Tradition to Military Cyber Operations." *Philosophy & Technology* 28 (2015): 387–405.
15. Mark Juergensmeyer. *Global Rebellion: Religious Challenges to the Secular State, from Christian Militias to Al Qaeda*. Berkeley: University of California Press, 2008.
16. Richard Sherlock. "Religious Terrorism and Monotheism." In *Religion and Terrorism: The Use of Violence in Abrahamic Monotheism*. Edited by Veronica Ward and Richard Sherlock. Lanham: Lexington Books, 2014, pp. 15–35.
17. Michael Walzer. *The Paradox of Liberation: Secular Revolutions and Religious Counterrevolutions*. New Haven: Yale University Press, 2015.

18. Alex Thurston. "Nigeria's Mainstream Salafis between Boko Haram and the State." *Islamic Africa* 6 (2015): 109–34.
19. Abdulbasit Kassim. "Defining and Understanding the Religious Philosophy of *jihadi*-Salafism and the Ideology of Boko Haram." *Politics, Religion & Ideology*, 2015. Available online: http://dx.doi.org/10.1080/21567689.2015.1074896 (accessed on 29 September 2015).
20. Sidney Tarrow. *The New Transnational Activism*. Cambridge: Cambridge University Press, 2005.
21. Audrey Kurth Cronin. "ISIS is not a Terrorist Group: Why Counterterrorism Won't Stop the Latesst Jihadist Threat." *Foreign Affairs* 94 (2015): 87–98.
22. David C. Rapoport. "The Four Waves of Modern Terrorism." In *Attacking Terrorism: Elements of a Grand Strategy*. Edited by Audrey Kurth Cronin and James M. Ludes. Washington: Georgetown University Press, 2004.
23. David Robinson. "Revolutions in the Western Sudan." In *The History of Islam in Africa*. Edited by Nehemia Levtzion and Randall L. Powells. Athens: Ohio University Press, 2000, pp. 131–52.
24. Philip D. Curtin. "Jihad in West Africa: Early Phases and Inter-relations in Mauritania and Senegal." *The Journal of African History* 12 (1971): 11–24.
25. John O. Hunwick, ed and trans. *Sharī'a in Songhay: The Replies of al-Maghīlī to the Questions of Askia al-Hājj Muhammad*. London: British Academy, 1985.
26. David Robinson. *Muslim Societies in African History*. Cambridge: Cambridge University Press, 2004.
27. John N. Paden. *Faith and Politics in Nigeria*. Washington: United States Institute of Peace Press, 2008.
28. David Cook. "The Rise of Boko Haram in Nigeria." *CTC Sentinal* 4 (2011): 3–5.
29. Jacob Zenn. "A Biography of Boko Haram and the Bay'a to al-Baghdadi." *CTC Sentinal* 8 (2015): 17–21.
30. Muhammad Umar Memon. *Ibn Taymiyya's Struggle against Popular Religion: With an Annotated Translation of his Kitab iqtida al-sirat al-mustaqin ashab al-jahim*. The Hague: Mouton 1976.
31. Natana DeLong-Bas. *Wahhabi Islam: From Revival and Reform to Global Jihad*. New York: Oxford University Press, 2004.
32. Yonina Talmon. "Millenarian Movements." *Archives Européennes de Sociology* 7 (1966): 159–200.
33. John O. Voll. "Muhammad Hayya al-Sindi and Muhammad ibn Abd al-Wahhab: An Analysis of an Intellectual Group in Eighteenth Century Madina." *Bulletin of the School of Oriental and African Studies* 38 (1975): 32–39.
34. John O. Voll. "Hadith Scholars and Tariqahs: An Ulama Group in the 18th Century Haramayn and their Impact in the Islamic World." *Journal of Asian and African Studies* 15 (1980): 264–73.
35. Uthman ibn Fudi. *Bayan Wujūb Al-Hijra 'ala al-Ibād*. Edited and translated by F. H. El Masri. Khartoum: Khartoum University Press, 1978.

36. Victoria Carty. *Social Movements and New Technology*. Boulder: Westview Press, 2015.
37. John Arquilla, and David Ronfeldt. "The Advent of Netwar (Revisited)." In *Networks and Netwars*. Edited by John Arquilla and David Ronfeldt. Santa Monica: RAND, 2001, pp. 1–25.
38. David Ronfeldt, and John Arquilla. "Emergence of Influence of the Zapatista Social Netwar." In *Networks and Netwars*. Edited by John Arquilla and David Ronfledt. Santa Monica: RAND, 2001.
39. Peter Clark. "Islamic Reform in contemporary Nigeria: Methods and aims." *Third World Quarterly* 10 (1988): 519–38.
40. Niels Kastfelt. "Rumors of Maitatsine: A Note on Political Culture in Northern Nigeria." *African Affairs* 88 (1989): 83–90.
41. S. N. Eisenstadt. "The Reconstruction of Religious Arenas in the Framework of 'Multiple Modernities'." *Millennium Journal of International Studies* 29 (2000): 591–611.
42. Robert W. Hefner. "Multiple Modernities: Christianity, Islam, and Hinduism in a Globalizing Age." *Annual Review of Anthropology* 27 (1998): 83–104.
43. Martha Crenshaw. *Explaining Terrorism: Causes, Processes and Consequences*. London: Routledge, 2011.
44. Angel Rabasa, Peter Chalk, Kim Cragin, Sara A. Daly, and Heather S. Gregg, Theodore W. Karasik, Kevin A. O'Brien, and William Rosenau. *Beyond al-Qaeda, Part 1. The Global Jihadist Movement*. Santa Monica: RAND, 2006.
45. Ben Hubbard. "Al Qaeda Tries a New Tactic to Maintain Power: Sharing It." *New York Times*, 10 June 2015.
46. John Campbell. *Nigeria: Dancing on the Brink*, updated ed. Lanham: Rowman and Littlefield, 2013.
47. Sean McFate. *The Modern Mercenary: Private Armies and What They Mean for World Order*. New York: Oxford University Press, 2014.
48. Fawaz A. Gerges. *The Far Enemy: Why Jihad Went Global*. Cambridge: Cambridge University Press, 2005.
49. Beverly B. Mack, and Jean Boyd. *One Woman's Jihad: Nana Asma'u, Scholar and Scribe*. Bloomington: Indiana University Press, 2000.
50. Norman Cohn. *The Pursuit of the Millennium: Revolutionary Messianism in Medieval and Reformation Europe and Its Bearing on Modern Totalitarian Movements*, 2nd ed. New York: Harper & Row, 1961.

Explaining Support for Sectarian Terrorism in Pakistan: Piety, Maslak and Sharia

C. Christine Fair

Abstract: In the discourse around sectarian violence in Pakistan, two concerns are prominent. The first is the contention that piety, or the intensity of Muslim religious practice, predicts support for sectarian and other forms of Islamist violence. The second is the belief that personal preferences for some forms of sharia also explain such support. As I describe herein, scholars first articulated these concerns in the "clash of civilizations" thesis. Subsequent researchers developed them further in the scholarly and policy analytical literatures that explored these linkages through qualitative and quantitative methodologies. I revisit these claims in the particular context of sectarian violence in Pakistan. To do so, I use several questions included in a recent and large national survey of Pakistanis to create indices of both piety and support for three dimensions of sharia. I use these indices as explanatory variables, along with other explanatory and control variables, in a regression analysis of support for sectarian violence, the dependent variable. I find that the piety index and dimensions of sharia support are significant only when district fixed effects are excluded; however, personal characteristics (*i.e.*, the particular school of Islam respondents espouse, ethnicity, several demographics) most consistently predict support for sectarian violence.

Reprinted from *Religions*. Cite as: Fair, C.C. Explaining Support for Sectarian Terrorism in Pakistan: Piety, Maslak and Sharia. *Religions* **2015**, *6*, 1137–1167.

1. Introduction

Pakistan concentrates the attention of policy-makers and scholars for numerous reasons. With over 196 million Muslims, Pakistan's population is larger than the populations of Iran (80.8 million), Egypt (86.9 million) and Saudi Arabia (27.3 million) combined [1–4]. Its location has long been of strategic importance to the international community, as it sits astride the Middle East, Central Asia and South Asia. Most recently, Pakistan has been an important—albeit problematic—US partner in the conduct of US and NATO-led military and stabilization operations in Afghanistan. Pakistan's madaaris (pl. of madrasah, religious schools) and institutions of higher Islamic studies attract scholars from the world over and thus Pakistan is an important leader in Islamic thought and scholarship across the Muslim world.

Pakistan is also a nuclear-armed state with the fastest growing arsenal in the world, inclusive of battlefield nuclear weapons [5,6]. As the revisionist state in the security competition with India, Pakistan has long sought to alter maps in Kashmir. To do so, Pakistan has started several wars with India in 1947–1948, 1965 and 1999 in effort to seize territory in that portion of Kashmir controlled by India. More worrisome, the Pakistani state has employed Islamist militants as tools to achieve the state's goals in India as well as Afghanistan since 1947, essentially when the state became independent from the erstwhile Raj [7–9]. With both India and Pakistan possessing nuclear weapons, analysts fear that such Pakistani provocations may incite the next war in South Asia with potential escalation to nuclear use.

While Pakistan sustains critical attention for all of these reasons, Pakistan is itself a site of Islamist militant activities. Pakistan's domestic Islamist terrorists have long targeted religious minorities, including Hindus and Christians, as well as others who consider themselves to be Muslims such as Shia, Barelvis and Ahmedis because these militant groups do not consider them to be Muslims. Disturbingly, it should be noted that many non-militants such as influential clerics, popular television talk show hosts and ordinary citizens in Pakistan share these views [10–13]. While Pakistanis are wont to blame the origins of these domestic militants upon the United States, India and even Israel; in fact, their origins are domestic. From late 2001 onward, many of Pakistan's one-time proxies began turning their guns against the state by taking on military, police and intelligence targets as well as civilian bureaucrats and political leaders [14].

As I detail herein, Pakistan's internal enemies have claimed more lives than all of Pakistan's wars combined, including the 1971 war in which Pakistan lost half of its territory and people. Given the lethal ferocity of Pakistan's internal enemies, in this paper I focus upon public support for groups who are the vanguard of such violence: sectarian militant groups. Sectarian militancy, defined as violence between different sects within Islam, began to emerge in 1979, as a result of domestic factors as well as regional and geopolitical developments. Since then, Pakistan has persistently experienced sectarian violence. While in the early 1980s sectarian groups included both Shia and Sunni militias, since the mid-1990s sectarian violence has almost exclusively been the purview of the anti-Shia organization, the Sipah-e-Sahaba and its related organization Lashkar-e-Jhangvi [15–18]. Both of these groups are now known as the Ahl-e-Sunnat wal Jamaat (ASWJ). While these groups are most known for their murdering of Shia, they also are the key perpetrators in the slayings of Ahmedis, Christians, Hindus, and Barelvis.

While Pakistan suffers a vast array of political violence with sanguinary consequences, in this paper I focus specifically upon Islamist militant violence generally and sectarian violence in particular within Pakistan itself [19]. The reasons for this particular focus are several. First, I hope to expand the debate about Pakistani Islamist violence. Contemporary discourse tends to frame Pakistan-based terrorist groups primarily in terms of the external threat they pose to Pakistan's neighbors and the international community, almost always at the behest of the Pakistani state. I want to remind analysts and scholars that many of the victims of Pakistan-based terrorist group are Pakistanis themselves, second only to the Afghans whose lives have been continuously imperiled by Pakistan's proxies since the early 1970s if not earlier [20].

Second, while Pakistan's sectarian killers continue to claim thousands of Pakistani lives, these sectarian groups, which are almost exclusively Deobandi, also share overlapping membership with other Deobandi militant groups including the Afghan Taliban, the Pakistani Taliban, and the so-called "Kashmiri tanzeems" that focus upon Kashmir and the rest of India, most notably the Jaish-e-Mohammad [16]. Pakistan's Deobandi sectarian terrorist groups have served as the principle sub-contractors for al-Qaeda in Pakistan as well [21]. These varied Deobandi militant groups also have important ties to the factions of the Deobandi Jamiat Ulema-e-Islami (JUI), which is a generally non-militant Islamist political party which regularly contests elections. This association with JUI leadership provides the militant groups with important political patrons and complicates government action against them.

Third, Pakistan's sectarian conflicts have long been inflected by extra-regional events such as the Iranian revolution, the Iran-Iraq war, and the anti-Soviet Jihad in Afghanistan and have had an adverse synergistic relationship with the Sunni Islamization of the state that began to unfold in the nation's earliest years [22]. This is currently the state of affairs with Saudi Arabia and Iran engaging in another bout of high-stakes sectarian brinkmanship in Iraq, Syria, Yemen and elsewhere. The consequences of these regional developments are significant because many of Pakistan's Deobandi sectarian militants have elected to join the Islamic State to kill Shia and Allawites in Iraq and Syria respectively [23–25].

In the discourse around sectarian violence in Pakistan and elsewhere, two prominent concerns come to the fore. The first is the notion that piety, or the intensity of Muslim religious practice, is a potential predictor for personal support for sectarian and other forms of Islamist violence. The second is the belief that individual conceptualizations of some forms of sharia also explain this support. As I describe herein, scholars first espoused these concepts in the "clash of civilizations" thesis [26,27]. Later writers advanced this discourse in scholarly and policy fora using qualitative and quantitative studies. In this paper, I use a new and large dataset collected by Fair *et al.* which is drawn from a recent and large national survey of Pakistanis [28]. The team's survey instrument collected several questions about different aspects of support for sharia as well as several dimensions of religious practice and piety. I use these various questions to create indices of both piety as well as support for three dimensions of sharia, described herein. I use these indices as explanatory variables, along with other explanatory and control variables such as sectarian background, in my regression analysis of support for sectarian violence, my dependent variable.

I find that the index of piety is a positive predictor of support for sectarian terrorism in Pakistan. In other words, persons who indicate greater piety are more likely to support sectarian violence than those with lower degrees of revealed piety. However, this significance disappears when I include district fixed effects in the model. (Including such fixed effects accounts for district-level characteristics for which I cannot explicitly control in my model). Those who espouse support for sharia in terms of good governance and restrictions upon women are less likely to support sectarian violence. Those who embrace the punitive dimensions of share are more likely to support this kind of violence. All three of these effects are not significant when district fixed effects are included in the model. In contrast, several other personal variables are more robust predictors than either piety or beliefs about sharia, including: the particular school of Islam (maslak) that respondents espouse, ethnicity and key demographics.

The remainder of this paper is organized as follows. In the second section, I provide a brief background to the problem of sectarian militants in Pakistan and the vast array of violence they produce. Next, I detail the literatures in which I root these present queries and derive several hypotheses which I test subsequently. In the fourth section of this paper, I describe the dataset and analytical methods I employ. Fifth, I present the empirical findings. I conclude this essay with a brief discussion of the implications of this analysis.

2. Sectarian and Other Violence in Pakistan: The Role of the Sipah-e-Sahaba-e-Pakistan

While many Pakistani security managers decry the purported threat from India, in fact, the most vicious threat to the Pakistani state and citizens alike comes from Islamist militant organizations that engage in a wide array of terrorist attacks against ordinary civilians as well as assaults on non-combatants (e.g., political leadership). Many of these crimes are explicitly sectarian or communally motivated. Additionally, these militant groups have perpetrated guerilla campaigns against Pakistan's security forces and intelligence agencies as well. According to data collected by Bueno de Mesquita *et al.* [29], between 1988 and 2011, terrorist attacks have claimed the lives of 5783 Pakistanis[1] while another 35,839 Pakistanis were killed in other kinds of political violence, which include insurgent attacks upon state forces, communal violence, ethno-nationalist violence, *etc.* [29]. In contrast, Pakistani battlefield deaths over four wars (1947, 1965, 1971 and 1999) are fewer than 9000—a full order of magnitude less than those killed in internal security events [30].

While most commentators on Pakistan's dire internal security situation tend to use the anodyne descriptors of "Islamist", "terrorist", or even "sectarian militants" to describe these groups, these expressions suffer from considerable under-specification. In fact, the groups that are primarily engaged in this kind of Islamist domestic violence against Pakistanis in and out of government are almost exclusively Deobandi, one of the five major interpretive traditions of Islam in Pakistan. Deobandis, like most Muslims in South Asia, follow the Hanafi School of fiqh, or jurisprudence[2]. This cluster of Deobandi militant organizations includes the sectarian (and communal) organization Ahl-e-Sunnat wal Jamaat (ASWJ), which is the name under which older Deobandi, sectarian groups such as Sipah-e-Sahaba-e-Pakistan (SSP) and Lashkar-e-Jhangvi (LeJ) now operate. These Deobandi groups have long-standing ties to the Afghan Taliban and consequently to al-Qaeda and to several Deobandi militant groups that the ISI groomed for operations in India (*inter alia* Jaish-e-Mohammad (JeM), Harkat-ul-Jihadi-e-Islami (HuJI), Harkat ul Mujahideen (HuA), Harkat ul Ansar (HuA)) [13,31,32]. These groups are often called "Kashmiri tanzeems" (Kashmiri organizations) even though few of their cadres are actually Kashmiri and they operate well beyond Kashmir.

The so-called Tehreek-e-Taliban-e-Pakistan (TTP or Pakistani Taliban) also emerged from this morass of Deobandi militant groups, including the SSP [33]. While the TTP is often understood as a "Pashtun insurgency", in fact Punjab-based groups such as the Deobandi SSP/LeJ and JM are core components of the TTP and conduct attacks in its name [34]. The roots of the TTP stretch back to 2002, when Pakistan's Deobandi militant organizations began a serious reorganization. First, Jaish-e-Mohammad (JeM) fissured over General and President Pervez Musharraf's decision (whether voluntary or not) to facilitate US operations in Afghanistan to overthrow the Afghan Taliban. After

---

[1] Per the so-called BFRS [29] dataset "terrorist attacks" are defined by attacks on noncombatants conducted by violent groups in effort to advance a political goal. Sectarian attacks are a sub-set of these terrorist incidents in the BFRS dataset. Between 1988 and 2011, the BFRS dataset records 1724 deaths. This is most certainly an under-estimate because the BFRS coders could code an attack as "sectarian" only if the article described the attack in such terms.

[2] In Pakistan, there are five main interpretative traditions of Islam (*masalik*, plural of *maslak*). In addition to the Shia maslak, which itself has multiple sects, there are four Sunni masalik: Barelvi, Deobandi, Ahl-e-Hadith, and Jamaat-e-Islami (which is also a political party that purports to be supra-sectarian). Each maslak has its own definition of sharia and looks to different sources of Islamic legitimacy.

all, the Taliban regime was, for most intents and purposes, the only extant Deobandi-inspired Islamist government. Masood Azhar, JeM's amir (leader) remained loyal to Pakistan while Jamaat-ul-Furqan, its breakaway rump, initiated suicide-operations against the state [14,35].

During the same period, important events began taking place in the Federally Administered Tribal Areas (FATA). After the US invasion of Afghanistan that began on 7 October 2001 many fighters associated with Al-Qaeda and the Taliban (*inter alia* Uzbeks, Uighers, Arabs, Afghans) sought sanctuary in the FATA and paid considerable amounts of money to locals who would support them and provide them with shelter and amenities. In 2002 when the Pakistan army began undertaking limited operations in FATA, specific tribal dimensions of the conflict began to manifest. At first, the Wazirs elected to fight the Pakistan army and later the Mehsuds—who had previously been loyal to the army—also enjoined the fight against the Pakistani army. By 2007, Mullah Nazir and Hafiz Gul Bahadur led a new formation called the "Muqami Tehreek-e-Taliban" (Local Taliban Movement). This group aimed to protect the interests of Wazirs in North and South Waziristan. Nazir and Bahadur formed this group "to balance the power and influence of Baitullah Mehsud and his allies, the Islamic Movement of Uzbekistan" ([14], p. 577). Notably both Nazir and Gul Bahadur forged a pact with the Pakistan army whereby they would desist from attacking the Pakistan army and focus all of their efforts upon ousting the US/NATO troops from Afghanistan and helping to restore the Afghan Taliban to power [36,37]. Other tribal lashkars (militias) also began forming to either challenge the Pakistan military or rivals. Some of the commanders began espousing the appellation of the "Pakistani Taliban".

These various Deobandi militias successfully forged a tentative archipelago of sharia (Islamic law) that arched across the Pashtun belt in the FATA and Khyber Pakhtunkhwa (KPK). Analysts generally cite 2007 as the year that the TTP formally coalesced. In November of that year, several Pakistani militant commanders, rallying under the leadership of Baitullah Mehsud, announced that they would henceforth operate under the banner of the Tehreek-e-Taliban-e-Pakistan (Pakistani Taliban Movement). Following Baitullah Mehsud's death in a 2008 drone strike, Hakimullah Mehsud took over the TTP. Under Hakimullah, the TTP became more coherent and intensified its campaign of suicide bombings of Pakistani security and intelligence agencies [38–40]. Under the leadership of Hakimullah, TTP campaigns against civilian targets also became more vicious, singling out Shia and Ahmedis (also spelled Ahmediyyas), who are considered munafiqin (Muslims who spread discord in the community) and murtad (liable to be killed), respectively [41].

The TTP has also attacked important Sufi shrines. While this is a new phenomenon that had no precedent in Pakistan, since 2005, militants have launched more than 70 suicide attacks on such sites, killing hundreds. These attacks against Sufis have intensified in recent years. For example, Lahore's prominent Datta Ganj Bakhsh—perhaps the most important Sufi shrine in the Punjab—was attacked in late June 2010 [42,43]. In October of that year, TTP attacked the shrine dedicated to a saint named Abdullah Shah Ghaz in Karachi [44]. In April 2011, suicide bombers assaulted a shrine dedicated to a Punjabi saint, Sakhi Sarvar, in Dera Ghazi Khan [45]. These and other Pakistani Taliban attacks have cumulatively served to deter Pakistanis from frequenting such shrines [46]. In May of 2015, gunmen from a sectarian group operating under the name of Jandullah boarded a bus of Ismailis (a Shia sect) and began gunning them down. Before the carnage was over, at least 43 were dead.

Jundullah is a confederate of the Pakistani Taliban and Lashkar-e-Jhangvi and pledged allegiance to the Islamic state in November 2014 [47,48].

The focus on sectarian violence against Shia, Barelvis, Ahmedis, and others no doubt reflected Hakimullah Mehsud's long-time association with the sectarian terrorist group SSP/LeJ [49]. In November 2013, a US drone strike killed Hakimullah [50]. Maulana Fazlullah became the amir of the TTP. Fazlullah had previously achieved notoriety with the moniker "Maulana Radio" and as head of the Tehreek-e-Nifaz Shariat-e-Muhammadi (TNSM), an Islamist militant group in Swat that first agitation for the imposition of sharia in Swat in the 1990s. After resuming these demands with a sustained campaign of terrorism that lasted several years, in 2009, the TNSM wrested an agreement (called Nizam-e-Adl, "System of Justice") from the Pakistani government for Swat and Malakand [51] However, when the TNSM broke the accord, the Pakistan army moved in quickly to crush the movement. Scholars believe that Fazlullah now resides in Kunar province in Afghanistan. He rarely issues statements [52]. The most sectarian commanders of the TTP, particularly those associated with the SSP/LeJ are turning away from their traditional allegiance to the Afghan Taliban leader, previously Mullah Omar and now Mullah Mounsour, and are embracing the Islamic State [53].

The SSP (aka LeJ and ASWJ) and virtually all other Deobandi militant groups in Pakistan and Afghanistan are not only networked with each other, they are all tightly aligned with Islamist political organizations, most notably various factions the Deobandi ulema political party, the Jamiat Ulema-e-Islami (JUI)-Fazlur Rehman and JUI-Sami ul Haq. These Deobandi militant groups also enjoy funding by wealthy Arab individuals and organizations [16,54]. In addition, the SSP itself is a political party, which makes it difficult to completely disambiguate violent Islamist politics and non-violent Islamist politics. Given the role of coalitions in forming a government in Pakistan, numerous parties have partnered with SSP including President Musharraf's "King's Party" the Pakistan Muslim-Qaid, the Pakistan Peoples' Party (a left-of-center national political party with many Shia leaders) as well as the Pakistan Muslim League-Nawaz among others [17,33,55].

While Deobandi terrorists groups are mostly responsible for sectarian violence in Pakistan, Ahl-e-Hadith organizations have also targeted Barelvis and others as well, albeit with far less frequency. It is important to note that the Lashkar-e-Taiba, an Ahl-e-Hadith terrorist group, has never attacked targets in Pakistan [56]. Notable anti-Sunni, Shia groups exist (Sipah-e-Mohamad Pakistani (SMP) and Tehrik-e-Jafria-Pakistan (TJP)) and enjoyed support from Iran in the past. These groups are not nearly as active as their Deobandi counterparts today and mostly engage in tit-for-tat killings in response to Shia assassinations. In the growing sectarian violence, observers worry that Iran may once again enter this arena of sectarian proxies with verve. In recent years, especially in areas like the tribal agency of Kurram where Sunni militants have targeted Shia, Shia militias have formed in small numbers ([24], pp. 9–11). In recent years, Pakistan's Barelvis have begun attacking Deobandis in retaliation. Barelvis are also often involved in acts of political violence centered on blasphemy issues in Pakistan [57]. Barelvis have taken up violence against Deobandis in Pakistan as well [17,57,58].

Unfortunately, the activities of these sectarian militant groups are directly and indirectly sustained by Islamist and right-of-center political parties that are not overly militant. For example, Prime

Minister Nawaz Sharif's Pakistan Muslim League (PML-N) has resisted cracking down on the sectarian groups for fear of alienating their sympathizers while Imran Khan's Pakistan Tehreek-e-Insaaf has advocated conciliatory policies towards the TTP [59][3].

3. Extent of the Problem?

To provide an overview of the trends of domestic violence in Pakistan, I employ data on Pakistan's political violence, which were collected by Bueno de Mesquita and his colleagues using Pakistani press reports. Henceforth, I refer to this as the BFRS dataset [29]. Unlike most datasets on Pakistan, which focus only upon "terrorism", the BFRS dataset collects information about virtually every kind of political violence in Pakistan from the beginning of 1988 (when the anti-Soviet war was concluding) to the end of 2011. The BFRS dataset defines terrorism as political violence against non-combatants. An event is coded as "sectarian" if the news account explicitly characterizes the attack as sectarian, which we define as violence committed by one sect of Islam against another. This is distinct from communal violence which, in Pakistan, invariably involves Muslims attacking non-Muslims. In the BFRS dataset, an event is coded as communal or sectarian if there is information in the news account that identifies the attack in such terms. The BFRS data set also includes guerilla attacks, which are those conducted by militant groups against security forces. The BFRS dataset offers a further refinement: ethno-nationalist attack. These are most commonly involving Baloch or Sindhi separatists. Because these are not Islamist events and because sectarian groups do not engage in these attacks, I do not deal with ethno-nationalist violence here.

In Table 1, I divide the various incidents in this dataset into two periods: before and after 9/11. As the data in Table 1 show, even before the events of 9/11, Pakistan was a dangerous place for Pakistanis. In Figures 1–5, I geographically depict terrorist events by type and year aggregated at the district level for 1988, 2001, 2002, 2006 and 2011. These figures demonstrate a few important points. First, while much of Pakistan has experienced some form of domestic political violence, some districts remain free of violence most of the time. Second, sectarian, communal and guerilla violence seem to be confined to specific provinces and even districts. In other words, these forms of violence, despite the prevalence of reports in the news cycle, do not occur everywhere. Sectarian violence is most intensely concentrated in the Punjab in most years. In some years, it also has also occurred in parts of Sindh and the FATA. Communal violence is also mostly concentrated in the Punjab. Guerilla violence is generally concentrated in Balochistan (where the state has been at war with ethno-nationalist Baloch separatists) and in the FATA and parts of KPK where the state has been at war with the TTP and their confederates. What these maps also show is that the intensity of guerilla violence is a relatively recent phenomenon after 9/11. And as discussed above, much of this violence is due to the Pakistan Taliban and their sectarian and other allies. These charts alone attest to the importance of understanding Pakistan as a victim of political violence as well as an active exporter of the same.

---

[3] Neither the PML-N nor the TTP are themselves directly purveyors of violence even if there are groups that may conduct political violence on their behalf on various occasions. It is common throughout South Asia for political parties to have armed militias and/or thuggish student wings [60].

Table 1. BFRS political violence.

Variable	1988–2001	2002–2011	Total: 1998–2011
Total Incidents, Terrorist Attacks	2087	3721	5808
Total Killed, Terrorist Attacks	2086	3697	5783
Total Wounded, Terrorist Attacks	6754	9025	15,779
Total Incidents, Sectarian Violence	690	427	1117
Total Killed, Sectarian Violence	865	859	1724
Total Wounded, Sectarian Violence	1861	1414	3275
Total Incidents, Other Political Violence	11,340	12,820	24,160
Total Killed, Other Political Violence	10,873	24,966	35,839
Total Wounded, Other Political Violence	12,886	20,924	33,810

Source: In-house tabulations of BFRS [29,61].

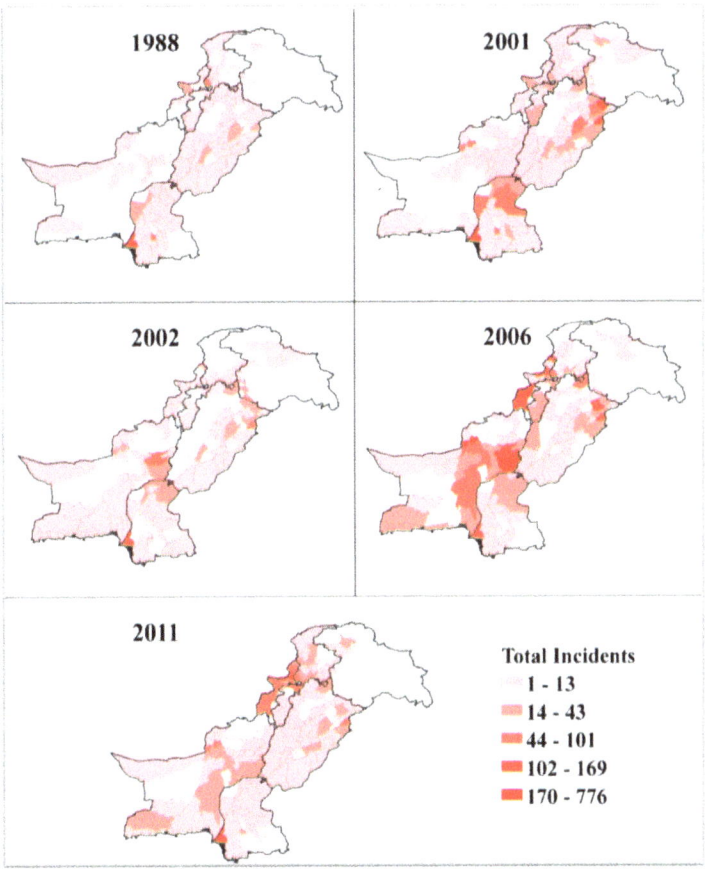

Figure 1. All Political Violence in Pakistan-Selected Years. Source: In-house manipulations of BFRS dataset [29,61] by Jesse Turcotte.

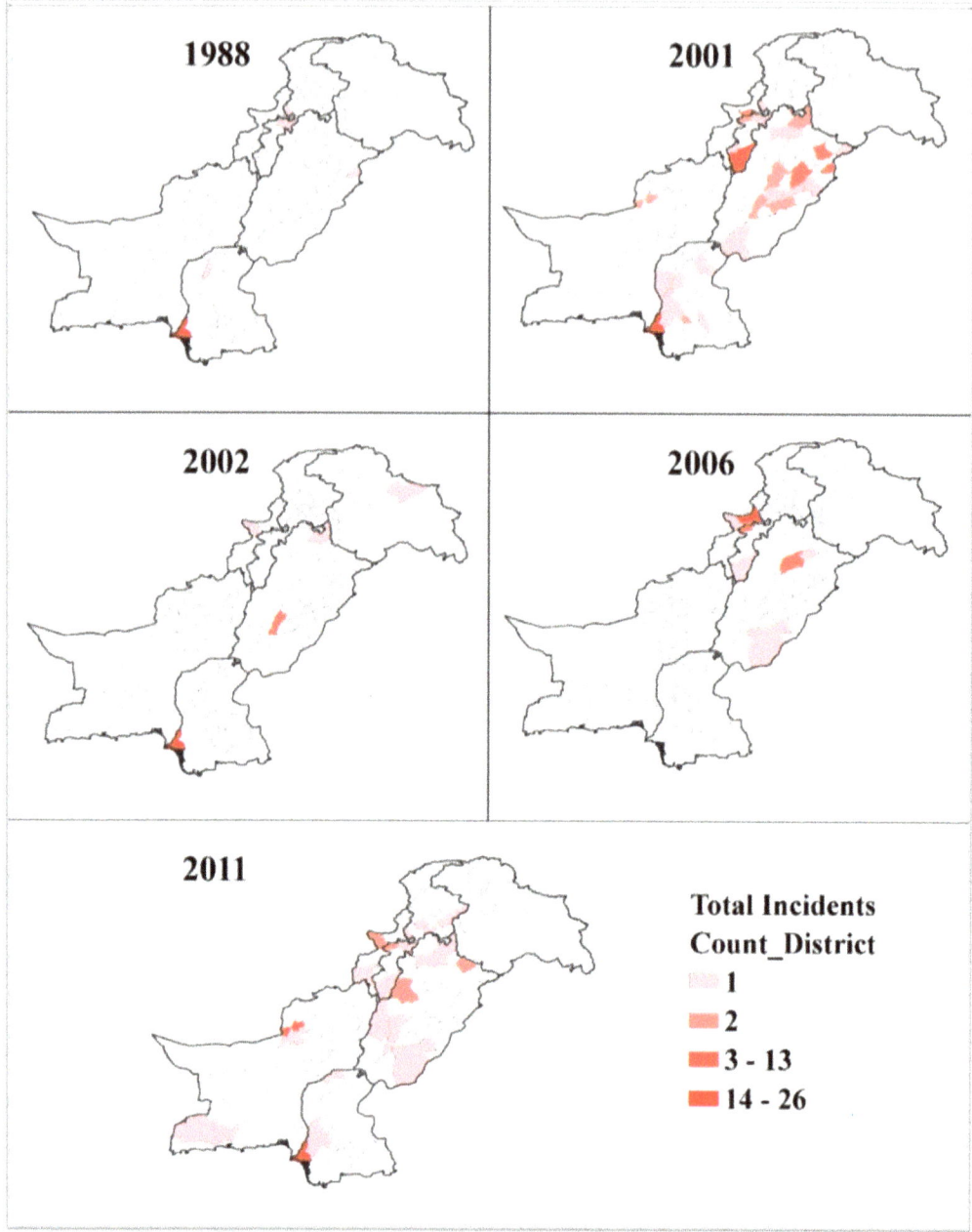

Figure 2. Sectarian Violence in Pakistan-Selected Years. Source: In-house manipulations of BFRS dataset [29,61] by Jesse Turcotte.

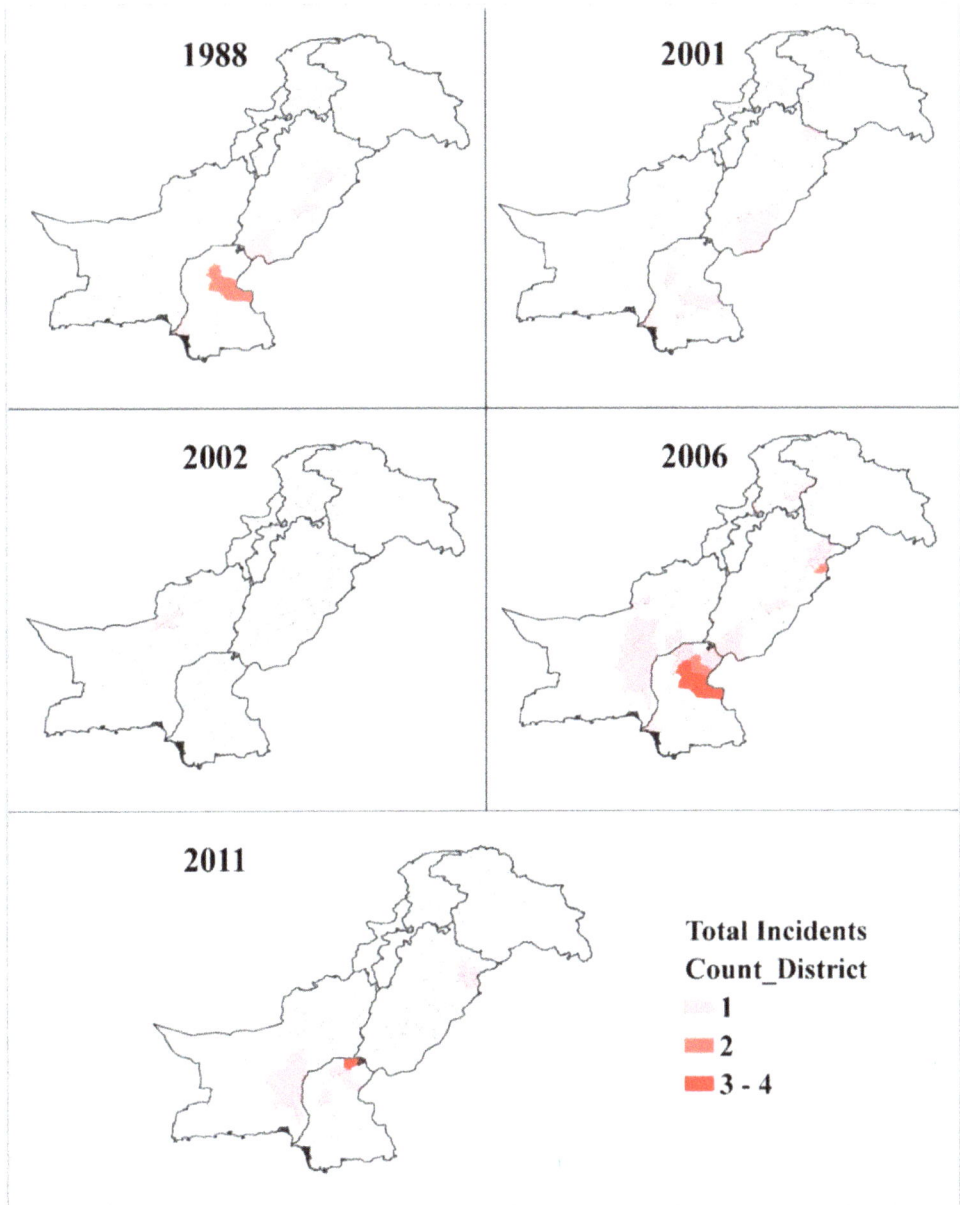

Figure 3. Communal Violence in Pakistan-Selected Years. Source: In-house manipulations of BFRS dataset [29,61] by Jesse Turcotte.

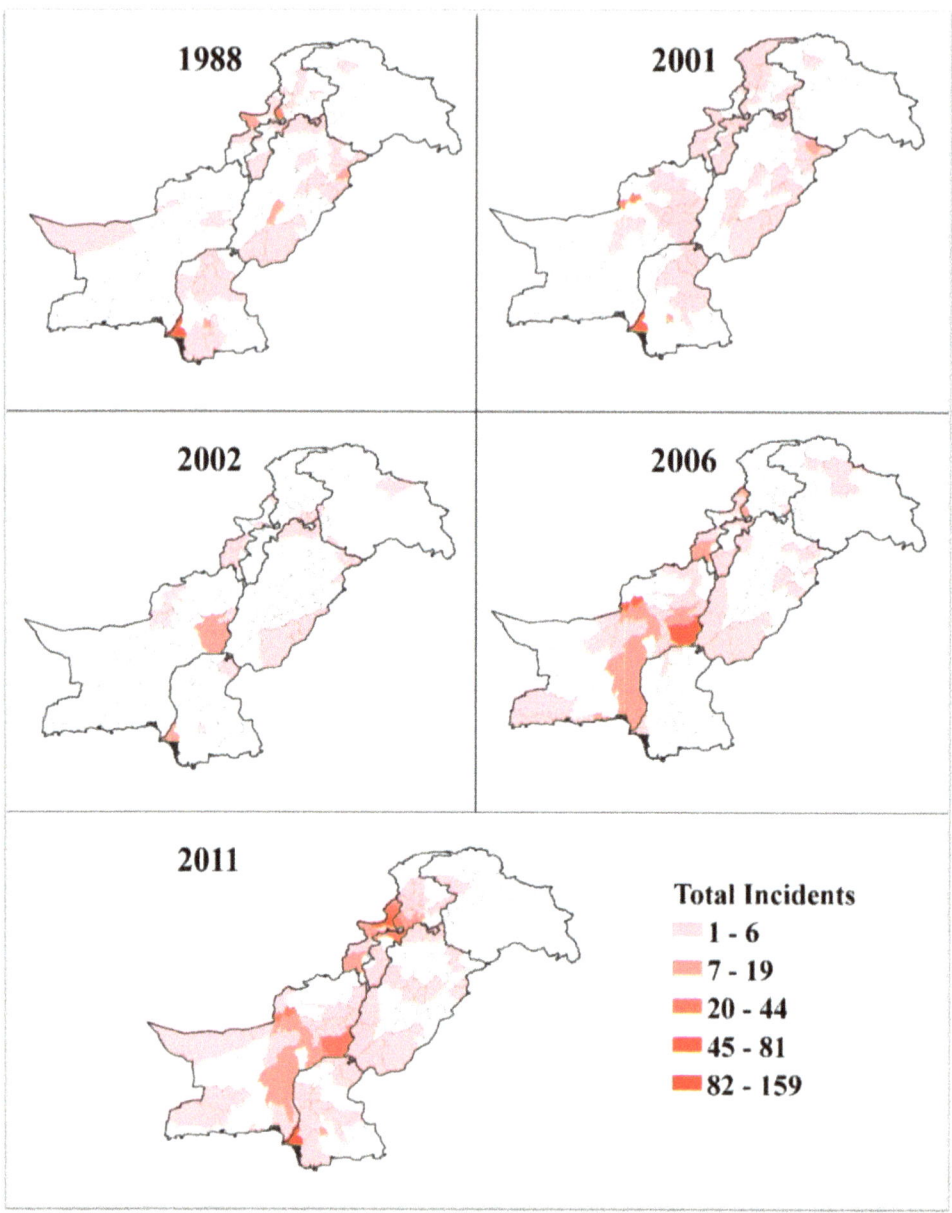

Figure 4. Terrorist Violence in Pakistan-Selected Years. Source: In-house manipulations of BFRS dataset by [29,61] Jesse Turcotte.

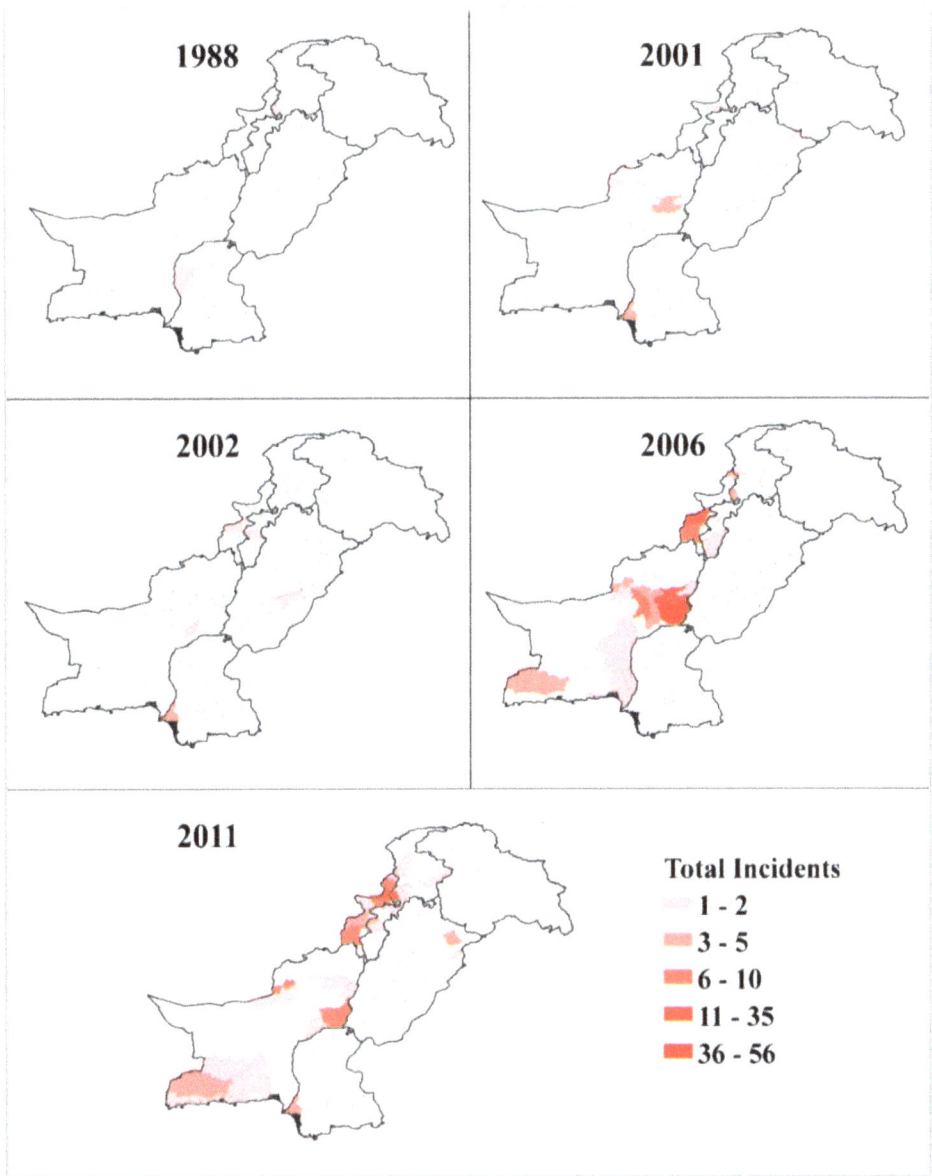

Figure 5. Militant/Guerilla Violence in Pakistan-Selected Years. Source: In-house manipulations of BFRS dataset [29,61] by Jesse Turcotte.

4. Literature Review and Hypotheses

To formulate testable hypothesis about the determinants of support for sectarian violence in Pakistan, I draw from several policy analytic and scholarly discourses about Islamist militancy. Specifically, I review the literatures that examine potential ties between support for Islamist violence and several aspects of Muslim identity politics in Pakistan and other Muslims countries namely: religious practice (piety), support for sharia, and adherence to a particular interpretative tradition or maslak[4].

4.1. Piety and Religious Practice

The "clash of civilizations" thesis advanced by Huntington [26] and Lewis [27] held that tensions between the Muslim world and the West derive from innate conflicts between Islam and Christianity. This provocative assertion galvanized a widening discourse that posited intrinsic ties between Islam and support for Islamist violence[5]. Public intellectuals contributed to this debate with their varied contentions that public support for violence against "the West" is inherently related to Muslim religiosity or faith [63–65] and renowned scholars pursued this line of empirical inquiry as well [66]. Juergensmeyer, for example, employing qualitative case studies concluded that the very theological foundations of religions are soaked in blood and that believers employ violence in elemental aspect of their religious corporate existence [67,68]. Weinberg, Pedahzur and Canetti-Nisim, using the Palestinian-Israeli conflict as a case study, argue that it is difficult to "deny that in the Palestinian-Israeli conflict a substantial majority of suicide bombings have been the work of shahids or religious self-martyrs belonging to Hamas and Palestinian Islamic Jihad, two organizations expressing Islamist ideas about the nature of the situation"([69], p. 141). Similarly, Hafez [70], taking the biographies and videos of suicide bombers in Iraq, details how al Qaeda goes to great pains to project the attackers at pious (e.g., frequently engaged in prayer). Taking a somewhat different stance and approach, Wiktorowicz [71], drawing on interviews with recruits in the militant British Islamist group al-Muhajiroun, found that persons who were more religious and engaged with Islam were actually less supportive of and more reistent to al-Muhajiroun's message.

While robust evidence of a link between religiosity and support for militancy is scant, there is mounting countervailing evidence for such a claim (see e.g., [72]). Tessler and Nachtwey [72], in their analysis of public opinion data from Egypt, Kuwait, Palestine, Jordan, and Lebanon, found that frequency of prayer is uncorrelated with attitudes toward conflict with Israel. Clingingsmith, Khwaja, and Kremer found that feelings of Muslim unity and intensified commitment to Islamic orthodoxy among Pakistani pilgrims after performing Hajj were co-extant with expanded tolerance towards non-Muslims [73]. Fair, Malhotra and Shapiro using survey data from Pakistan and an endorsement experiment to measure such support similarly find no ties between support for Islamist militancy and piety [74].

Given that the evidence on the relationship between religious piety and practice on the one hand and support for militant groups on the other is weak or ambiguous, I put forward H1 as a testable hypothesis:

---

[4] The first two correspond to Hypotheses 1 and 2 in [62].

[5] Advocates of this view often reference "the verse of the sword" in the Quran (Sura 9:5) to justify the link between religious practice and militancy: "Then, when the sacred months have passed, slay the idolaters wherever ye find them, and take them captive, and besiege them, and prepare for them each ambush."

H1: Religious piety and practice is not positively related to support for sectarianism in Pakistan.

4.2. Islamist Politics

Some scholars who have sought to exposit the determinants of individual support for Islamism and terrorism generally have found no significant positive or, I some cases, negative correlation between the two. Ginges, Hansen and Norenzayan [75] report that while a 2003–2004 survey of Indonesian Muslims did not show an association between religious devotion and prayer frequency and support for suicide attacks, their own research concluded that attendance at religious services did predict support for such attacks among Palestinian Muslims. Similarly, Kaltenthaler, Ceccoli, Gelleny, and Miller [76] analyze survey Pakistanis from 2007 and conclude that there is no correlation between individual beliefs about the extent to which Islam should play a more important and influential role in the world on the one hand and whether they justify terrorist attacks on civilians on the other. Tessler and Nachtwey [72] conclude find that "politicized Islam", measured via responses to four binary questions about the role of Islam in politics, was negatively associated with peaceful attitudes; however, Furia and Lucas [77], analyzing data derived from the 2002 Arab Values Survey, conducted in Egypt, Jordan, Lebanon, Kuwait, Morocco, Saudi Arabia, and the UAE, conclude that Arab Muslims with higher levels of "Islamic consciousness" were no more hostile to Western countries than others. Similarly, Fair, Ramsay, and Kull [78] find no relationship between views on sharia law and support for violence[6].

Looking across these varied studies and the countries from which they draw, the evidence that ties support for political Islam (variously instrumented) and Islamist violence is not robust. Nonetheless there are several reasons why we might observe a relationship between support for Islamist politics and militancy in Pakistan. First, many avowedly Islamist parties in Pakistan take positions that are explicitly tolerant of some forms of Islamist violence. The two most important Islamist political parties not only vocally support "jihadi" actions but also have direct command and control over key militant groups themselves. For example, Jamaat-e-Islami (JI) not only offers its political support to the Afghan Taliban and opposes military action against the Pakistani Taliban, it also has direct ties to the Hizbul Mujahideen, a so-called "Kashmiri jihadi tanzeem" (organization) that is active in

---

[6] Kaltenthaler *et al.* [76] similarly find that Pakistanis who were more accepting of the imposition of extreme Islamist views (often called "Talibanization") were more likely to believe that attacks on civilians could be justified. There have been other studies that focus upon political beliefs that are not easily classified as "political Islam." Specific political grievances are one of the few reliable determinants of support for militant actions. Chiozza [79] finds that among Muslims in Jordan and Lebanon, the strongest predictor of support for suicide bombings against American forces in Iraq was disaffection towards the American people, not religiosity, and that religiosity was associated with support for attacks only when accompanied by fear for Muslim identity. Similarly, research on Palestinian public opinion towards Israel has repeatedly found that the perception of Israel as posing a threat is strongly associated with support for violence, but that support for political Islam exhibits no association [80–82]. National surveys of Algeria and Jordan in 2002 also showed that while higher levels of religious involvement did not make individuals more likely to approve of terrorist acts against the US, there was a significant relationship between respondents' attitudes towards their government and US foreign policy and their support for terrorism [62].

Indian-administered Kashmir. The other key Islamist party is the Deobandi Jamiat Ulema-e-Islami (JUI) vocally supports an array of Deobandi Islamist militant groups, including the Pakistani and Afghan Taliban as well as numerous Kashmiri groups and the SSP/LeJ, and has direct command and control over them [9,21,31,54, 58,83,84]. Second, these two parties frequently align with other Pakistan-based terrorist organizations such as the Jamaat-ud-Dawa (previously known as Lashkar-e-Taiba) to form political pressure groups around specific issues (*inter alia* Pakistan's ties with the United States; closure of the ground lines of control for the US military operations in Afghanistan; opposition to the US-led war in Afghanistan, support for Saudi Arabia's actions in Yemen). It is not unreasonable to assume therefore that a vote for such Islamist parties should be tantamount to supporting the party's jihadi politics[7]. Third, these groups, with their very visible ties to Islamist militancy generally and sectarian militancy in particular, also vocally advocate for the implementation of sharia along the lines of their own particular maslak. Incidentally, disagreement about which form of Sharia should form the basis of Pakistani law leads precludes lasting political alliances in and beyond the ballot box.

Previous empirical work by Fair, Malhotra and Shapiro on Pakistan finds that Pakistanis conceptualize sharia in various ways, with many more seeing sharia as a mechanism for good governance and rule of law rather than punitive measures [86]. Fair, Nugent and Littman, expanding upon those findings and using a larger dataset (described below) that asks more expansive questions of Pakistanis about their beliefs about sharia, find that there are three broad categories into which their beliefs fall: sharia as a form of good governance; sharia as a set of punitive regimes such as hudud ordinances; and sharia as a set of rules that govern women's public role in particular [74]. Presumably, persons who believe sharia is fundamentally about rule of law and good governance should oppose organizations and activities that undermine both. This gives rise to the first of three inter-related hypotheses:

> H2a: Support for sharia defined as good governance is negatively related to support for sectarian militancy.

With respect to hudud punishments, many Islamist militant organizations embrace hudud punishments. For example, the Afghan Taliban with whom the SSP collaborated, were in power in Afghanistan and established a sharia government based upon their Deobandi interpretation of Sharia. The Afghan Taliban, both in and out of power, have used hudud ordinances inclusive of stoning adulterers to death, whipping men and women who do not wear "Islamic" dress, punishing men who shave their beards among other physical punishments. The SSP use similar rationale to kill Shia, Barelvis, and Ahmedis as well as non-Muslims arguing variously that they are apostates, blasphemers and kufar (non-believers), all of whom should be killed [12]. It stands to reason that if one rejects hudud notions as a part of sharia, one should also be disinclined to support the militant groups that embrace them. This suggests another hypothesis:

---

[7] While some of the Ahl-e-Hadith ulema in Pakistan have rejected militarized jihad waged by any actor other than the state, Lashkar-e-Taiba (now known as Jamaat ud Dawa) is the only jihadi group in Pakistan that is associated with the Ahl-e-Hadith masalik [85].

H2b: Support for sharia defined as hudud is positively related to support for sectarian militancy.

Finally, while many militant and non-militant Islamist organizations in Pakistan maintain that women should observe veiling and restrict their presence in public, many women themselves see veiling as a means of expanding their access to the public space while retaining their respectability. Thus for some women, veiling is a liberating mechanism rather than a mechanism of confinement. For other women in Pakistan, different kinds of veiling take on different kinds of social signaling altogether, a full discussion of which is beyond this paper[8]. Given these different interpretations about veiling and its contested relationship to various notions of sharia, there are no empirical reasons to suspect that support for aspects of sharia that restrict women should have any correlation with support for terrorism. This gives rise to the third hypothesis in this cluster:

H2c: Support for sharia defined as rules governing women's public role is unrelated to support for sectarian militancy.

4.3. Maslak and Militancy

In Pakistan, there are four key Sunni interpretative traditions called masalik (pl. of maslak): Ahl-e-Hadith, Deobandi, Barelvi, and Jamaat-e-Islami. All but Ahl-e-Hadith adherents ascribe to the Hanafi School of Islamic jurisprudence (fiqh). Those of the Ahl-e-Hadith tradition follow no fiqh and refer to themselves accordingly as "ghair muqalid", or one who does not follow any fiqh. In addition to these four Sunni masalik, the fifth maslak encompasses Shia Islam and its variants in Pakistan. While Jamaat-e-Islami is technically supra-sectarian and even denounces sectarianism in its public posturing, JI does align itself politically with the sectarian militant groups and their Deobandi supporters in the JUI among others as noted above and has long supported an array of jihadi causes. The Ahl-e-Hadith maslak also espouses a very sectarian world view. (Note that while Lashkar-e-Taiba follows this school, the terrorist organization is at odds with the mainstream Ahl-e-Hadith ulema) [85]. As noted above, Barelvis have militarized in recent years largely in response to being attacked by Deobandis and even Ahl-e-Hadith adherents. In the past, Shia ulema have aligned with Shia militants who targeted their Sunni Deobandi rivals. These groups are now defunct.

In Pakistan, the production of these different ideological positions is the job of the madaris and the religious scholars they train irrespective of any particular madrassah's maslak[9]. As a fraction of

---

[8] Among various Muslim women's blogs the issue of the "ho-jabi" is a serious affair. The etymology is a play on words of the original "hejab" and the misogynist epithet of "ho" or "hoe" for a promiscuous woman. A thorough discussion of this social phenomenon is beyond the scope of the paper. But this serious debate among young women is a testament to the varying valence of "hejab" as a not-so-entirely pietic marking. See blog posts variously from [87–89] among numerous others including microblogs on Facebook, Twitter, Instagram, Pinterest and the like.

[9] This is not to say that madaris are the only sites of religious education in Pakistan. In fact, Pakistanis receive such education in the public schools as well and many private schools also teach religious and non-religious subjects. In some cases, private schools have even blended the entire madrassah curriculum such that students will have attained the title of alim upon completion of either ten or twelve years of schooling [90].

the overall market of full-time enrolled children, less than one percent attends a madrasah full-time. However, many more children and young adults attend a madrasah in addition to their other schools (public or private). One of the dominant functions of madaris is to argue for the legitimacy of each school's maslak. Thus, madaris stand accused of fostering support for sectarianism in Pakistan or at least world views that espouse the superiority of one maslak over another [90,91]. In principle, JI madaris should be an exception as JI claims to repudiate such sectarian divides.

One of the most important function of madaris is the production of ulema (pl. of alim, scholar) and less-accomplished religious leaders who deliver sermons, most notably during Friday prayer and on major Muslim holidays. Association with a specific maslak will expose a person to a particular set of sectarian commitments. However, despite the deepening of sectarian divides in Pakistan, not all Pakistanis will readily or openly identify with a particular tradition; survey work indicates that most respondents will prefer to simply say that they are "Ahl-e-Sunnah", or generically "Muslim". Thus, I anticipate that persons who espouse a particular commitment to one of the main Sunni masalik that have been tied to sectarian violence in Pakistan either directly or indirectly (Ahl-e-Hadith, Deobandi) will support sectarian violence while those who identify as "Ahl-e-Sunnah" will be less likely support this violence.This category includes those who espouse Jamaat Islami as well as Barelvi as their maslak of preference. This discussion gives rise to a third testable hypothesis:

> H3: Support for sectarian militancy should vary according to the maslak to which the respondent adheres.

5. Data and Research Methods

To explore the determinants of support for purveyors of sectarian violence and to test the above-posited hypotheses, I use a dataset originally collected by Fair, Malhotra and Shapiro [91]. That research team fielded a face-to-face survey with a sample of 16,279 people. This included 13,282 interviews in the four main provinces (Punjab, Sindh, Balochistan, and Khyber Pakhuntkhwa), as well as 2997 interviews in six of seven agencies in FATA (Bajaur, Khyber, Kurram, Mohmand, Orakzai, and South Waziristan). The survey was fielded in January and February 2012 in the four main provinces and in April 2012 in FATA.

Analytical Methods

My dependent variable measures explicit support for one of the key providers of sectarian terrorism in Pakistan, the Sipah-e-Sahaba-e-Pakistan (SSP). As noted above, the SSP not only commits sectarian attacks, it is also involved in communal violence, and it is an important collaborator in violence perpetrated by the Pakistani Taliban, or TTP, and even al-Qaeda. In recent years, its cadres have also left to fight in Syria and Iraq abroad and, domestically, have thrown support to the Islamic State. The question I use for my dependent variable is "How much do you support Sipah-e-Sahaba-e-Pakistan (SSP) and their actions?" Respondents could answer "not at all", "a little", "a moderate amount", "a lot", or a "great deal".

Per H1, I require a measure that instruments for individual piety. Thus I constructed an index that would measure the intensity of person's religiosity or intensity of religious practice. This index is a straightforward, additive index of the several variables that tap aspects of intensity of, or frequency of, religious practice. To derive this index, I used several questions from the survey noted below.

- Do you attend dars-e-Quran? (if yes, then 1)
- If yes: How many times do you go to dars-e-Quran per week on average? (scaled from 0 to 1)
- How often per week do you pray Namaz? (range scaled from 0 to 1)
- How many times did you pray Namaz in congregation in the Mosque last Sunday?[10] (range scaled from 0 to 1)
- Do you pray "Tahajjud Namaz?" (if yes, 1)

To obtain the respondent score for this index, these five items are summed and then divided by five. The largest possible value for this index is one while the smallest possible value is zero.

Next I developed a cluster of independent variables that instrument for respondent support for different conceptualizations of sharia, derived from the empirical work of Fair, Littman, and Nugent and Fair, Malhotra, and Shapiro find that Pakistanis conceive of sharia in at least three key dimensions: good governance (access to services, minimization of corruption, *etc.*); "hudud" punishments for crimes (whipping, stoning *etc.*); and pertaining to women (veiling, presence in public, *etc.*) [74,86]. Following and, at times modifying, their approaches, I use several survey items to construct three additive indices which reflect these different dimensions of sharia. Specifically, the survey asks respondents "Here is a list of things some people say about sharia. Tell us which ones you agree with. Sharia government means:...". Respondents can agree or disagree with each item presented.

The first sharia index I calculate pertains to respondent's support for the notion that sharia has specific provisions for women. It is derived from the following two survey items:

- A government that restricts women's role in the public (working, attending school, going out in public) (If agree, 1)
- A government that requires women to veil in public. (If agree, 1)

To obtain the value for this index, I add these two measures and divide by two. Thus the maximum possible value of this index is 1 and the smallest value is zero.

The second measure of sharia is an additive index that reflects the degree to which the respondents view sharia essentially in terms of good governance. I derive this index from following four survey items:

- A government that provides basic services such as health facilities, schools, garbage collection, road maintenance. (If agree, 1)
- A government that does not have corruption. (If agree, 1)
- A government that provides personal security. (If agree, 1)

---

[10] As is well known, the most important day of prayer is Friday. For many men, they only got to a mosque on a Friday. For this reasons, we deliberately chose an "off day" to measure prayer attendance in a mosque. In Pakistan, few women are encouraged to prayer in a mosque and thus they do their prayers at home.

- A government that provides justice through functioning non-corrupt courts. (If agree, 1)

To obtain this index value, I add the values for the above items and then divide by four. This index has a possible of range of zero to one.

The third measure of sharia reflects the degree to which the respondents view sharia essentially in terms of physical punishments. It is derived from the following survey item:

- A government that uses physical punishments (stoning, cutting off of hands, whipping) to make sure people obey the law. (If agree, 1).

This value is zero if the respondent disagrees and 1 if they agree.

The third set of independent variables refers to the maslak of the respondent. Due to fears of respondent social desirability bias, Fair *et al.* [92] do not ask respondents directly about the maslak they embrace. Rather, they ask this indirectly by querying the respondent "If a child in your house were to study hifz-e-Quran or nazira, what kind of madrassah or school would you like them to attend?" (Hifz-e-Quran is the memorization of the Quran while Nazira is learning to recite the Quran properly). I similarly use this question to instrument for respondent maslak. In this open-ended question, respondents gave the following answers "Sunni" (which includes Jamaat Islami and Barelvi), "Deobandi", "Ahl-e-hadith", "Shia", "Non-Muslim", and "Don't Know".

In addition to these independent variables, following Shafiq and Sinno [93], I include several control variables including marital status (single/never married, married, divorced, widowed), age group (18–29, 30–49, 50+), educational attainment (less than primary, primary (6th grade), middle (8th grade) matriculate (10th grade), higher education (above 10th grade)), and income quartiles. In addition, I include ethnicity due to the observed geographical patterns in the kinds of violence evidenced and documented in this paper. In Table 2, I present the summary statistics for the dependent, independent, and control variables.

To conduct the analysis, I ran ordinary least squares regression on the dependent variable that captures support for SSP and its actions, using the above noted list of variables for Muslim respondents only. I categorized respondent as "non-Muslim" if they indicated that they were non-Muslim when asked about the kind of madrassah they would use for their children. If respondents did not answer the question or said "did not know," their responses were coded as "missing". To capture any district-level characteristics for which I cannot control directly, I ran this model both with and without district fixed-effects. Because the original survey sample was drawn at the level of the Primary Sampling Unit (PSU), standard errors are clustered at the PSU (for details about the survey execution, see discussion in [28,74]). In Table 2, I indicate with an "*" the reference group, within a particular variable cluster, which I used as the "omitted group" in the regression.

Table 2. Summary Statistics of Dependent and Independent Variables.

	Categories	Frequency	Percentage
Dependent Variable			
	Not at all	6176	37.9%
	A little	2238	13.7%
How much do you support Sipah-e-Sahaba-e-	A moderate amount	2521	15.5%
Pakistan (SSP) and their actions?	A lot	1287	7.9%
	A great deal	1268	7.8%
	No answer	2789	17.1%
Total		16,279	100%
Independent variables			
	0.00	912	5.60%
	0.04	1121	6.89%
	0.08	694	4.26%
	0.12	543	3.34%
	0.16	721	4.43%
	0.2	1332	8.18%
	0.24	480	2.95%
	0.28	1345	8.26%
	0.32	675	4.15%
	0.36	742	4.56%
	0.4	1152	7.08%
	0.44	1123	6.90%
	0.48	714	4.39%
Piety Index (0.00–1.00)	0.52	603	3.70%
	0.56	647	3.97%
	0.6	564	3.46%
	0.64	656	4.03%
	0.68	396	2.43%
	0.72	404	2.48%
	0.76	635	3.90%
	0.8	107	0.66%
	0.84	259	1.59%
	0.88	141	0.87%
	0.92	92	0.57%
	0.96	220	1.35%
	1.00	1	0.01%
Total		16,279	100%
	0.00	415	2.55%
	0.25	600	3.69%
Sharia Good Governance Index (0.00–1.00)	0.5	1164	7.15%
	0.75	2925	17.97%
	1.00	11,175	68.65%
Total		16,279	100%

Table 2. *Cont.*

	Categories	Frequency	Percentage
Sharia Hudud Index (0.00–1.00)	0.00	6913	42.47%
	1.00	9366	57.53%
Total		16,279	100%
Sharia Women Index	0	3547	21.79%
	0.5	6622	40.68%
	1	6110	37.53%
Total		16,279	100%
Maslak: Type of Madrassah	Shia *	601	3.69%
	Sunni	7394	45.42%
	Deobandi	5928	36.42%
	Ahl-hadith	585	3.59%
	Non Muslim	384	2.36%
	Don't know/No response	1387	8.52%
Total		16,279	100%
Control Variables			
Ethnicity	Other *	818	5.03%
	Punjabi	5325	32.71%
	Muhajiir	1073	6.59%
	Pashtun	5718	35.13%
	Sindhi	1673	10.28%
	Baloch	1566	9.62%
	No response/don't know	106	0.65%
Total		16,279	100%
Marital Status	Married	12,481	76.67%
	Divorced	38	0.23%
	Widowed	424	2.33%
	Single/never married *	3292	20.22%
	Don't know/ no answer	44	0.27%
Total		16,279	100%
Level of Education	Less than Primary *	6354	39.03%
	Primary	1951	11.99%
	Middle	2189	13.45%
	Matriculate	2875	17.66%
	Higher Education	2732	16.78%
	Don't know/no response	178	1.09%
Total		16,279	100%
Age Group	18–29 *	5945	36.52%
	30–49	7896	48.50%
	50+	2396	14.7%
	Don't know/no response	42	0.26%
Total		16,279	100%

Table 2. *Cont.*

	Categories	Frequency	Percentage
Income Quartiles	First quartile *	5640	34.65%
	Second quartile	4272	26.24%
	Third quartile	1974	12.13%
	Fourth quartile	3162	19.42%
	Don't know/no response	1231	7.56%
Total		16,279	100%

Note: * denotes regression reference level.

6. Discussion of Regression Results

As the regression results in Table 3 show, many of the independent variables are significant in the full model (without fixed effects). For example, with respect to H1 which posits ties between piety and support for sectarianism, I find that increased piety is significantly and positively associated with higher support for sectarianism contrary to what I had had hypothesized based upon the existing literature. Turning to respondent perceptions of sharia on the one hand and support for sectarian militancy on the other, I find mild support for H2a that respondents who believe sharia implies good governance are less approving of sectarian militancy. Consistent with H2b, I also find that respondents who interpret sharia in terms of hudud offences exhibit greater support for sectarian militancy. With respect to H2c, I find that those who interpret sharia as imposing strictures on women's public life are less supportive of sectarianism. However, all of these results dissipate when I control for district fixed effects. In other words, district-level characteristics for which I cannot explicitly control for in this model "absorb" the effects of these independent variables for piety and interpretations of sharia.

The third hypothesis concerns the respondents' professed maslak. It turns out that a person's maslak is a far more stable predictor of support for various aspects of sharia or evidenced piety. Relative to those who are Shia, the reference category in this regression, those who identify with one of the Sunni masalik are strongly associated with support for sectarian militancy. Contrary to my expectations, even those who simply identify as "Sunni—in contrast to "Deobandi" or "Ahl-e-Hadith"—are more inclined to support sectarian militancy. These results persist as significant and positive even when district fixed effects are included. This outcome tends to support the findings of Fair (2008) and Ali (2009) that sectarianism in Pakistan is tightly related to the production of identities associated with adherence to particular masalik [83,90].

One of the primary institutions that produces these identities is the madrasah which educates Pakistan's religious scholars and preachers who in turn disseminate and reproduce these ideologies and identities within institutions tied to these masalik (e.g., mosques, madaris, *etc.*). Unfortunately, Pakistan's madaris have fiercely fought off any sort of reform that could possibly attenuate the sectarian worldviews that they generate and sustain far and beyond the numbers of students who pass through their doors. Madaris, of course, are not the only institutions that reproduce ties to a particular maslak and the sectarian outlooks they create and reinforce. Other sources of sectarian influence include, *inter alia*: family and social networks [94]; public schools [95]; civil society organizations which have been inflected by Islamic movements [96]; proselytization efforts that many Islamist and Islamic groups encourage [97]; Islamic revival organizations such as al Huda [98]; Islamist political parties [97]; religious television and radio programming [99]; internet-based religious content and programming [99]; as well as religious print materials. Unfortunately, it is beyond the data used to here to identify the various sources that contribute to a respondent's embrace of a particular maslak and the sectarian worldviews that identification seems to inculcate.

Most of the control variables (including marital status, education, income and age) are not significant when I control for district characteristics. There is one important exception: those in the oldest age category (50 years and older) are significantly less likely to support sectarian militancy. In many cases ethnicity is significant in explaining variation support for sectarian violence. Controlling for all other factors noted above and relative to those who identified their ethnicity as "other" (e.g., Kashmiri), Punjabis, Sindhis, and Baloch are less likely to support sectarianism in both models. This is likely due to the fact that Punjab, Sindh and Balochistan have experienced considerable amounts of violence perpetrated by Islamists militants, as Figures 1 and 2 attest.

Table 3. Regression Results (How much do you support Sipah-e-Sahaba-e-Pakistan (SSP) and their actions?

	No District Fixed Effects	With District Fixed Effects
Independent Variables		
piety_ind_rounded	0.400 (3.84) **	0.174 (1.82)
sharia_gg_ind	−0.457 (−4.61) **	−0.172 (−1.74)
sharia_h_ind	0.125 (2.57) *	−0.026 (−0.54)
sharia_wom_ind	−0.223 (−3.88) **	−0.079 (−1.54)
madrasa_sunni	0.754 (8.94) **	0.516 (4.23) **
madrasa_deobandi	0.953 (10.59) **	0.708 (5.38) **
madrasa_ahl_e_hadis	0.823 (6.16) **	0.646 (4.04) **
Control Variables		
maritalstatus_married	0.079 (1.78)	0.092 (2.29) *
maritalstatus_divorced	0.200 (0.57)	0.233 (0.73)
maritalstatus_widowed	0.140 (1.32)	0.132 (1.33)
ethnicity_punjabi	−0.283 (−2.45) *	−0.294 (−2.27) *
Control Variables		
ethnicity_muhajir	−0.560 (−4.30) **	−0.129 (−0.94)
ethnicity_pashtun	−0.153 (−1.29)	−0.162 (−1.13)
ethnicity_sindhi	−0.691 (−5.40) **	−0.492 (−3.17)**
ethnicity_baloch	−0.537 (−3.81) **	−0.343 (−2.16)*
educ_primary	−0.098 (−2.04) *	−0.064 (−1.46)

Table 3. *Cont.*

	No District Fixed Effects	With District Fixed Effects
educ_middle	−0.070 (−1.44)	−0.039 (−0.90)
educ_matric	−0.084 (−1.67)	−0.036 (−0.77)
educ_higher	−0.158 (−2.97) **	−0.084 (−1.70)
age_30to49	−0.062 (−1.71)	−0.041 (−1.27)
age_50plus	−0.296 (−5.85) **	−0.218 (−4.74) **
quartile_second	0.008 (0.20)	−0.012 (−0.34)
quartile_third	0.011 (0.20)	−0.035 (−0.72)
quartile_fourth	0.072 (1.45)	−0.031 (−0.64)
_cons	1.049 (5.84) **	1.022 (5.21) **
R2	0.08	0.21
N	11,601	11,601

Notes: * $p < 0.05$; ** $p < 0.01$.

7. Conclusions and Implications

While analysts and scholars of security studies typically view Pakistan as a perpetrator and exporter of Islamist terrorism; this analysis shows that Pakistanis are perhaps the largest group of victims of these Pakistan-based groups apart from the Afghans; whose country has been the object of considerable Pakistani predations from the 1950s onward [20,100]. Unfortunately; the roots of these groups savaging Pakistanis are predominantly domestic and tied to the state's security policies towards India and Afghanistan [14]. After all; there would be no Pakistan Taliban had there been no Afghan Taliban and the myriad other Deobandi groups that the state has supported has supported from the mid-1970s. Alarmingly; even Pakistan's sectarian groups; such as SSP/LeJ; have been important allies of segments of the state at various times.

The durability of these Deobandi sectarian groups should motivate the Pakistani government to rethink its policies not only due to the toll they have exacted from Pakistanis, but because Pakistan's sectarian groups are likely to become ever more enmeshed in contemporary sectarian conflicts far beyond South Asia, as Saudi Arabia and Iran continue to carry out their sectarian proxy wars in Bahrain, Yemen, Syria, Iraq and elsewhere. Given that sectarianism in Pakistan has its origins from Iranian and Arab Gulf State sectarian competition in late 1970s, Pakistan should be deeply concerned. Indeed, it seems that the challenges of sectarianism in Pakistan are poised to deepen rather than retract given these developing realities and the insouciance and ambivalence that Pakistan's civilian and military entities exhibit towards the purveyors of sectarian violence.

Pakistan's will to eradicate sectarian militancy is constrained by the overlapping nature of the various militant groups and their membership. For example, Pakistan cannot tackle the Pakistani Taliban and their sectarian collaborators while it still fosters the Afghan Taliban and other Deobandi groups, such as the Jaish-e-Mohammad, that operate in India. Even if the state had the will to counter all forms of Islamist militancy including those that have external utility in Afghanistan and India, the evidence is not encouraging that Pakistan has the capacity. Pakistan's law enforcement institutions—

including the judiciary—are woefully ill prepared for this task. All of Pakistan's rule of law institutions are riven with corruption and have suffered neglect at the hands of federal and provincial governments for decades [101,102].

The survey data analyzed here offer little hope either. The most consistent and positive predictors of support for sectarian violence are sectarian commitments as expressed through their maslak. These characteristics—unlike education levels or poverty—cannot be easily influenced over time either by Pakistan policy actions or by international actors. More challenging yet, commitments to a particular maslak and the sectarian views they encourage are deeply rooted to multiple facets of Pakistan's educational landscape as well as social and cultural practices. However, the good news is that most ethnic groups are less likely to support sectarian violence relative to those who identified their ethnicity as "other." It is beyond this paper and the data analyzed here to exposit this mechanism. It is possible that Punjabis, Sindhis and Baloch may oppose sectarian violence most because their provinces have witnesses much of this kind of violence. However, in recent years, so has KPK and Pashtun ethnicity is not a significant predictor of support. Understanding the drivers of these ethnicity effects may offer some future promise in dampening support for this violence if the Pakistani state is ever motivated to do so. It seems that Pakistan is going to continue to bleed for the foreseeable future.

Acknowledgments

I am thankful to Jessica Bluestein and Ali Hamza who did the statistical programming for this project and Jesse Turcotte, who did the geo-coded mapping. I am also thankful to Georgetown's School of Foreign Service and the Security Studies program which have supported this effort generously by funding the work of Bluestein and Hamza. The original survey data used here were collected with funding from the US Embassy in Islamabad, Public Affairs Section. I am also grateful to my collaborators on related work, in alphabetical order: Graeme Blair, Patrick Kuhn, Rebecca Littman, Neil Malhotra, Elizabeth Nugent, and Jacob Shapiro.

Conflicts of Interest

The author declares no conflict of interest. However the survey data used here were collected under a grant from the US Embassy in Islamabad (Pakistan), Department of Public Affairs.

References

1. US Central Intelligence Agency. "The World Factbook: Pakistan." 24 June 2015. Available online: https://www.cia.gov/library/publications/the-world-factbook/geos/pk.html (accessed on 1 September 2015).
2. US Central Intelligence Agency. "The World Factbook: Iran." 24 August 2015. Available online: https://www.cia.gov/library/publications/the-world-factbook/geos/ir.html (accessed on 1 September 2015).

3. US Central Intelligence Agency. "The World Factbook: Saudi Arabia." 26 August 2015. Available online: https://www.cia.gov/library/publications/the-world-factbook/geos/sa.html (accessed on 1 September 2015).
4. US Central Intelligence Agency. "The World Factbook: Egypt." 25 August 2015. Available online: https://www.cia.gov/library/publications/the-world-factbook/geos/eg.html (accessed on 1 September 2015).
5. Koblentz, Gregory D. "Strategic Stability in the Second Nuclear Age." *Council on Foreign Relations*, 19 November 2014. Available online: http://www.cfr.org/nonproliferation-arms-control-and-disarmament/strategic-stability-second-nuclear-age/p33809# (accessed on 31 August 2015).
6. Sankaran, Jaganath. "Pakistan's Battlefield Nuclear Policy: A Risky Solution to an Exaggerated Threat." *International Security* 39 (2015): 118–51.
7. Fair, C. Christine. *Fighting to the End: The Pakistan Army's Way of War*. New York: Oxford University Press, 2014.
8. Nawaz, Shuja. "The First Kashmir War Revisited." *India Review* 7 (2008): 115–54.
9. Swami, Praveen. *India, Pakistan and the Secret Jihad: The Covert War in Kashmir, 1947–2004*. London: Routledge, 2007.
10. Hussain, Irfan. "In the name of faith." *The Dawn*, 27 September 2008. Available online: http://www.dawn.com/news/421131/in-the-name-of-faith (accessed on 31 August 2015).
11. Tanveer, Rana. "In broad daylight: Ahmadi leader gunned down in Gujranwala." *Express Tribune*, 28 December 2014. Available online: http://tribune.com.pk/story/813329/in-broad-daylight-ahmadi-leader-gunned-down-in-gujranwala/3 (accessed on 1 September 2015).
12. Lashkar-e-Jhangvi. "Shia Wajib Ul Qatal Kiyon (Why Are Shia Deserving of Being Killed)?" December 2008. Idara-e-Inteqam-e-Haq. Available online: http://www.mediafire.com/download/oiv665tqtvsfve2/Shia+Wajib+Ul+Qatal+Kiyon.pdf (accessed on 3 September 2015).
13. Ispahani, Farahnaz. "Cleansing Pakistan of Minorities." *Current Trends in Islamist Ideology*, 31 July 2013. Available online: http://www.hudson.org/research/9781-cleansing-pakistan-of-minorities (accessed on 1 September 2015).
14. Qazi, Shehzad H. "Rebels of the frontier: origins, organization, and recruitment of the Pakistani Taliban." *Small Wars & Insurgencies* 22 (2011): 574–601.
15. Abou Zahab, Mariam. "The Regional Dimensions of Sectarian Conflict in Pakistan." In *Pakistan: Nationalism Without a Nation*. Edited by Christophe Jaffrelot. London: Zed Books, 2002, pp. 115–30.
16. Abou Zahab, Mariam, Olivier Roy. *Islamist Networks: The Afghan-Pakistan Connection*. London: C. Hurst and Co., 2004.
17. Nasr, Seyyed Vali Reza. "The Rise of Sunni Militancy in Pakistan: The Changing Role of Islamism and the Ulama in Society and Politics." *Modern Asian Studies* 34 (2000): 139–80.
18. Zaman, Muhammad Qasim. "Sectarianism in Pakistan: The Radicalization of Shi'i and Sunni Identities." *Modern Asian* Studies 32 (1998): 689–716.

19. Kfir, Isaac. "Sectarian Violence and Social Group Identity in Pakistan." *Studies in Conflict & Terrorism* 37 (2014): 457–72.
20. Hussain, Rizwan. *Pakistan and the Emergence of Islamic Militancy in Afghanistan*. Burlington: Ashgate, 2005.
21. Fair, C. Christine. "Militant recruitment in Pakistan: Implications for Al-Qai'da and Other Organizations." *Studies in Conflict and Terrorism* 27 (2004): 489–504.
22. Haqqani, Husain. *Pakistan: Between Mosque and Military*. Washington: CEIP, 2005.
23. Mehsud, Saud, and Mubasher Bukhari. "Pakistan Taliban Splinter Group Vows Allegiance to Islamic State." *Reuters*, 18 November 2014. Available online: http://www.reuters.com/article/2014/11/18/us-pakistan-militants-is-idUSKCN0J20YQ20141118 (accessed on 1 September 2015).
24. Ur Rehman, Zia. "Pakistani Fighters Joining the War in Syria." *Combating Terrorism Center*, 9 September 2013. Available online: https://www.ctc.usma.edu/posts/pakistani-fighters-joining-the-war-in-syria (accessed on 9 September 2015).
25. Al-Salhy, Suadad. "Syria War Widens Rift Between Shi'ite Clergy in Iraq, Iran." *Reuters*, 20 July 2013. Available online: http://www.reuters.com/article/2013/07/20/us-iraq-politics-syria-idUSBRE96J04120130720 (accessed on 1 September 2015).
26. Huntington, Samuel P. *The Clash of Civilizations and the Remaking of the World Order*. New York: Simon & Schuster, 1996.
27. Lewis, Bernard. "The roots of Muslim rage: Why so many Muslims deeply resent the West and why their bitterness will not be easily mollified." *Atlantic Monthly* 266 (1990): 47–60.
28. Fair, C. Christine, Rebecca Littman, Neil Malhotra, and Jacob N. Shapiro. "Relative Poverty, Perceived Violence, and Support for Militant Politics: Evidence from Pakistan." 2013. Available online: http://www.princeton.edu/~jns/papers/FLMS_2013_Poverty_Violence_Support_for_Militancy.pdf (accessed on 1 September 2015).
29. Bueno de Mesquita, E., C. Christine Fair, Jenna Jordan, Rasul Bakhsh Rais, and Jacob N. Shapiro. "The BFRS Political Violence in Pakistan Dataset." 2013. Available online: https://webspace.princeton.edu/users/esocweb/ESOC%20website%20publications/BFJRS_2013_PK_Data_v10.pdf (accessed on 31 August 2015).
30. Sarkees, Meredith Reid, and Phil Schafer. "The Correlates of War Data on War: An Update to 1997." *Conflict Management and Peace Science* 18 (2000): 123–44.
31. Fair, C. Christine. "The Militant Challenge in Pakistan." *Asia Policy* 11 (2011): 105–37.
32. Mahsud, Mansur Khan. "The Battle for Pakistan Militancy and Conflict in South Waziristan." *New America Foundation*, 2010. Available online: http://www.operationspaix.net/DATA/DOCUMENT/4799~v~The_Battle_for_Pakistan___Militancy_and_Conflict_in_South_Waziristan.pdf (accessed on 1 September 2015).
33. Rafiq, Arif. *Sunni Deobandi-Shi`i Sectarian Violence in Pakistan (Explaining the Resurgence Since 2007)*. Washington: Middle East Institute, 2014. Available online: http://www.mei.edu/sites/default/files/publications/Arif%20Rafiq%20report.pdf (accessed on 1 September 2015).
34. Roggio, Bill. "Suicide Bomber Kills 60 at Mosque in Pakistan's Northwest." *Long War Journal*, 5 November 2010. Available online: http://www.longwarjournal.org/archives/2010/11/suicide_bomber_kills_40.php (accessed on 1 September 2015).
35. Mir, Amir. *True Face of the Jehadis*. Lahore: Mashall, 2004.

36. Fair, C. Christine, and Seth G. Jones. "Pakistan's War Within." *Survival* 51 (2010): 161–88.
37. BBC.com. "The Afghan-Pakistan militant nexus." 5 February 2013. Available online: http://www.bbc.com/news/world-asia-21338263 (accessed on 31 August 2015).
38. Pak Institute for Peace Studies. *PIPS Security Report 2009*. Islamabad: PIPS, 2009. Available online: http://san-pips.com/download.php?f=29.pdf (accessed on 1 September 2015).
39. New York Times. "Hakimullah Mehsud." 29 April 2010. Available online: http://topics.nytimes.com/topics/reference/timestopics/people/m/hakimullah_mehsud/index.html (accessed on 1 September 2015).
40. PBS Newshour. "Pakistan Blast Sharpens Concern on Taliban." *PBS Newshour*, 1 April 2010. Available online: http://www.pbs.org/newshour/bb/military-jan-june10-pakistan_01-01/ (accessed on 1 September 2015).
41. Siddique, Qandeel. "The Syria Conflict and Its Impact on Pakistan." 2014. Available online: http://strategiskanalyse.no/Publikasjoner%202014/2014-02-20_SISA15_The-Syria-Conflict-Pak_QS.pdf (accessed on 1 September 2015).
42. Tohid, Owais. "In Pakistan, Militant Attacks on Sufi Shrines on the Rise." *Christian Science Monitor*, 5 November 2010. Available online: http://www.csmonitor.com/World/Asia-South-Central/2010/1105/In-Pakistan-militant-attacks-on-Sufi-shrines-on-the-rise (accessed on 1 September 2015).
43. Tavernise, Sabrina. "Suicide Bombers Strike Sufi Shrine in Pakistan." *The New York Times*, 1 July 2010. Available online: http://www.nytimes.com/2010/07/02/world/asia/02pstan.html (accessed on 1 September 2015).
44. Gul, Imtiaz. *The Al Qaeda Connection: The Taliban and Terror in Pakistan's Tribal Areas*. London: Penguin, 2009.
45. Masood, Salman, and Waqar Gillani. "Blast at Pakistan Shrine Kills Dozens." *The New York Times*, 3 April 2010. Available online: http://www.nytimes.com/2011/04/04/world/asia/04pakistan.html?partner=rss&emc=rss (accessed on 31 August 2015).
46. Karimjee, Mariya. "Crocodile Tears: Taliban Attacks on Sufi Shrines Lead to Unlikely Victims." *Al Jazeera*, 15 December 2014. Available online: http://america.aljazeera.com/articles/2014/12/15/sufi-shrine-crocodiles.html (accessed on 31 August 2015).
47. Hassan, Syed Raza. "Gunmen kills 43 in bus attack in Pakistan's Karachi." *Reuters*, 13 May 2015. Available online: http://www.reuters.com/article/2015/05/13/us-pakistan-attack-idUSKBN0NY0FH20150513 (accessed on 1 September 2015).
48. Bin Perwaiz, Salis. "Jundullah, LeJ worked together to target SSP Farooq Awan." *The News*, 27 September 2014. Available online: http://www.thenews.com.pk/Todays-News-4-275158-Jundullah-LeJ-worked-together-to-targe (accessed on 31 August 2015).
49. Siddique, Qandeel. "Tehrik-e Taliban Pakistan: An Attempt to Deconstruct the Umbrella Organization and the Reasons for Its Growth in Pakistan's North-West." 2010. Available online: http://diisinfo.dk/graphics/Publications/Reports2010/RP2010-12-Tehrik-e-Taliban_web.pdf (accessed on 1 September 2015).

50. Craig, Tim. "Drone kills Taliban chief Hakimullah Mehsud; Pakistan accuses U.S. of derailing peace talks." *Washington Post*, 2 November 2013. Available online: http://www.washingtonpost.com/world/asia_pacific/pakistani-official-accuses-us-of-sabotage-as-drone-targets-taliban-leaders-in-northwest/2013/11/01/1463d0c2–431d-11e3-b028-de922d7a3f47_story.html (accessed on 31 August 2015).
51. Hashim, Asad. "The iron fist of Maulana Fazlullah." *Al Jazeera*, 8 November 2013. Available online: http://www.aljazeera.com/indepth/features/2013/11/iron-fist-maulana-fazlullah-20131171538269715.html (accessed on 31 September 2015).
52. Khan, Zia. "Pakistani Spies Trace Fazlullah to Kunar Province." *The Express Tribune*, 26 July 2010. Available online: http://tribune.com.pk/story/31093/pakistani-spies-trace-fazlullah-to-kunar-province/ (accessed on 31 August 2015).
53. Nazish, Kiran. "The Islamic State's Potential Recruits in Pakistan." *The Diplomat*, 3 October 2014. Available online: http://thediplomat.com/2014/10/the-islamic-state-arrives-in-pakistan/ (accessed on 1 September 2015).
54. Fair, C. Christine. "Militant Recruitment in Pakistan: A New Look at the Militancy-Madrasah Connection." *Asia Policy* 4 (2007): 107–34.
55. Nasr, Seyyed Vali Reza. "International Politics, Domestic Imperatives, and Identity Mobilization: Sectarianism in Pakistan, 1979–1998." *Comparative Politics* 32 (2000): 171–90.
56. Fair, C. Christine. "Lashkar-e-Tayiba and the Pakistani State." *Survival* 53 (2011): 29–52.
57. Khan, Ismail. "The Assertion of Barelvi Extremism." *Current Trends in Islamist Ideology* 12 (2011): 51–72.
58. Jamal, Arif. *Shadow War: The Untold Story of Jihad in Kashmir*. Brooklyn: Melville House, 2009.
59. Naqvi, Feisal H. "An Unholy Alliance." *Express Tribune*, 25 February 2013. Available online: http://tribune.com.pk/story/512400/an-unholy-alliance/ (accessed on 1 September 2015).
60. Staniland, Paul. "Armed Groups and Militarized Elections." *International Security Studies*, 15 March 2015. Available online: http://onlinelibrary.wiley.com/doi/10.1111/isqu.12195/abstract (accessed on 1 September 2015).
61. BFRS Dataset. Available online: https://esoc.princeton.edu/files/bfrs-political-violence-pakistan-dataset (accessed on 1 September 2015).
62. Tessler, Mark, and Michael D. H. Robbins. "What Leads Some Ordinary Arab Men and Women to Approve of Terrorist Acts Against the United States?" *Journal of Conflict Resolution* 51 (2007): 305–28.
63. Laqueur, Walter. *The New Terrorism: Fanaticism and the Arms of Mass Destruction*. New York: Oxford University Press, 1999.
64. Calvert, John. "The Islamist syndrome of cultural confrontation." *Orbis* 46 (2002): 339–49.
65. Mendelsohn, Barak. "Sovereignty under Attack: The International Society Meets the Al Qaeda Network." *Review of International Studies* 31 (2005): 45–68.
66. Jackson, Richard. "Constructing Enemies: Islamic Terrorism in Political and Academic Discourse." *Government and Opposition* 42 (2007): 394–426.
67. Juergensmeyer, Mark. *Terror in the Mind of God: The Global Rise of Religious Violence*. Berkeley: University of California Press, 2003, vol. 13.

68. Juergensmeyer, Mark. *Global Rebellion: Religious Challenges to the Secular State, From Christian Militias to Al Qaeda*. Berkeley: University of California Press, 2008, vol. 16.
69. Weinberg, Leonard, Ami Pedahzur, and Daphn Canetti-Nisim. "The Social and Religious Characteristics of Suicide Bombers and Their Victims." *Terrorism and Political Violence* 15 (2003): 139–53.
70. Hafez, Mohammed M. "Martyrdom Mythology in Iraq: How Jihadists Frame Suicide Terrorism in Videos and Biographies." *Terrorism and Political Violence* 19 (2007): 95–115.
71. Wiktorowicz, Quintan. *Radical Islam Rising: Muslim Extremism in the West*. Lanham: Rowman & Littlefield Publishers, 2005.
72. Tessler, Mark, and Jodi Nachtwey. "Islam and attitudes toward international conflict: Evidence from survey research in the Arab world." *Journal of Conflict Resolution* 42 (1998): 619–36.
73. Clingingsmith, David, Asim Ijaz Khwaja, and Michael R. Kremer. "Estimating the impact of the Hajj: Religion and tolerance in Islam's global gathering." *Quarterly Journal of Economics* 124 (2009): 1133–70.
74. Fair, C. Christine, Rebecca Littman, and Elizabeth Nugent. "Pakistani Conceptualization of Shari's and Support for Militancy and Democratic Values: A New Empirical Approach." 2014. Available online: http://papers.ssrn.com/sol3/papers.cfm?abstract_id=2482547 (accessed on 1 September 2015).
75. Ginges, Jeremy, Ian Hansen, and Ara Norenzayan. "Religion and support for suicide attacks." *Psychological Science* 20 (2009): 224–30.
76. Kaltenthaler, Karl, William J. Miller, Stephen Ceccoli, and Ron Gelleny. "The Sources of Pakistani Attitudes toward Religiously Motivated Terrorism." *Studies in Conflict & Terrorism* 33 (2010): 815–35.
77. Furia, Peter A., and Russell E. Lucas. "Arab Muslim Attitudes toward the West: Cultural, Social, and Political Explanations." *International Interactions* 34 (2008): 186–207.
78. Fair, C. Christine, Clay Ramsay, and Steve Kull. *Pakistani Public Opinion on Democracy, Islamist Militancy, and Relations with the US*. Washington: United States Institute of Peace, 2008.
79. Chiozza, Giacomo. "How to Win Hearts and Minds? The Political Sociology of the Support for Suicide Bombing." 2010. Available online: http://www.elecdem.eu/media/universityofexeter/elecdem/pdfs/giacomochiozzatraining/How_to_Win_Hearts_and_Minds.pdf (accessed 16 September 2015).
80. Tessler, Mark. "Arab and Muslim Political Attitudes: Stereotypes and Evidence from Survey Research." *International Studies Perspectives* 4 (2003): 175–81.
81. Tessler, Mark. "The nature and determinants of Arab attitudes toward Israel." In *Contemporary Anti-Semitism: Canada and the World*. Edited by Michael Robert Marrus, Derek Jonathan Penslar and Janice Gross Stein. Toronto: University of Toronto Press, 2004, pp. 96–121.
82. Shikaki, Khalil. "Willing to Compromise: Palestinian Public Opinion and the Peace Process." U.S. Institute of Peace, Special Report 158. 2006. Available online: http://www.usip.org/publications/willing-compromise-palestinian-public-opinion-and-the-peace-process (accessed 16 September 2015).

83. Ali, Saleem H. *Islam and Education: Conflict and Conformity in Pakistan's Madrassahs*. Karachi: Oxford University Press, 2009.
84. Haqqani, Husain. "The Ideologies of South Asian Jihadi Groups." *Current Trends in Islamist Ideology* 1 (2005): 12–26.
85. Rana, Muhammad Amir. *The A to Z of Jehadi Organizations in Pakistan*. Translated by Saba Ansari. Lahore: Mashal, 2004.
86. Fair, C. Christine, Neil Malhotra, and Jacob N. Shapiro. "Islam, Militancy, and Politics in Pakistan: Insights from a National Sample." *Terrorism and Political Violence* 22 (2010): 495–521.
87. Jahan, Muska. "Stop Calling Each Other Hojabis—Hijabi Problems." 28 March 2015. Available online: http://muskajahan.com/2015/03/stop-calling-each-other-hojabis-hijabi-problems/ (accessed on 1 September 2015).
88. Khan, Zeba. "Red Wine and Hojabis: A Judgment on Being Judgmental." *Muslimmatters.org*, 10 February 2014. Available online: http://muslimmatters.org/2014/02/10/red-wine-hojabis-judgment-judgmental/ (accessed on 1 September 2015).
89. Tanda. "The Myth of the 'Hojabi'; a Ramadan Reminder." *The Alternative Muslim*, 3 August 2011. Available online: https://thealternativemuslim.wordpress.com/2011/08/03/the-myth-of-the-hojabi-a-ramadan-reminder/ (accessed on 1 September 2015).
90. Fair, C. Christine. *The Madrassah Challenge: Militancy and Religious Education in Pakistan*. Washington: United States Institute of Peace, 2008.
91. Fair, C. Christine, Rebecca Littman, Neil Malhotra, and Jacob N. Shapiro. "Relative Poverty, Perceived Violence, and Support for Militant Politics: Evidence from Pakistan." 2015. Available online: http://www.princeton.edu/~jns/papers/FLMS_2013_Poverty_Violence_Support_for_Militancy.pdf (accessed on 16 September 2015).
92. Fair, C. Christine, Neil Malhotra, and Jacob N. Shapiro. "Faith or Doctrine? Religion and Support for Political Violence in Pakistan." *Public Opinion Quarterly* 76 (2012): 688–720.
93. Shafiq, M. Najeeb, and Abdulkader H. Sinno. "Education, income and support for suicide bombings: Evidence from six Muslim countries." *Journal of Conflict Resolution* 54 (2010): 146–78.
94. Asal, Victor C., Christine Fair, and Stephen Shellman. "Consenting to a Child's Decision to Join a Jihad: Insights from a Survey of Militant Families in Pakistan." *Studies in Conflict and Terrorism* 31 (2008): 973–94.
95. Hussain, Azhar, Ahmad Salim, and Arif Naveed. *Connecting the Dots: Education and Religious Discrimination in Pakistan A Study of Public Schools and Madrassas*. Washington: United States Commission on International Religious Freedom, 2011. Available online: http://www.uscirf.gov/sites/default/files/resources/Pakistan-ConnectingTheDots-Email(3).pdf (accessed on 1 September 2015).
96. Qadeer, Mohammad. *Pakistan—Social and Cultural Transformations in a Muslim Nation*. New York: Routledge, 2006.
97. Shaikh, Farzana. "Islamisation to Shariatisation: Cultural transnationalism in Pakistan." *Third World Quarterly* 29 (2008): 593–609.

98. Ahmad, Sadaf. *Transforming Faith: The Story of Al-Huda and Islamic Revivalism among Urban Pakistani Women*. Syracuse: Syracuse University Press, 2009.
99. Khan, Zafarulla. "Cyberia: A New Warzone for Pakistan's Islamists." In *Pakistan's Counterterrorism Challenge*. Edited by Moeed Yusuf. Washington: Georgetown University Press, 2014, pp. 69–186.
100. Rubin, Barnett. *The Fragmentation of Afghanistan: State Formation and Collapse in the International System*, 2nd ed. New Haven: Yale University Press, 2002.
101. International Crisis Group. "Reforming Pakistan's Criminal Justice System." 2010. Available online: www.crisisgroup.org/en/regions/asia/south-asia/pakistan/196-reforming-pakistanscriminal-justice-system.aspx (accessed on 31 August 2015).
102. Abbas, Hassan. *Reforming Pakistan's Police and Law Enforcement Infrastructure: Is it Too Flawed to Fix*? Washington: US Institute of Peace, 2011.

Islam and Political Violence

John L. Esposito

Abstract: The global threat of Al Qaeda post 9/11 and ISIL, increased Sunni-Shia conflicts, and violence in the Middle East and Pakistan dominate headlines and challenge governments in the region and globally. Both Muslim extremists and some Western experts and observers speak of a clash of civilizations or a culture war in Muslim-West relations. Both the discourse and violence yet again raise questions about the relationship of Islam to violence and terrorism: is Islam a particularly violent religion? Critics cite Quranic passages, doctrines like jihad and events in Muslim history as strong indicators and proof that Islam is the primary driver of Muslim extremism and terrorism. What do the Quran and Islamic law have to say about violence, jihad and warfare? What are the primary drivers of terrorism in the name of Islam today? This article will address these questions in the context of development of global jihadist movements, in particular Al Qaeda and ISIL, their roots, causes, ideology and agenda.

Reprinted from *Religions*. Cite as: Esposito, J.L. Islam and Political Violence. *Religions* **2015**, *6*, 1067–1081.

The global threat of Al Qaeda post 9/11 and ISIL, increased Sunni-Shia conflicts and violence in the Middle East and Pakistan, Boka Haram terror in Nigeria, and domestic attacks in France and the U.S. dominate headlines and challenge governments in the region and globally. Both Muslim extremists and Western experts and observers, speak of a clash of civilization or a culture war in Muslim-West relations. Both the discourse and violence yet again raise questions about the relationship of Islam to violence and terrorism: is Islam a particularly violent religion? Critics cite Quranic passages, doctrines like jihad and events in Muslim history as strong indicators and proof that Islam is the primary driver of Muslim extremism and terrorism.

1. The Quran and Violence

Islam, like its monotheistic cousins Judaism and Christianity, is a religion whose sacred scripture, history and tradition include both peace and violence [1–3]. The prophets of the Bible and Quran (Joshua, David, Saul, and Muhammad) were also warriors/military leaders. Historically, all three monotheistic religious traditions, Judaism, Christianity and Islam, have justified violence in the name of self-defense, but followers have also legitimated both holy and unholy wars, wars of conquest and imperial expansion and made religious claims to the occupation of land in the name of God. While the great majority of believers read violent texts in their historical contexts, religious extremists and terrorists continue to site them as justification for their actions. Mainstream believers also, in the words of Philip Jenkins, often have "Holy Amnesia" when it comes to their sacred texts *versus* those of others. Thus, for example, while many (including hardline Christian ministers and political commentators) rush to refer to violent passages in the Quran as if this were a specific problem of Islam, they overlook much the much greater number of passages that command violence, murder and even genocide, in the Bible [4]. As Jenkins has noted: "Much to my surprise, the Islamic scriptures in the Quran were actually far less bloody and less violent than those in the Bible. ... By the standards of the time, which is the 7th century A.D., the laws of war that are laid down by the Quran are actually reasonably humane...Then we turn to the Bible, and we actually find something that is for many people a real surprise. There is a specific kind of warfare laid down in the Bible which we can only call genocide" [5–7].

Understanding violence in Quranic texts, as with all religious texts, requires reading the text within its historical context. In Arabia's tribal society and environment, tribal raids and warfare were considered normal and lawful unless a truce had been concluded between tribes. Chivalry forbade killing noncombatants like children, women, religious leaders and old people. These rules were later incorporated into Islamic law and the doctrine of jihad.

From 622 until his death ten years later, Muhammad very successfully consolidated his power in Medina and united the feuding tribes of Arabia. At critical points throughout these years, Muhammad received revelations from God that provided guidelines for the jihad. As the Muslim community grew, questions about who had religious and political authority, how to handle rebellion and civil war, what was proper behavior during times of war and peace, how to rationalize and legitimate expansion and conquest, violence and resistance—all quickly emerged. Answers to these questions were developed by referring to Quranic injunctions.

The Quran provides detailed guidelines and regulations regarding the conduct of war: who is to fight and who is exempted (48:17, 9:91), when hostilities must cease (2:192), how prisoners should be treated. (47:4) Verses such as Quran 2:194 emphasize proportionality in warfare: "whoever transgresses against you, respond in kind." Other verses provide a strong mandate for making peace: "If your enemy inclines toward peace then you too should seek peace and put your trust in God" (8:61) and "Had Allah wished, He would have made them dominate you and so if they leave you alone and do not fight you and offer you peace, then Allah allows you no way against them" (4:90). From the earliest times, it was forbidden to kill noncombatants as well as women and children and monks and rabbis, who were given the promise of immunity unless they had taken part in the fighting.

Under the leadership of Muhammad and then his early successors (caliphs), the Islamic community spread rapidly, creating a vast empire greater than Rome at its zenith and stretching from North Africa to India. Muslim armies, motivated both by economic rewards from the conquest of richer, more developed societies, and religious zeal, the promise of reward in heaven, successfully overran the Byzantine and Persian empires which had become exhausted from endless warring with each other.

The religious rationale (as distinct from the practical political and economic motives) for conquest and expansion was not to force conversion to Islam upon other faiths who had their own prophets and revelations. The Quran states clearly "There is no compulsion in religion" (2:256) but rather to spread its righteous order so that ignorance and unbelief could be replaced by just societies throughout the world. The religious justification made for a jihad to propagate the faith is connected to Islam's universal mission to spread the word of God and the just reign of God's will for all humanity: "So let there be a body among you who may call to the good, enjoin what is esteemed and forbid what is odious. They are those who will be successful" (3:104) and "Of all the communities raised among men you are the best, enjoining the good, forbidding the wrong, and believing in God" (3:110).

2. Jihad and Violence

The history of the Muslim community from Muhammad to the present can be read within the framework of what the Quran teaches about jihad. There is no single doctrine of jihad that has always and everywhere existed or been universally accepted. Muslim understanding of what is required by the Quran and the practice of the Prophet regarding jihad has changed over time. The doctrine of jihad is not the product of a single authoritative individual or organization's interpretation. It is rather the product of diverse individuals and authorities interpreting and applying the principles of sacred texts in specific historical and political contexts. Muslims throughout the ages have discussed and debated and disagreed about the meaning of jihad, its defensive and expansionist as well as legitimate and illegitimate forms. Terrorists have hijacked Islam and the doctrine of jihad much as Christian and Jewish extremists have committed their acts of terrorism in their own unholy wars in the name of Christianity or Judaism.

The importance of jihad is rooted in the Quran. The Quranic meaning of jihad refers to the obligation incumbent on all Muslims to struggle or exert (jihad) oneself, to follow and realize God's will: to lead a virtuous life, to fight injustice and oppression, reform and create a just society and, if necessary, engage in armed struggle to defend one's community and religion. Quranic passages referring to jihad as armed struggle fall into two broad categories: defensive, those that emphasize fighting against aggression, and offensive or expansionist, a more general command to fight against all unbelievers and spread the message and public order, or *Pax Islamica*, of Islam. Muslims throughout the ages have discussed, debated and disagreed about the meaning of jihad, its defensive and expansionist, legitimate and illegitimate forms ([8]; [9], p. 119).

The Quran does not command or condone illegitimate violence and terrorism. At the same time, early Quranic verses did affirm the right to respond to aggression, and to counter persecution and attack by Meccan rivals: "Permission is given to those who fight because they were wronged. Surely Allah is capable of giving them victory. Those who were driven out of their homes unjustly, merely for saying 'Our Lord is Allah'." Q. 22:39–40. Muslims are urged to fight with great commitment so that victory will come and battle will end: "If you meet them in battle, inflict on them such a defeat as would be a lesson for those who come after them, and that they may be warned" (8:57). However, as is noted in the same passage, if they propose peace, then the fighting must end: "But if they are inclined to peace, make peace with them, and have trust in God for he hears all and knows everything" (8:61). A similar message is found in the passage: "Fight for the cause of God with those who fight you, but do not be aggressive: God does not like aggressors" (2:190).

But what about the so-called "sword verses? The term "sword-verse" is not found in the Quran, or in major Prophetic traditions (hadith). This term represents a later interpretation of the Quran and Islamic law, developed by late eighth/early ninth century religious scholars (ulema), many of whom enjoyed royal patronage. Religious scholars annulled earlier Meccan Quranic verses in favor of the more militant verses revealed in Medina and then rulers employed these verses in Islamic law to legitimate their military jihads of conquest and imperial expansion in the name of defending and spreading Islam.

Quran 9:5 is the major sword-verse cited: "When the sacred months have passed, slay the idolaters wherever you find them, and take them, and confine them, and lie in wait for them at every place of ambush." [10]. Quran 9:5 responded to the context in which it was revealed; it was referring to Meccan non-Muslims, the pagans or polytheists of Arabia, not to Jews and Christians whom the Qur'an always refers to as the "People of the Book" ("*Ahl al-Kitāb*"). In contrast to the earliest commentators, as noted above, later medieval commentators reinterpreted this verse and expanded its meaning to justify wars of imperial expansion, a jihad against all non-Muslims.

Today, the meaning and intent of Q. 9:5 is distorted by both polemical critics of Islam and Muslim terrorists alike. Critics cite this verse to demonstrate that the religion of Islam is a violent religion that commands the killing of Jews and Christians. Muslim extremists and terrorist groups, past and present, like Al Qaeda, ISIS and Boka Haram, have used this verse to justify unconditional warfare against all unbelievers, non-Muslims as well as Muslims who do not accept their militant beliefs. Both conveniently overlook or reinterpret the end of Q. 9:5 which clearly states that, while Muhammad's followers had permission to fight to defend themselves, they were to stop if the enemy stopped its aggression: "But if they repent, perform the prayer and pay the zakat, then let them go their way, for God is forgiving and kind" (9:5).

3. Muslims Attitudes towards Jihad Today

The multiple meanings of jihad across the Muslim world today are reflected in Muslim responses to a worldwide Gallup Poll's open-ended question, "Please tell me in one word (or a very few words) what 'jihad' means to you." Personal definitions of jihad included (in decreasing order of frequency) references to: "a commitment to hard work" and "achieving one's goals in life"; "struggling to achieve a noble cause"; "promoting peace, harmony or cooperation, and assisting others"; and "living the principles of Islam."

In four Arab nations (Lebanon, Kuwait, Jordan, and Morocco), the most frequent response was: "duty toward God", a "divine duty", or a "worship of God"—with no explicit militaristic connotation at all. In four non-Arab countries (Pakistan, Iran, Turkey, and Indonesia), a significant minority reported—"sacrificing one's life for the sake of Islam/God/a just cause", or "fighting against the opponents of Islam" and in Indonesia, it was expressed by an outright majority ([11], p. 33).

4. Islam in Modern Muslim Politics and Its Relationship to Violence

In the late twentieth century, Islamically-informed or buttressed ideologies, replaced Arab nationalism/socialism in the Arab world as the primary political ideology. During the 1950s and 1960s widespread dissatisfaction with Western-inspired liberal nationalism took its toll as monarchs and governments tumbled from power in Egypt, Libya, Syria, the Sudan, Iraq, and Algeria. All were based upon some form of Arab nationalism/socialism with its populist appeals to Arab-Islamic roots, stress on Arab unity, criticism of the failures of liberal nationalism and the West, and promise of widespread social reforms. Arab nationalist leaders like Egypt's Gamal Abd al-Nasser and his admirers like Sudan's Jafar al-Numeiry and Libya's Muammar Qaddafi came to power. Arab nationalism/socialism was discredited by the disastrous Arab defeat in the 1967 Arab-Israeli war, the failure of economic policies, and government corruption. Israel's crushing victory over the combined forces of Egypt, Jordan and Syria in the 1967 Six-Day War symbolized the depth of Arab and Muslim impotence and the failure of modern nation states in the Muslim world. Israel seized major pieces of territory, including the Sinai Peninsula and Gaza Strip from Egypt, the Golan Heights from Syria, and the West Bank and East Jerusalem from Jordan. The loss of Jerusalem, the third holiest city of Islam, was particularly devastating to Muslims around the world, making Palestine and the liberation of Jerusalem an Islamic, not just an Arab or Palestinian, issue.

1967 proved a turning point for many in the Arab world but also in South and Southeast Asia. Critics blamed Western political and economic models for their moral decline and spiritual malaise. Disillusionment with the West, and in particular with the United States, its pro-Israel policy, and its support for authoritarian rulers fed anti-Western feelings. Muslim religious leaders and activists believed their message had been vindicated, maintaining that the failures and troubles of Muslims were a result of turning away from God's revealed path and relying on the West. Many urged a return to the Islamic principles and values that had made Muslim countries so powerful throughout history. Muslims must reclaim their Arab-Islamic identity and heritage, history, culture and values. This quest for identity, a more historic and authentic identity, triggered a resurgence of religion in politics and society across the Muslim world, a force that continues to impact Muslim politics today [12].

From the 1970s onwards, Islam and Islamic movements became a major force in Muslim politics that has continued for decades, informed as much by politics as by religion, taking many shapes and forms.

From Africa, across the Middle East to South, Southeast and Central Asia, Islam became the primary language of political discourse and mobilization in many Muslim countries. Muslim rulers have appealed to Islam to enhance their legitimacy, rule, and policies. Mainstream Islamist movements and political parties appealed to Islam for legitimacy and to mobilize popular support. Islamists in subsequent years were elected president, prime minister, deputy prime minister, parliamentarians, and mayors. At the same time, extremist Islamist (also commonly referred to as jihadist or militant Salafi movements) organizations used violence and terrorism in the name of Islam to threaten and destabilize governments, attack government institutions, and terrorize populations. However different mainstream Islamists were from militants in their specific agendas and tactics, the primary drivers were political grievances with the appeal to religion as a source of identity, ideology, legitimation, and mobilization. The Muslim Brotherhood in Egypt, Jamaat-i Islami in Pakistan, Ennahda in Tunisia, the FIS in Algeria, Turkey's Welfare Party, and later the Justice & Development Party (AKP) participated in elections as opposition parties; Hizbollah emerged in response to the Israeli invasion and occupation of southern Lebanon and HAMAS was founded soon after the first intifada in Palestine; Islamic Jihad (Egypt) in 1980 and Islamic Jihad Palestine in 1981.

5. Roots and Development of Today's Global Jihadist Movements

Since the last half of the 20th century, a globalization of jihad has occurred in religious thought and in armed struggles. On the one hand, jihad's primary Quranic religious and spiritual aspects—the "struggle" or effort to follow God's path, to lead a good life—remains central to Muslim spirituality. On the other hand, the concept of jihad has been used and misused; used by resistance and liberation movements and hijacked and misused by extremist and terrorist organizations to legitimate, recruit, and motivate their followers. The trajectory of jihadist movements has moved from a national to a transnational or global agenda.

From the late 1970s to the early 1990s, militant Muslim groups focused locally, within their own nations. With the exception of bombings at the World Trade Center in 1993 and in Paris in 1995, most movements, their members and targets were national (the near enemy), using violent attacks to destabilize and in time overthrow specific Muslim governments. America and Europe remained secondary targets, "the far enemy," due to their military and economic support for oppressive regimes. Why the transformation from a local to a global jihad?

The 1979–1989 Soviet-Afghan war marked a turning point; jihad went global to a degree never seen in the past. The war was waged during the Cold War at the very time that Western and many Muslim nations feared not only Communism but also Ayatollah Khomeini and Iran's export of its Islamic revolution. An unforeseen consequence and outgrowth of the Afghan war was the development of a global jihad ideology and movement(s) that came to see Afghanistan as but one step in a global war against what were seen as un-Islamic Muslim governments and the West. The policies of authoritarian Muslim regimes proved to be catalysts for radicalization, violence and terrorism not only nationally but also transnationally.

11 September 2001 heralded the global threat of Osama bin Laden and Al-Qaeda and the genesis of global movements and networks with a global agenda and use of violence and terror in the name of Islam. The global jihad by Osama bin Laden and Al-Qaida (The Base) against corrupt Muslim governments and the West emerged as the primary movement and model for others that subsequently emerged, including ISIL ISIS. Afghan Arabs moved on to fight other jihads in their home countries and in Bosnia, Kosovo, and Central Asia. Others stayed on or were trained and recruited in the new jihadi madrasas and training camps [13,14]. Al Qaeda, its affiliates and other terrorist groups represented a new form of terrorism, transnational in its identity and recruitment and global in its ideology, strategy, targets, and network of organizations, as well as economic transactions. Individuals and groups, religious and lay, have seized the right to declare and legitimate unholy wars in the name of Islam.

The globalization of jihad was reflected in Bin Laden's fatwa signed by Ayman Al-Zuwahiri, his deputy and now leader of Al Qaeda, and two other radical Muslim leaders from Pakistan and Bangladesh: "Killing the Americans and their allies—civilians and military—is an individual duty for every Muslim who is capable of it and in every country in which it is possible to do so. This will continue until al-Aqsā Mosque and the Holy Mosque in Mecca have been liberated from their grip, and their armies have moved out of all the lands of Islam, being defeated and unable to threaten any Muslim" [15].

After the Afghan-Soviet War, in which Bin Laden was on the same side as the U.S. and many in the Arab world and global community, he became a sharp critic of American foreign policy, radicalized by the prospect of an American-led coalition in the 1991 Gulf War, the danger of substantial American military and economic involvement and a subsequent increased presence and influence of America in Saudi Arabia. Although Bin Laden appealed to Islam, his primary justification and appeal was to the grievances and popular causes of many in the Arab and Muslim world.

In his "A Declaration of War against the Americans" in 1996, Bin Laden declared he was fighting U.S. foreign policy in the Middle East and, in particular, American support for the House of Saud and the state of Israel. His goal, he said, was to unleash a clash of civilizations between Islam and the Zionist crusaders of the West. Bin Laden sought to provoke an American backlash that would radicalize the Muslim world and would topple pro-Western Muslim governments.

Al Qaeda and their affiliates, as ISIS and other militants today, go beyond classical Islam's criteria for a just jihad and recognize no limits but their own, employing any weapons or means, which they rationalize as due to the overwhelming force of the enemy, Muslim governments and their Western allies. They reject Islamic law's regulations regarding the goals and means of a valid jihad, that violence must be proportional, that only the necessary amount of force should be used to repel the enemy, and that innocent civilians should not be targeted, and that jihad must be declared by the ruler or head of state. Acts normally forbidden—such as stealing, murdering noncombatants, and terrorism—against non-believers and unsupportive fellow believers now seen as the enemies of God alike are seen as necessary and required, religiously legitimated in a cosmic war between good and evil, between the armies of God and Satan. For these extremists, Muslims who remain apolitical or resist—individual Muslims or governments—are no longer regarded as Muslims but rather as atheists or unbelievers, or enemies of God, against whom all true Muslims must wage holy war, or jihad.

6. Islam and Suicide Terrorism

Historically, suicide bombing is not exclusively associated with Islam, but is also associated with secular political groups who used it as a means to fight against a stronger enemy, be it in military, technological, or economic terms (the Tamil Tigers for whom suicide bombing was their primary weapon are a case in point). As witnessed in Northern Ireland, Sri Lanka, Israel, India, Lebanon, Palestine, Pakistan, post Saddam Iraq, Kashmir, Chechnya, the major goal has often been nationalist, to end the occupation of lands, force "foreign" military forces from what these movements regarded as their homeland. Two major types of Muslim suicide bombers can be distinguished: those who embrace martyrdom to achieve national goals identified as supported by Islam (Palestinian, Chechnyan, and Kashmiri activists) and transnational terrorist movements, in particular al-Qaida and ISIS.

However, while terrorists use religious appeals to recruit volunteers, is religion the key catalyst? Contrary to the conventional wisdom, Robert Pape's groundbreaking study of suicide terrorism incidents from 1980 to 2003, concluded:

"From Lebanon to Sri Lanka to Chechnya to Kashmir to the West Bank, every major suicide-terrorist campaign—over 95 percent of all the incidents—has had as its central objective to compel a democratic state to withdraw" [16–18].

Suicide bombing and terrorism were not, and are not, simply driven by blind religious, ethnic or cultural hatred, but by real or perceived injustices, especially associated with occupation. Both self-described religious and even secular groups have framed their terrorist acts within a powerful religious medium. The Tamil Tigers, a non-religious Marxist-Leninist group, whose main tactic was suicide bombings, appealed to Tamil Hindu religious identity in their struggle for independence against Sinhalese Buddhists in Sri Lanka. Hamas, an acronym for the Islamic Resistance Movement (Ḥarakat al-Muqāwamah al-'Islāmiyyah), which originated primarily to resist Israeli occupation and Hizbollah which emerged in response to the Israeli occupation in southern Lebanon repression appealed to religion to legitimate its actions. Even the Al-Aqsa Brigade, a secular Palestinian militia, like Hamas, used religion to legitimate its suicide bombings, choosing the name Al-Aqsa (a major mosque and religious site in Jerusalem) as well as calling its attacks "jihads" and its fallen "jihadists" or martyrs. In Iraq: suicide terrorism was unknown in Iraq before its invasion and occupation by the United States and Great Britain. However, suicide bombing became a widespread tactic, used by Sunni and Shii militias, in sectarian conflicts over power and to end American occupation.

7. ISIS and Its Self-Proclaimed Caliphate

ISIS, with its proclaimed global agenda and wanton use of violence and terror, is the most recent iteration of militant globalism. ISIS stands for the Islamic State of Iraq and Syria, also called the Islamic State of Iraq and the Levant or ISIL, and, more recently, just IS or Islamic State. Political conditions in Syria and Iraq, ethnic-religious/sectarian divisions in the region, and the failures of the U.S. and international community contributed to ISIS stunning if barbaric success. Bashar al-Assad's brutal military response to the "threat" of the Arab uprisings or Spring's seeming democratization wave and the slaughter of moderate Syrian opposition groups, paved the way for outside jihadist groups and heightened Sunni-Shia sectarian warfare. Saudi Arabia, Qatar and Turkey's initial support for militant Sunni jihadist groups like including ISIS rather than moderate anti-Assad groups, to fight a primarily political-driven proxy war in Syria against Assad, compounded the situation. In Iraq, Nouri al-Maliki's installing a Shiah-dominated government and political marginalizing Sunnis increased an already polarized situation and sectarian violence that resulted in former Sunni military officers joining ISIS and alienated some Iraqi Sunnis welcoming ISIS ([19], p. 339).

8. But What about ISIS Islamic Pedigree and Vision?

As an organization, ISIS originated from Al-Qaeda's group in Iraq, the Islamic State of Iraq (ISI). While there are similarities between ISIS and other terrorist groups like Al-Qaeda in their religious/ideological worldview and tactics, there are also distinctive differences. Terrorist groups and networks usually consist of relatively small numbers of fighters who strike and move on; their primary targets are the "near enemy" with the "far enemy" a distant second. Estimates of ISIS membership and fighters vary from 30,000 to 70,000 and, in contrast to Al-Qaeda, ISIS seeks to take and hold territory and create a proto-state. ISIS invades, occupies and governs areas as part of its version of a transnational caliphate. Populations are forced to publically pledge their allegiance (baya) to the caliphate in exchange for which they are offered a mafia-like version of "protection". For example, after driving out Iraqi security forces and capturing Ramadi, a predominantly Sunni city, in May 2015, ISIS consolidated its power and proceeded to govern and administer its would-be state, as it had from Raqqa and Deir al-Zour in Syria to Mosul, imposing its brutal version of law and order. Those who resisted were killed, often beheaded, mosques were seized and regulated; male residents were required to attend and pray. However, at the same time, ISIS operated as an efficient government providing jobs, goods and services, rebuilding the city's infrastructure, public works projects, repairing roads, restoring medical services, and providing food, fuel, and electricity [20].

ISIS offers a new and unique militant Salafi ideology/religious rationale to justify, recruit, legitimate and motivate many of its fighters to achieve its goals. Baghdadi has mythologized and reinvented his own idiosyncratic brand of Islam to legitimate, recruit and mobilize fighters for his military ideological movement. He has blended religion and politics into a more comprehensive religious ideology, with its symbols, slogans and discourse and promoted it through social media, and to a degree that neither AQ nor any other Islamist movement has done in modern times. On 29 June 2014, ISIS proclaimed itself a worldwide caliphate, the Islamic State (IS), with Abu Bakr al-Baghdadi its caliph. Baghdadi's commitment to the restoration of the Caliphate identified his movement and proto-state with an idealized period of history that many Muslims see as the Golden Age of Islam religiously, politically and culturally. The Caliphate symbolizes Muslim unity, governance and social justice that still evoke the glories of Islamic history, in the face of more recent centuries of Western invasions, occupation and colonialism [21]. ISIS (or IS) now extended its claim to religious, political and military authority over all Muslims globally. Implied in the creation of the Islamic State as a restoration of the caliphate was the illegitimacy of post WWI European colonial creation of modern Arab states and their rulers and thus the legitimacy of the Islamic State's expansionist agenda.

Baghdadi's Islam is religiously and organizationally monolithic, authoritarian and exclusivist: "One leader, One authority, One mosque: submit to it, or be killed." [22]. For Baghdadi, he as Caliph has sole and absolute decision-making authority over all Muslims, Muslim groups, movements and institutions. All mujahedeen and Islamic factions or affiliates are expected to swear allegiance to him as caliph and to the Islamic state. There is but one interpretation of sharia with no recognition of diverse schools of Islamic law. Sunni imams/religious leaders who resist ISIS occupation and disagree with its violent brand of Islam are crushed. ISIS takes over all mosques, often replaces the local preachers and imposes its hardline exclusivist interpretation of Islam with brutal consequences for Shiah and non-Muslims. Indeed, for Baghdadi Shiah are not true Muslims nor are Sunnis who disagree with him.

ISIS has been unrelenting in its persecution of Shia Muslims, Christians and Yazidis with hundreds of thousands killed and forced to flee from the villages. Driven by a ruthless indiscriminate anti-Shia sectarianism, ISIS targets Shiah with a vengeance, making no distinction between Shiah fighters and ordinary civilian Shiah. This policy is reinforced by senior ISIS officers, Sunni members of Saddam Hussein's military who lost their positions after the U.S. invasion and occupation of Iraq post Saddam Shiah rule, non-Muslim religious minorities, Yazidis and Christians, have been expelled from their villages in Iraq where they had lived for 14 centuries. Christians only other choice for survival is conversion to Islam.

ISIS has used total war without limits: extreme public violence, beheading and gruesome images to worn, subdue and punish captured populations as well as attract international media coverage, attention and ransom [23]. Historically, beheading was an all too common form of punishment, an instrument employed in early Islamic, European (in particular the guillotine in France) and Asian history by governments and terrorists. Public beheadings of criminals remains common in Saudi Arabia today and, although not common, it has been used by AQ in the beheading of American journalist Daniel Pearl and recently by Mexican cartels.

Ironically, Ayman al-Zawahri, Al-Qaeda's leader, has criticized Baghdadi's premature creation of a caliphate as well as Baghdadi's excessive and indiscriminate use of violence: the slaughter of ordinary (non-combatant) Shia and use widespread policy of beheadings.

9. Religion as a Cause and Catalyst for Political Violence and Terrorism

Major polls have consistently reported that Islam is a significant component of religious and cultural identity in Muslim countries and communities globally and thus the use of Islam by violent extremists as an instrument for legitimation and mobilization is not surprising. As the Gallup World Poll of Muslims (2001–2007) in some 35 countries reported, the most frequent response by those polled as to what they admire most about themselves was "faithfulness to their religious beliefs." The top statement they associated with Arab/Muslim nations was that "attachment to their spiritual and moral values is critical to their progress" [24]. However, a primary catalyst for extremism, often seen as inseparable from the threat to Muslim religious and cultural identity, is the threat of political domination and occupation.

While religion/Islam does play a significant role, political grievances also play a significant role, often intertwined with religion. ISIS execution videos, released (October 2006–April 2013 Al-Furqan Media Foundation), when ISIS called itself the Islamic State of Iraq, underscore the importance of political grievances as motivations to join: Western military invasion, occupation and support for authoritarian regimes, the Iraqi and Syrian governments' killing of tens of thousands of civilians and "crimes" committed by individuals/groups (Iraqi soldiers, police, and government workers). Both the Iraqi and Syrian governments and their oppositions have conflated political grievances and violence with Sunni-Shia sectarianism. "The Syrian and Iraqi regimes have deliberately and successfully portrayed the conflict as sectarian to discredit the opposition and unify non-Sunnis around the governments. Many in the opposition in turn have embraced sectarianism…British officials noted that ISIS atrocities have played well with certain segments among Muslim youth, particularly those already involved in criminal activity. ISIS also offers its fighters uniforms, has English-language media, and otherwise appeals to young Westerners" [25].

As in the recent past, so too today, these grievances have remained powerful among some 20,000 foreign recruits, including more than 5000 Europeans and Americans.

10. Legitimate *vs.* Illegitimate Uses of Violence

A critical issue is the distinction between legitimate *vs.* illegitimate uses of religion and of violence. The role of Pope John Paul II and Catholicism in Eastern Europe or of U.S. chaplains and Christianity and Judaism in support of WWII and other wars was welcomed as constructive in contrast to the role of some Christian leaders in Serbia and Muslim leaders who supported extremist groups. Similarly, while it is common to say we reject any group that advocates or uses violence, most Muslims, like Jews and Christians and others, in fact accept as legitimate the use of defensive violence and violence in "just wars".

The line between movements of national liberation and terrorist organizations is often blurred or dependent upon one's political vantage point. America's revolutionary heroes were rebels and traitors for the British crown. We find many recent examples among people of many faiths: Catholics and Protestants in Northern Ireland; Bosniaks (Muslims), Serbian Orthodox and Croat Catholics in the Balkans; Christians and Muslims during the Lebanese civil war; and Sunni and Shii in post Saddam Iraq. The complexity of the issue of legitimate *vs.* illegitimate violence is reflected in the changing perceptions and fortunes of leadership. In the recent past, Menachem Begin and Yitzak Shamir, Jomo Kenyatta, Nelson Mandela, and Yasser Arafat and the PLO, were regarded by their opposition as terrorists leading terrorist movements. Yesterdays' terrorists may be just that—terrorists; or they may be judged by history as freedom fighters, statesmen, and even Nobel Laureates.

Religion becomes a vehicle for expressing moral outrage at the invasion and occupation of Muslim lands, repression by authoritarian "un-Islamic" governments, sectarian conflicts and legitimation for the use of force and violent. However, the profiles of militant Muslim groups in recent decades reveals diverse personal, religious, and socioeconomic profiles and motivations. Within weeks after 9/11, media reported, what they regarded to be a "stunning discovery" that the attackers were not all from the poor, uneducated or oppressed sectors of society nor were they all particularly religious.

Profiles of terrorists, from the 9/11 attacks to the London bombings of 7/7 reveal that many were educated individuals from middle- and working-class backgrounds. Some were devout; others were not—some had frequented bars, red light distracts, *etc*. Most were not graduates of madrasas or seminaries but of private or public schools and universities, among them: Osama Bin Laden, Ayman al-Zawahiri, Muhammad Atta, and British-born Omar Sheikh, the terrorist kidnapper of the executed Wall Street Journal reporter Daniel Pearl.

Studies on radicalization, terrorism and global suicide bombings by the EC's European Network of Experts on Violent Radicalization (of which I was a member) post 9/11 and 7/7 on radicalization in Europe on terrorism and others have found that in most cases religion is not the primary source of most extremists' behavior. The drivers of radicalization are diverse and influenced by specific contexts. For example, the vast majority of Muslim populations in Europe are members of a visible ethnic minority. Their narratives are shaped by experiences such as xenophobia, anti-Islam and anti-Muslim bias and racism, lower employment and educational levels, lack of a sense of dignity and self-esteem. The results often include a sense of marginalization and alienation, moral outrage, and search for a new identity with a sense of meaning, purpose and belonging. In many cases, terrorists are neither particularly religiously literate nor observant though their issues may overlap. As the UK's MI5 briefing report on radicalization (2008), concluded, "far from being religious zealots, a large number of those involved in terrorism do not practice their faith regularly. Many lack religious literacy and could be regarded as religious novices." Contrary to conventional wisdom, the report concluded that, "a well-established religious identity actually protects against violent radicalization".

Many of the above characteristics can be found among ISIS foreign recruits. Like many recruits to other militant Muslim movements, Europeans and Americans who join ISIS are often not necessarily religiously literate or devout. The case of Yusuf Sarwar and Mohammed Ahmed, two jihadi wannabes who in July 2014 pled guilty to terrorism offences, are a not uncommon example. Before they set out from Birmingham to fight in Syria last May, they ordered two books online from Amazon, *Islam for Dummies* and *The Koran for Dummies* [26]. Similarly, "Overall, security officials believe that the decision to go fight in a foreign conflict is usually less an act of religious commitment than of young male rebellion and thirst for adventure. One intelligence official notes that many recruits "just want to fight in Syria" but are vague on why. "Only one percent know a theologian" or are informed on dogma in any way." ([25], p. 5; [27], pp. 53–94).

ISIS has attracted a diverse group of fighters, including: former senior Iraqi Sunni military officers, tribal leaders and anti-U.S. insurgents who have been alienated and radicalized by the policies of Iraq's Shii dominated government; Tunisians, Egyptians, and Uighurs; Americans and Europeans. ISIS message of brotherhood, community, purpose and meaning, fighting for an alleged noble and higher cause find a ready audience among European and American recruits, many of whom feel alienated and marginalized in their societies and seek a more meaningful and exciting life and cause. While Bin Laden and Al-Qaeda fighters have lived a life of more itinerant ascetic warriors of Islam, always on the move or on the run, often living in primitive conditions, away from wives, ISIS offers it members and new recruits not only a strong sense of identity, community, power, agency, adventure, and meaning but also paid salaries, the opportunity to meet and marry female recruits and raise a family, and other tangible benefits [28].

ISIS has been remarkably successful in tapping into these needs and benefits in their use of the Internet for recruitment globally. Its extraordinarily professional and effective use of the Internet, social media (Facebook and twitter), video games and magazine's such as Islamic State News-online to preach its message and attract followers has brought recruits, women as well as men, from Tunisia to the Philippines and Europe to America. Like recruits to other effective social movements, many of ISIS recruits, are drawn by a message and lifestyle that romanticizes and legitimates their mission and their brutality and excessive use of force. The slaughter and savagery of ISIS fighters are normalized by images of heroic jihadist warriors, their cause and exploits, in victoriously routing of the enemy or "enemies of Islam".

Like AQ and other militant Muslim groups or movements, ISIS is a symptom of much deeper systemic problems in the Arab world that must be addressed by Arab political and religious leaders,

Arab societies and the West. There is a direct linkage between the spread of extremism and authoritarian and repressive governments on the one hand and Western double standards on the other. The fallout from the failure of the Arab Spring, crushing hopes for democratization; Egypt's military-led coup which overthrew a democratically elected president and restoration of authoritarianism with the massacre of civilians, brutal repression of the Muslim Brotherhood and secular activist opposition; the U.S. and European Union's ambivalent response; and restoration of aid to the Abdel Fatah el-Sisi regime have all been a gift to ISIS and other terrorists' propaganda and recruitment. U.S. and European strengthening of ties with authoritarian Arab allies to defeat ISIS at the expense of their espoused principles and support for the right to self-determination, democracy and human rights reinforces the image and reality of a Western double standard. The suppression of moderate Islamist and secular groups and parties by authoritarian regimes with the acquiescence or support of Western allies fuels political violence and the rise and spread of AQ, ISIS and their lookalikes.

Violence and terrorism in the name of Islam by a host of militant Muslim movements in recent decades is a product of historical and political factors, not simply religion or a militant Islamic theology/ideology. Focusing on reading the Quran or violent passages in the Quran can obscure the importance of the policies of authoritarian and oppressive regimes and their Western allies. Many contemporary Muslim religious scholars and leaders have denounced extremists' appeals to Islam and their acts of violence and terrorism, issued fatwas, supported madrasa reforms and de-radicalization programs [29]. However, in the long run, to break the cycle of Muslim violence and terrorism, Muslim governments and their Western allies must address the political conditions that terrorist movements exploit. Addressing real grievances of the population (such as occupation, authoritarianism, repression, tyranny, and corruption) will suck the air from the extremist organizations and ideologies.

Conflicts of Interest

The author declares no conflict of interest.

References and Notes

1. For discussions of the relationship between monotheism and violence, see Rodney Stark. *One True God: Historical Consequences of Monotheism*. Princeton: Princeton University Press, 2007.
2. Mark Jurgensmeyer. *Terror in the Mind of God: The Global Rise of Religious Violence*. Los Angeles: University of California Press, 2003.
3. Jessica Stern. *Terror in the Name of God*. San Francisco: HarperOne, 2009.
4. For mass killings and genocide passages, see, for example, 1 Samuel 15:1–9, Joshua 6:20–21, Deuteronomy 2:32–35 and 3:3–7.
5. Philip Jenkins, as quoted in Barbara Bradley. "Is the Bible more Violent than the Quran." *NPR*, 18 March 2010. Available online: http://www.npr.org/templates/story/story.php?storyId=124494788 (accessed on 31 August 2015).

6. Philip Jenkins. *Jesus Wars*. San Francisco: HarperOne, 2011.
7. John Shelby Spong. The Sins of Scripture: Exposing the Bible's Texts of Hate to Reveal the God of Love. San Francisco: Harper Collins, 2006.
8. For a major recent study of jihad, see Asma Asfaruddin. *Striving in the Path of God: Jihad and Martyrdom in Islamic Thought*. New York: Oxford University Press, 2013.
9. M. Cherif Bassiouni. "Evolving Approaches to Jihad: From Self-Defense to Revolutionary Regime-Change Political Violence." *Chicago Journal of International Law* 8 (2007): Article 8.
10. Others verses include 2:191, 193; 4:89, 91; 8:39; 9:29, and 66:9.
11. John L. Esposito, and Dalia Mogahed. "Battle for Muslims' Hearts and Minds: The Road Not (Yet) Taken." *Middle East Policy* 14 (2007): 27–41.
12. John L. Esposito. *The Future of Islam*. New York: Oxford University Press, 2010, p. 61.
13. For excellent coverage of the origin and development of Al-Qaeda, see Peter L. Bergen. *Holy War, Inc.: Inside the Secret World of Osama Bin Laden*. New York: Free Press, 2002.
14. Lawrence Wright. *The Looming Tower: Al-Qaeda and the road to 9/11*. New York: Knopf, 2006, p. 122.
15. John L. Esposito. *Unholy War: Terror in the Name of Islam*. New York: Oxford University Press, 2002, pp. 2–21.
16. Robert Pape. "Why the Bombers are so angry at us." *The Age*, 2005. Available online: http://www.theage.com.au/news/opinion/why-the-bombers-are-so-angry-at-us/2005/07/22/1121539145036.html (accessed on 31 August 2015).
17. Robert Pape. Dying to Win: The Strategic Logic of Suicide Terrorism. New York: Random House, 2010.
18. Robert Pape. Cutting the Fuse: The Explosion of Global Suicide Terrorism and How to Stop It. Chicago: University of Chicago, 2010.
19. Fawaz Gerges. "Isis and the Third wave of Jihadism." *Current History*, 2014. Available online: http://currenthistory.com/Gerges_Current_History.pdf (accessed on 31 August 2015).
20. Erin Cunningham. "Islamic State converting Ramadi into stronghold." *The Washington Post*, 2015, A08.
21. Graham Fuller. "Who's afraid of the Caliphate." *Huffington Post*, 2015. Available online: http://www.huffingtonpost.com/graham-e-fuller/isis-caliphate-meaning_b_5562600.html (accessed on 31 August 2015).
22. Alastiar Crooke. "You Can't Understand ISIS if you don't know the history of Wahhabism in Saudi Arabia." *Huffington Post*, 2014. Available online: http://www.huffingtonpost.com/alastair-crooke/isis-wahhabism-saudi-arabia_b_5717157.html (accessed on 31 August 2015).
23. Fawaz Gerges quoted in, "The Islamic State, can its savagery be explained?" *BBC News*, 9 September 2014. Available online: http://www.bbc.com/news/world-middle-east-29123528 (accessed on 31 August 2015).
24. John L. Esposito, and Dalia Mogahed. *Who Speaks For Islam? What a Billion Muslims Really Think*. New York: Gallup Press, 2008, p. 86.

25. Daniel Byman, and Jeremy Shapiro. "Be Afraid. Be A Little Afraid: The Threat of Terrorism from Western Foreign Fighters in Syria and Iraq." *Foreign Policy at Brookings* 34 (2014): 12–13. Available online: http://www.brookings.edu/~/media/research/files/papers/2014/11/western-foreign-fighters-in-syria-and-iraq-byman-shapiro/be-afraid--web.pdf (accessed on 31 August 2015).
26. Mehdi Hasan. "What the Jihadists Who Bought 'Islam for Dummies' on Amazon Tell Us about Radicalisation." *Huffington Post UK*, 2014. Available online: http://www.huffingtonpost.co.uk/mehdi-hasan/jihadist-radicalisation-islam-for-dummies_b_5697160.html?utm_hp_ref=tw (accessed on 31 August 2015).
27. Thomas Hegghammer. "The Rise of Muslim Foreign Fighters: Islam and the Globalization of Jihad." *International Security* 35 (2010): 53–94. Available online: http://www.mitpressjournals.org.proxy.library.georgetown.edu/doi/pdf/10.1162/ISEC_a_00023 (accessed on 31 August 2015).
28. Audrey Kurth Cronin. "ISIS is Not a Terrorist Group Why Counterterrorism Won't Stop the Latest Jihadist Threat." *Foreign Affairs*, 2015. Available online: http://cf.linnbenton.edu/artcom/social_science/clarkd/upload/ISIS%20Is%20Not%20a%20Terrorist%20Group.pdf (accessed on 31 August 2015).
29. Charles Kurzman. "Islamic Statements against Terrorism." Available online: http://kurzman.unc.edu/islamic-statements-against-terrorism/ (accessed on 31 August 2015).

Comparative Framework for Understanding Jewish and Christian Violent Fundamentalism

Arie Perliger

Abstract: Although most scholars agree that in the last couple of decades, religious fundamentalism has become the dominant ideological feature in the landscape of modern terrorism, many prefer to ignore the fact that this is not a development which is restricted to the Islamic world, and that other religious traditions have also experienced growth in groups which prefer to use violent strategies to promote their sacred visions. The current chapter strives to fill this gap by analyzing the emergence of violent religious groups in two distinct, non-Islamic, religious traditions. At first glance, the Christian Identity and the Religious-Zionist movements have very little in common. However, both movements served as a breeding ground for the emergence of violent fundamentalist groups aspiring to facilitate an apocalyptic/redemption scenario by engaging in illegal violent campaigns. Moreover, in both cases, the role of spiritual leaders was crucial in shaping the radicalization of the groups and their target selection, and the violence had a clear symbolic narrative. In other words, for the members of these violent groups, the violence served a clear role in the mobilization of potential supporters, and the branding and dissemination of the movement's ideology. Finally, while in general, terrorism is perceived as the weapon of the weak, in these two cases it was perpetrated by individuals/groups affiliated to communities belonging to the dominant religious framework in their respective polities (*i.e.*, the Religious-Zionist and Christian Identity movements are perceived by their members as branches of Judaism and Christianity). Hence, by utilizing a comparative framework, the article will not just analyze the violent manifestations that emerged from these two movements, but also try to identify the unique factors that characterize and facilitate the emergence of religious groups within religious communities belonging to the dominant religious tradition in their societies.

Reprinted from *Religions*. Cite as: Perliger, A. Comparative Framework for Understanding Jewish and Christian Violent Fundamentalism. *Religions* **2015**, *6*, 1033–1047.

1. Introduction

On the morning of Tuesday, 10 August 1999, the North Valley Jewish Community Center in Los Angeles was crowded with more than 250 playing children. A few minutes before 11 am, Buford Oniel Furrow parked a Chevrolet van that he had purchased a few days earlier, at the entrance to the Community Center. He proceeded into the lobby carrying an Israeli Uzi-type submachine-gun and started shooting at the crowd. When he left the building a few minutes later, three kids, a receptionist, and a camp counselor were lying wounded on the floor [1]. But these were not his last victims that day. A short time later, in the town of Chatsworth, he shot and killed Joseph Ileto, a USPS worker. Ileto had just delivered mail to a home and was returning to his postal truck when Furrow asked him to mail a letter for him and immediately after that, shot him with his Glock 9mm handgun [1]. Furrow eventually surrendered at the Las Vegas FBI office. During the investigation of the event, Furrow's association with the *Aryan Nations* and the Christian Identity movement at large was uncovered, as well as the fact that he had been motivated by racial sentiments, a core element of the movement's ideology.

Despite events such as the one described above, and the fact that the Christian Identity movement continues to proliferate (today including more than 70 active ministries in over 34 states, with approximately 50 thousand followers and/or members) ([2], p. 139), it has received little attention from contemporary students of political violence. Although most scholars agree that in the last couple of decades, religious fundamentalism ("Strict adherence to certain theological doctrines, in reaction against modernist theology" [3]) has become the dominant ideological feature in the landscape of modern terrorism [4–6], many prefer to ignore the fact that this is not a development which is restricted to the Islamic world, and that other religious traditions have also experienced growth in groups which prefer to use violent strategies to promote their sacred visions.

The current article strives to fill this gap by analyzing the emergence of violent religious groups in two distinct, non-Islamic, religious traditions. At first glance, the Christian Identity and the Religious-Zionist movements have very little in common. However, especially from the late 1970s and early 1980s, both movements served as a breeding ground for the emergence of violent fundamentalist groups aspiring to facilitate an apocalyptic/redemption scenario by engaging in illegal violent campaigns. Moreover, in both cases, the role of spiritual leaders was crucial in shaping the radicalization of the groups and their target selection, and the violence had a clear symbolic narrative. In other words, for the members of these violent groups, the violence served a clear role in the mobilization of potential supporters, and the branding and dissemination of the movement's ideology. Finally, while in general, terrorism is perceived as the weapon of the weak, in these two cases it was perpetrated by individuals/groups affiliated to communities belonging to the dominant religious framework in their respective polities (*i.e.*, the Religious-Zionist and Christian Identity movement are perceived by their members as branches of Judaism and Christianity). Hence, by utilizing a comparative framework, the next sections will not just analyze the violent manifestations that emerged from these two movements, but also try to identify the unique factors that characterize and facilitate the emergence of religious groups within religious communities belonging to the dominant religious tradition in their societies.

2. Ideology

Before discussing the violent manifestations of the religious-Zionist and Christian Identity movements, a concise introduction to their ideological tenets will be presented, followed by an attempt to identify how their ideological structures facilitate violence by some members of these movements.

2.1. Christian Identity Movement

The ideology of the Christian Identity movement is rooted in the writings of a radical Irish weaver, John Wilson, who asserted in the mid-nineteenth century, that the lost biblical Israeli tribes migrated from Palestine and settled in northern Europe to become the Anglo-Saxon nations. Hence, he believed that since the Anglo-Saxons are the true chosen people, the "British Israelite" had a divine obligation to dominate the earth, in the spirit of the biblical prophecies given to the people of Israel [7]. These ideas were spread in the U.S. during the late nineteenth and early twentieth century via the *British-Israelite World Federation*, which had several branches on the East Coast. When William J. Cameron and Howard Rand gained dominancy over the movement before World War II, they identified the Zionist movement and Jews as the main adversaries of the British-Israelite movement; hence, they gradually embraced anti-Semitic and racial rhetoric. Cameron and Rand's followers, preachers such as Wesley Swift, Richard Butler, and William Porter Gale, continued to integrate similar theological analyses via their respective identity churches and groups (such as *the Church of Jesus Christ Christian*, and *The US Christian Posse Association*) and emphasized anti-Semitic notions, principles of white supremacy and racial segregation, as well as related apocalyptic visions [8–10].

Several core beliefs characterize the Christian Identity movement. First, Jews are the direct biological offspring of the devil or Satan, who are using various manipulations in order to gain dominancy in financial arenas all over the world as a tool for promoting the destruction and decomposition of Aryan civilizations. Thus, the Jews are not just the natural "threat" of the identity movement (because of their perception that they are the chosen people), but they aim to destroy or control other religious traditions ([8], pp. 34–39); [9,10]. The second core belief of the movement could be described as an apocalyptic perception that humanity is in its final days, hence, all believers should be ready for the second coming and the restoration of the dominancy of the true people of Israel. However, the movement emphasizes the active, rather than the passive, role of the believers. While many fundamentalist Protestants have asserted that during the time of the "rapture" and tribulation at the end of days and towards the second coming of the Messiah (times which will be characterized by violence, persecution and war), the "saved" will be taken from earth (hence, will not be directly involved in the struggle between forces of light and darkness), Identity scholars maintain that the true believers will embrace the opportunity to actively engage in the fight against the forces of evil. Therefore, believers will be fighting a war between the children of light and the children of darkness (Jews), which will end with divine intervention, and the establishment of Christ's Kingdom ([8], pp. 79–81). The third ideological pillar of the Identity movement is the support for racial segregation, which should be imposed to maintain the superiority of the Aryan race and to prevent racial mixing. These perceptions are an extension of the movement's unique interpretation of the biblical story of Genesis, in which Adam was not the first man, but the first white man. Before him (pre-Adamic), people of color were created by God, who had lesser qualities. The white people as well could be divided into superior and inferior "seed-lines": those who are descendants of Adam and Eve (Aryans), and all others (non-Aryans), who are descendants of Eve and the serpent (the reflection of the devil) ([8], pp. 162–63); [11]. Accordingly, Identity leaders asserted that race mixing was the original sin that led to the expulsion of the white man from the Garden of Eden. It should be noted that these kinds of distinctive interpretations of religious texts are not unique, as Identity leaders consistently produce interpretations of religious texts that can justify and rationalize the ideological pillars of the movement. While the relations between the various ideological components of the movement are complicated, from an analytical perspective, it is useful to see it as a religious movement, in which ethno-centric and racist attitudes are part of its theological pillars.

2.2. Religious Zionist Community

As in the case of the Identity movement, the foundational notions of Religious-Zionist ideology appeared first in the mid-nineteenth century, and gained momentum, becoming a mass movement, in the early twentieth century. The major gap between the Jewish Ultra-Orthodox (Haredi Jews) and the Religious-Zionists relates to their views regarding the circumstances that will lead to the foundation of Jewish religious kingdom in the Land of Israel. While the former believe that Jews should wait passively until the arrival of the Messiah, which will be followed by the establishment of a Jewish Kingdom, Religious Zionists preached a more active role. They too believed that a Jewish religious kingdom would be established following the arrival of the Messiah, but the founding fathers of the Religious-Zionist movement advocated that by settling the land of Israel, working the land, and restoring the Hebrew language, this redemption process could be expedited [12–14]. Thus, in contrast to the ultra-Orthodox, the Religious-Zionists have historically made efforts to find ways to bridge the gap between Jewish Orthodoxy and secular Zionist ideology. Moreover, in many ways, they accepted the dominancy of the secular Zionist streams, believing that the establishment of the State of Israel should be the end point of their efforts to expedite the redemption process. However, the implications of the war of 1967 changed this dynamic. Following the war, parts of the religious-Zionist community adopted beliefs which regarded the realization of the vision of the Greater Land of Israel by Jewish settlement in the West Bank as a decisive phase in the salvation of the People of Israel, and in the establishment of a religious Jewish state. In other words, they see the establishment of the State of Israel in 1948, the decisive Israeli victory of 1967 and the Israeli settlement of the West Bank, as stages in the redemption process [13,14]. As a consequence, any attempt to backtrack this process, for example by conceding lands to the Palestinians in the West Bank, is seen by them as a direct violation of God's will and should be prevented. Almost 50 years after the 1967 war, this vision has become dominant in the Religious-Zionist community, which comprises the decisive majority of the settler population and is today almost entirely ideologically homogenous [15].

Another important process has characterized the Religious-Zionist movement in the last couple of decades. After the establishment of the Israeli state, the movement was comfortable in taking a back seat, and accepting the dominancy of secular Zionism in the Israeli civilian and social spheres, while focusing on ensuring the prosperity of its own cultural and social infrastructures (schools, religious institutions, *etc.*). Since the early 1980s however, there has been a growing desire by the movement to have a more influential role in shaping the public and social sphere in Israel, and pushing its values to the mainstream. Hence, the community does not accept the liberal assumption that religion is a private matter [14,16], and that the collective does not have the right to impose religious practices on its members. Accordingly, the leaders of the Religious-Zionist movement seek to enforce their values not only within their own community, but on all Jews in Israel. Practical manifestations of their attitude can be seen in the aspirations of the movement to shape state legislation in the spirit of the Halacha (Jewish religious law), to impose religious components in secular schools' curriculum, and to prevent harm to the status of religion in the state's institutions and procedures (such as in the Israeli Defense Forces (IDF)), by any means [17]. As will be made clear later, violent manifestations of the movement aimed to both promote the movement's value system, as well as to prevent policies that were perceived as delaying or posing an obstacle to progress in the redemption process.

2.3. Ideology-Comparative Analysis

When analyzing the ideology of the two movements, and especially the way their ideological framework has been structured, several important similarities emerge, which can provide some initial ideas about how they became a breeding ground for violent actors.

The first is related to the *avant-garde* nature of the Identity and Religious-Zionist movements. While the supporters/members of both movements are a small minority within their respective societies, they see the implementation of their movement's vision as crucial for the survival of their entire respective nation/culture. Thus, the fact that members of these movements feel responsible for the "well-being" of their entire nation may push them to act via radical means to insure the promotion of policies that are necessary for the implementation of their movement's goals. Moreover, both movements see themselves as a transformative *avant-garde*, responsible to promote social/cultural transformation of mainstream culture by advocating their norms and morals. In this regard, during the past 40–50 years, there have been times in which there were indications that (at least in the public sphere) the respective American and Israeli societies are moving further away from the movements' belief system and core principles. That may explain the escalation of some elements within these movements to illegal and violent practices, as movement members feel that radical means must be exercised to overturn what they see as the societal moral decline. To illustrate, In Israel, especially during the 1990s, polls consistently showed that the majority of the public is supportive of the two state solution, and willing to make territorial compromises in the West Bank [18]. In the U.S., ideas of racial segregation, white supremacy and de-legitimization of non-Christian communities are increasingly perceived as illegitimate in the mainstream public sphere, probably more than at any time in the past.

Another characteristic that is shared by both movements is a flat and a pluralistic power structure, which provides flexibility in the interpretation of the movements' religious texts and core principles. In other words, the movements are comprised of a relatively high number of spiritual leaders, each promoting and disseminating his own interpretation of the movement's core religious texts to his group of followers ([2], pp. 31–36). While some of these spiritual leaders are more influential than others, there is no strong mechanism that enables enforcement of consensus within the movements. This structure lends itself to internal competition between the various "chapters" of the movements, and may encourage some leaders to adopt extreme interpretations of the texts, so to distinguish themselves from other leaders, and to appeal to more activist constituencies. It is therefore understandable how some segments may slide into illegal and violent activities when the movement's values seem to be threatened by external actors or are ignored by mainstream society. Simply put, members of the movements who are interested in engaging in extreme activities in order to "protect" movement values and way of life, can usually find at least some leaders who provide interpretations that may justify such acts. It is not a coincidence, for example, that the founders of *The Order*, the most well organized violent framework that emerged from the Identity movement, were members of Richard Butler's *Aryan Nations Church of Jesus Christ Christian* (mostly known just as *Aryan Nations* or *AN*) which for years pushed its members both to cooperate with other actors within the violent far right landscape (Neo-Nazis, KKK to name a few) and promoted ideas which presented the federal authorities as the ultimate representative of the dark forces. As the words of Pastor August Kreis (the current formal leader of *AN*) illustrate—"We, as you elect, will carry out your wrath against your enemies (Satan's forces and anti-Christ) in this, the great battlefield, called earth…We look forward to the destruction of your enemies on this earth and to the establishment of your kingdom" [19].

Within the Religious-Zionist movement we can find similar dynamics. Before its first attack in 1980 (in retaliation for the killing of a Jewish student in Hebron), members of the most well organized violent group to emerge from the Religious-Zionist movement, the *Jewish Underground*, approached at least two spiritual leaders, whom they felt would be able to provide moral support to their actions. Indeed, both leaders were willing to support some kind of retaliation attack ([12], p. 51).

Lastly, it is important to note that both movements endorse the view that they play a role in a progressive historical process that will end with an apocalyptic event, leading to the realization of their vision. Hence, in both we see strong emphasis on the active role of the individual believer. Each member of the community is responsible via his personal behavior and actions for promoting and maintaining the historical process and the vision to which the movement aspires. This empowering environment, which encourages individual activism, entrepreneurship, and responsibility, also provides a space of legitimacy for those interested in engaging in more extreme activities. To illustrate, during the implementation of the Oslo process, as well as during the implementation of the Israeli "Disengagement Plan" from the Gaza Strip, various leaders within the Religious-Zionist movement called for IDF soldiers who were religious Zionists to refuse to participate in any military activity that directly or indirectly assisted the evacuation of Jewish settlements in the West Bank or the Gaza Strip, emphasizing that every individual had to do whatever he could to support the ideological tenets of the movement [20]. Similar emphasis can be found in one of the most popular and well-known publications of the *AN*, which is basically a story of individual empowerment. The "Turner Diaries" which was initially published in serial form by the *AN*'s "Attack" magazine, and in 1978 as a book, tells the story of Earl Turner, who joins a revolutionary group which fights against the growing racial integration and gun control legislation by engaging in insurgency warfare against the authorities, including radical violent attacks against symbols of the federal government. Interestingly, the book, which was published 23 years before 9/11 attacks, ends with Turner crashing his airplane into the Pentagon [21].

Who were the people and groups who actually translated this mind set of empowerment into a campaign of violence? The following section will examine them and analyze the similarities in the operational dimensions of the violent manifestations of the movements.

3. Violent Manifestations

Before discussing the violence that was perpetrated by members of the Christian Identity and the Religious-Zionist movements, it is important to note, that in both cases we are dealing with a small minority. The majority of the members and leaders of these movements did not participate in or endorse violence. This partially explains the fairly limited violence that was committed by the two movements, and its infrequent nature.

3.1. The Violent Aspects of the Christian Identity Movement

Probably the first violent group which emerged from the Identity movement was the above mentioned The Order. Founded in 1983 by an Identity activist by the name of Robert Matthews, it aimed to engage in guerrilla warfare against the federal government (or what members of the group referred to as ZOG—Zionist Occupation Government), hoping to ignite a mass uprising [22]. Comprised mostly of AN members, The Order initiated a campaign of counterfeiting, armed robberies and violent attacks between 1983 and 1986. Among the group's violent attacks, worth mentioning are the robbery of a Brinks armored vehicle near Ukiah, California, which netted $3.8 million, the assassination of Alan Berg, a Jewish liberal radio host at KOA radio, the bombing of a pornographic theater in Seattle, Washington and of a synagogue in Boise, Idaho in April 1984 [22]. The limited operational experience of the group's members, probably explains the FBI's quick success in penetrating the group and detaining most of its members in less than a year after its initial attacks.

The quick elimination of The Order probably had some deterrent effect, since only in the early 1990s was it possible to identify the resurfacing of violent acts by members of Identity groups. Most perpetrators came from four specific groups: Aryan Republican Army, Creativity Movement/World Church of the Creator (also known as WCOTC), Phineas Priests, and AN. While the Aryan Republican Army was engaged in a systematic campaign of robberies between 1994 and 1995, attacks by members of the three other groups were mainly spontaneous, opportunity based, by lone wolves or small groups ([2], p. 79). Examples are the shooting attacks by Benjamin Smith, member of WCOTC who, during the weekend of July 4, 1999, filled his Ford Taurus with guns and ammunition and during a three-day, two-state shooting spree killed two people and wounded nine others [23]; or the attacks perpetrated by Jules Fettu, a member of Phineas Priests, who, fully armed with two guns and a pipe bomb, attacked a youth service at the Wedgwood Baptist Church and killed seven people, while shouting anti-religious statements [24]. This wave of attacks continued until the early 2000s before declining significantly in the last decade.

To conclude, attacks by Identity group members focused on minorities and financial institutions. The former were naturally linked to the movement's ideological tenets. The second were explained by members of The Order and Aryan Republican Army, as a necessity for funding of the groups' recruitment activities and future operations.

3.2. The Violent Aspects of the Religious Zionist Movement

As pointed out by Perliger and Pedahzur [15], most of the violence that was produced by members of the Religious-Zionist movement was in response to two types of pressure: (a) an escalation in the security situation in the West Bank, and especially an increase in Palestinian violence against the settler population (*i.e.*, the first and the second Palestinian uprisings, also known as Intifadas); (b) peace initiatives which might potentially lead to Israeli territorial concessions. In both cases the settlers' leaders were concerned that the violence/peace processes, would pressure Israel to make territorial concessions to the Palestinians, hence diverting Israel from the path of implementing its sovereignty over the "Greater Land of Israel", which is a core element of the Religious-Zionist theology, as explained above.

Several specific examples can illustrate the dynamics mentioned above. In the early 1980s, the combination of Israeli agreement (via the Camp David accords) to provide autonomy to the Palestinian population in the West Bank, and an increase in Palestinian violence, led to the emergence of groups such as the Jewish Underground and the Lifta Gang, which by attempting to bomb and destroy the Al-Aqsa Mosque on the Temple Mount, hoped to promote regional instability that would halt the peace process between Israel and Egypt ([12], pp. 51–52, 141–43). Similarly, the emergence of the Bat-Ayin group, which was engaged in a violent campaign of ambushing Palestinian vehicles and which was eventually exposed after a failed attempt to place an improvised bomb at the entrance to a Palestinian school, is attributed to the outbreak of the second Palestinian uprising [15]. Lastly, the assassination of Prime Minister Itzhak Rabin in 1995, by Yigal Amir (who had his own supporting network), was a direct result of Rabin's attempt to push forward the Oslo Peace process, and his willingness to promote territorial concessions ([12], pp. 101–10).

The examples above also illustrate the two major targets that were preferred by violent groups affiliated with the Religious-Zionist community. The first, and by far the most popular, is the Palestinian population in the West Bank, as their residence in the West Bank and their struggle for political independence were perceived as the most acute threat to the implementation of the vision of the Greater Land of Israel. Moreover, the first and second Palestinian uprisings, also positioned the Palestinian population as a direct security threat in the eyes of the settlers. Lastly, the religious symbols used by the Palestinian population to legitimize their political demands for Palestinian independence, such as the Dome of the Rock or Al-Aqsa Mosque, were perceived as an abomination and a direct obstacle to progress towards redemption in the eyes of many leaders of the Religious-Zionist movement. The second preferred target was Jewish leaders and/or public figures, who were known to be supporters of the peace process. The most notable examples are the above mentioned assassination of Prime Minister Rabin and the attempted assassination of Prof. Zeev Sternhell, a well-known Israeli academic and one of the most furious critics of the settlement movement, by Jacob Title, a resident of the Shvut Rachel settlement, who was also responsible for killing two Palestinians, on other occasions [25].

3.3. Radicalization and Violence-Comparative Analysis

When looking into the operational characteristics of the violence that was perpetrated by groups affiliated with the Religious-Zionist and Identity movements, several interesting similarities can be detected. To begin with, in both cases the majority of the attacks were directed against specific ethnic/religious groups, the "absolute" outsiders in the eyes of movement members, while a minority of the attacks was aimed at what can be termed "internal" dissents. This reflects the fact that in both cases, specific external communities/outsiders are portrayed as the foremost threat to the ability of the movement to realize its vision, and to maintain its way of life. The de-legitimization, and sometimes, de-humanization, of these external communities, seems to help the more radical members of the movements to cross the psychological threshold that prevents most members from engaging in violent activism. In other words, the selective nature of the targets helps the perpetrators to legitimize their actions more effectively, as they can draw a direct association between their actions and the movement's ideological framework.

In addition, the violent acts provided an opportunity for these movements to shape the discourse related to their objectives/ideological agenda. Terrorism is a method of symbolic violence, in which groups try to overcome the gap in resources (between them and the polity) by utilizing violence which they hope will shape the political perceptions and attitudes of the public and/or policy makers. In the cases of the movements discussed in this article, the careful selection of targets seems to demonstrate the understanding of the perpetrators of the importance of utilizing the various components of the violent acts in order to crystalize a clear ideological massage, which will both facilitate recruitment, but also enhance in-group cohesion and solidarity.

Another similarity is related to the structure and the radicalization of the violent groups. While the classical literature on terrorism tends to portray a clear linkage between the emergence of a terrorist group and the emergence of a social or political deprivation [26], reversed dynamics can be perceived in the movements at the center of this discussion, as in many cases the networks existed before the decision to resort to violence. To begin with, unlike other ideological movements, a significant number of the Religious-Zionists, as well as members of the Identity movement, reside and spend time together in isolated spaces, where they are consistently exposed to a single ideological perspective, and can easily share and interact (just) with people who have similar views. As Perliger and Pedahzur [15] demonstrated, most members of the Religious-Zionist violent groups resided in ideological settlements in the West Bank. In the same manner, most of the more radical members of the identity movement spend time in compounds such as the one which was established by Richard Butler, *AN*'s founder, near Hayden Lake, Idaho. On the one hand, these isolated environments facilitated effective indoctrination and commitment, and allowed effective control over members of the movement; on the other hand, prolonged ideological exposure, combined with strong peer interaction and positive feedback, may facilitate extremist interpretation of the movement's ideology, and a mindset which demands personal sacrifice for the group via violent activities. These circumstances can also explain why most of the groups are based on preexisting social networks, which existed before their members resorted to violence. Hence, in many cases the attacks were a more spontaneous response to perceived threats/hostilities against the community, opportunity based, perpetrated by social networks in which none of the members was what we can describe as a "professional" or "career" terrorist.

The fact that these groups were not comprised of "career" terrorists, may also explain their limited durability and "productivity". Many of these groups/perpetrators can be described as "one hit wonders", who were caught shortly after their "inaugural" attack, and failed to construct any organizational infrastructure that would enable a long term campaign. Even groups such as the *Jewish Underground*, which was active for several years, perpetrated just two attacks, and was involved in the planning of two additional operations (which eventually did not materialize). Groups who conducted double digit attacks (*Bat-Ayin* or *Aryan Republican Army*) were usually apprehended in a couple of years; far different from many of the left wing and Islamic groups that have populated the terrorism landscape in the last few decades, and which have been able to construct a durable operational infrastructure.

Finally, it seems that in both cases, the violent campaigns did not just fail to promote the ideological objectives of the movements, but in many ways undermined their efforts to gain legitimacy. This does not mean that both movements failed to promote their political agendas. Actually, the opposite is true in the case of the Religious-Zionist movement. The following section will further elaborate on the movements' political effectiveness.

4. Political Effectiveness

How did the violence described above affect the ability of the Identity and Religious-Zionist movements to promote their ideological framework, to gain political influence, and to mobilize support? The current section will try to answer these questions while attempting to explain the significant gap between the two movements in terms of their political capital. Or in other words, why did the violent manifestations of the Identity movement further enhance its marginal status, while the violent manifestations of the Religious-Zionist movement did not prevent it from continuing to expand its political influence within the Israeli political system, and ensure the ongoing support of the Israeli authorities in the settlement project in the West Bank.

4.1. The Political Irrelevancy of the Identity Movement

The Identity movement has always held a marginal status within American society. Unlike some of the other far right movements, such as the Skinheads in the 1990s, or the KKK in the 1920s and later in the 1950s, it was never able to develop a mass following and construct an effective nationwide organization. Moreover, since its ideological transformation in the 1920s and 1930s, which included the gradual integration of anti-Semitic notions and practices, and more focus on sentiments of white supremacy, the movement was also increasingly associated with other controversial elements within the far right landscape, a process which further undermined the movement's ability to mobilize mass support.

The cooperation between the Identity movement and other far-right movements could be traced to the appearance of the first "modern" Christian Identity groups/churches on the West Coast in the late 1940s. A series of conventions that were organized in the early and mid-1940s in the North

Pacific by a British-Israelite association from Vancouver led to the formation of a network of groups on the Pacific coast that departed from the traditional British-Israelite ideological tradition, emphasizing racial conspiracy theories and apocalyptic visions ([2], p. 74). The most well-known of these is probably Wesley Swift's *The Church of Jesus Christ Christian*, founded in 1948 in Lancaster, California, which, under the charismatic leadership of Swift, became the center of the movement. Swift's anti-Semitic rhetoric left no doubt that the movement was ideologically in line with the other white supremacy groups in America, as exemplified by a statement he made in the early 1950s in one of his lectures: "All Jews must be destroyed. I prophesy that before November 1953 there will not be a Jew in the United States, and by that I mean a Jew that will be able to walk or talk" [27].

In the 1980s and 1990s the ideological similarities eventually led to direct cooperation between the Identity movement and other white supremacy groups, especially via the attempts of Richard Butler, *AN*'s founder, to transform the group's compound into "The International Headquarters of the White Race" [19]. Indeed, in the 1990s the *AN*'s compound became a safe haven for leaders of various white supremacy groups. It was isolated and remote enough to discourage the interference of law enforcement and the media, but at the same time provided the ambience of the outdoors, wild freedom, and intellectual stimulation. Hence, some of the more known ideologues of the American far right, figures such as KKK's Louis Beam, WAR's Tom Metzger, and even the founder of the Montana Militia Jon Trochman, felt comfortable to utilize the compound in order to operate and further develop their ideological visions, to forge ties to improve coordination and cooperation, and to mobilize new recruits ([2], p. 77).

From a political perspective, the transition of the Identity movement from a religious group with a specific interpretation of biblical texts regarding the identity of the chosen Hebrew people, into another stream of the American white-supremacy community, meant that the movement had limited capabilities to develop any meaningful political power, as white supremacy notions, especially in the religious context, were never even close to being perceived as legitimate by any meaningful part of the American electorate or mainstream political leadership (the ongoing failure of the former KKK leaders to be elected to political offices is a case in point). The violent manifestations of some Identity groups naturally positioned the movement, even further to the right in the eyes of the public and policy makers, in the same category of groups such as the *KKK*, the American Nazi *Party*, and the *Hammeskins Nation*.

Another aspect which probably undermined the Identity movement's ability to develop political influence is its focus on "localism". Losing hope that they could operate via the legitimate political channels, the *AN* promoted the idea of creating a network of Aryan farm communities, which would be run according to the local "Biblical/Aryan" laws, independent of federal authorities ([8], pp. 231–32). Whether this vision was driven by hostility towards the authorities or by the desire to promote racial segregation, it represented a clear dissent from the mainstream political arena.

To conclude, despite the rise in the last few years of more moderate versions of the old Identity groups, and the fact that some of them were able to use modern technology to expand their mobilization efforts (Pete Peters' *La Porta Church of Christ* is a case in point) there is no indication that the movement has been able to amass any significant political capital.

4.2. The Political Success of the Religious-Zionist Movement

In contrast to the Identity movement, the Religious-Zionist movement was able to develop powerful political mechanisms in the last 40 years, which enable it, in the eyes of many, to effectively manipulate the Israeli political system, despite never gaining more than 10%–15% of the seats in the Israeli parliament or in the executive branch. This success is manifested mainly via its ability to expand the settlement project in the West Bank—including at times when Israeli left-wing parties dominated the executive branch—despite it being a disputed issue within the Israeli political system and society.

Several factors contributed to the political effectiveness of the Religious-Zionist movement. To begin with, acknowledging that the majority of the secular Israeli public would not be willing to support Israel's control over the West Bank based on the Religious-Zionist narrative of the redemption process, the movement adopted a complementary narrative which focused on the need to maintain Israeli control over the West Bank for security reasons, and that the settlements themselves are an important tool for enhancing Israel's security. Hence, the rhetoric of many (political) Religious-Zionist leaders, while emphasizing the historical/religious right of the Jewish people to the land of Israel, has also traditionally focused on the importance of maintaining control of the West Bank from a national security angle (providing Israel with greater strategic depth). They have also concentrated on the role of the settlements as a buffer zone between Palestinian terrorism and the Israeli population (a belief that was shared by some within the security establishment) [28], and the risks the settlers have been taking in order to serve national goals [28]. The effectiveness of this rhetoric is illustrated by the ability of the Religious-Zionists to garner significant support from the Israeli secular electorate and secular parties for maintaining some Israeli control over parts of the West Bank [28].

The religious Zionist leaders have also been highly effective in developing symbolic rhetoric based on the traditional and popular Zionists terminology and legacy. More specifically, they tend to portray the settlers as true pioneers, who are willing to undergo significant hardships and costs, for the sake of the Jewish nation. This romantic image can easily parallel the common image of Zionist pioneers who arrived in Palestine in the late nineteenth and early twentieth centuries and founded most of the modern Zionist (Israeli) political movements/parties [14]. Hence, the Religious-Zionist leaders were also able to legitimize the settlements in the West Bank by presenting them as a continuation of the Zionist project at large, and in line with the traditional methods used by the founding fathers of the state to promote Jewish sovereignty.

Another factor that contributed to the success of the Religious-Zionist movement was its ability to build effective networks of influence within the Israeli governmental bureaucracy and political institutions, especially in organizations which were essential for the survival and expansion of the settlement project. Pedahzur [28] has effectively illustrated how the "political networks" of the Religious-Zionist movement within the Israeli military (via the NAHAL—Fighting Pioneer Youth), in relevant ministries (Defense, Housing, Tourism, Industry) and in semi-governmental organizations (which were the executive pillar of the Zionist movement prior to the establishment of the state, *i.e.*, Jewish Agency) among others, allowed them to manipulate policy decisions and to create comfortable conditions for continuing expansion of the settlement project. As such, they were able not just to overcome the problem of having limited electoral power, but also to efficiently undermine policy decisions that were counterproductive to their ideological objectives [28].

The leaders of the Religious-Zionist community developed complex strategies to deal with the occasional manifestation of violence by members of the community and in order to ensure that these would not harm the movement's political brand. In general, most of the Religious-Zionist leaders have publicly rejected the use of violence (at least not through the legitimate state apparatuses). In most cases, they have been successful in creating a separation (in public opinion) between the perpetrators and the Religious-Zionist community at large. Moreover, in many cases, the movement has been able to portray the perpetrators as negative elements, operating on the margins of the community, suffering from mental illnesses, and/or suffering from the significant pressure of the security situation in the West Bank. Furthermore, the flat structure of the movement has allowed linking the occasional perpetrator with a specific, extreme segments, of the movement, and thus avoiding significant harm to the movement's image at large. A related factor, which has also probably mitigated the impact of violent manifestations on the legitimacy of the movement in the eyes of the Israeli public, has been the growing dominancy of hawkish views among the Israeli public. When a growing number of Israelis feel that a peace process/territorial concessions are not a viable option, that the conflict is escalating, and that the situation in the Middle East in general demands more aggressive security policies on the part of Israel, a potential by-product is more tolerance towards acts of violence against Palestinians. Lastly, in the last couple of decades, the Religious-Zionist movement has made a concentrated effort to increase its influence/presence within the IDF and the Israeli media. As for the former, today many of the IDF's elite units are dominated by Religious-Zionist youth. Emphasizing this direct contribution of the movement to the nation's security allows the movement leaders to counter the perception that views the movement as a threat to Israel's democratic nature or security. As for the latter, it has allowed the movement more effectively to socialize its norms and practices, and presents them as part of the new Israeli identity. In both cases, it has enabled the movement to further distance itself from a more militant image.

5. Concluding Remarks

In the last couple of decades, a growing number of religious streams preferred to manifest their departure from the mainstream of their religious tradition via violent campaigns. However, so far the investigations of these dynamics focused on the Islamic realm, or on religious streams that were associated with ethnic or religious minorities. By looking specifically at the Christian Identity and the Religious-Zionist movements, both relatively unknown, I have tried to provide some initial ideas to explain how structural and contextual factors may facilitate the emergence of violent segments within religious movements, which are not part of a minority segment of society.

Several conclusions can be drawn based on the analysis above. First, while political violence has been a feature of both movements, their distinct reaction to these manifestations of violence has had an impact on the long-term success of the movements. Moreover, while the ideological tenets of the contemporary Identity movement cannot coincide with democratic values, the Religious-Zionist movement has always emphasized its willingness to operate within the confines of the Israeli democratic framework, even though its long-term objective was not compatible with the idea of a Jewish democracy. Hence, despite the movements' lack of success in mitigating the emergence of violent elements from within, the general public in both societies has reflected differently on these acts of violence, marginalizing one movement (Christian Identity), while willingly accepting the legitimacy of the other (Religious-Zionists). Second, the analysis emphasizes the important role of social enclaves and the physical isolation of the members of the movements from mainstream society, as facilitators of radicalization. It seems that in both movements, the social networks that eventually slide into violence emerged from isolated spaces, with limited exposure to alternative interpretations of social and political reality. Hence, state policies that promote social integration may be part of the solution to counter radicalization within such movements. Third, the majority of the perpetrators of the violence were not "professional" terrorists; this is a partial explanation for the limited effectiveness of the attacks of members of the movements. Nonetheless, as relevant military technology and knowledge become more accessible than in the 1980s and 1990s, we cannot assume that future attacks will not be more effective. Fourth, some correlation exists between the organizational structure of the movements and the type of violence they produce. The flat and cellular structure of these movements, as well as the lack of formal ideological consensus, provides small social networks or individuals, space to identify potential rationalization and justification for militant activism. At the same time, the fragmentation of the movement also prevents, or makes it more difficult, to create a more long-term infrastructure for a violent campaign. Fifth, the focus of the violence on "illegitimate" outsiders helps the perpetrators to portray their acts as a self-defense, aimed at protecting the movement from external threats, as well as limiting the amount of internal criticism. It is no coincidence that many of the attacks were in what can be described as the first point of contact between members of the movements and "outsiders". Finally, it is interesting, and somewhat surprising, to note that the level of success of the movements in influencing mainstream society, and state policies, had no direct impact on the level of violence they produced. Hence, while perceived external threats to the well-being of the movement, may push some members to act violently, the level of success of the movement in garnering political capital, had limited impact on the decision whether to use violence or not, at least from initial review of the violence that was produced by both movements.

As for the future of the movements' violent bursts, cautious optimism is in place. As mentioned above, there are signs that the violence produced by members of the Identity movement is in decline. It seems that as long as future Israeli territorial concessions will be a remote possibility, the incentive for organized violence by members of the Religious-Zionist movement will be limited.

Conflicts of Interest

The author declares no conflict of interest.

References

1. Frank Gibney, Jr. "The Kids Got in the Way." *Time Magazine*, 23 August 1999. Available online: http://content.time.com/time/magazine/article/0,9171,991784,00.html (accessed on 20 July 2015).
2. Arie Perliger. *Challengers from the Sidelines: Understanding America's Violent Far-Right*. New York: Combating Terrorism Center at West Point, 2013.
3. George M. Marsden. *Fundamentalism and American Culture*. New York: Oxford University Press, 1980, pp. 4–5.
4. Walter Laqueur. *The New Terrorism: Fanaticism and the Arms of Mass Destruction*. New York: Oxford University Press, 1999.
5. Andrew Tian Huat Tan, and Kumar Ramakrishna. *The New Terrorism: Anatomy, Trends, and Counter-Strategies*. Singapore: Eastern Universities Press, 2002.
6. Thomas R. Mockaitis. *The "New" Terrorism: Myths and Reality*. Westport: Praeger Security International, 2007.
7. John Wilson. "British Isealism: The Ideological Restraints on Sect Organization." In *Patterns of Sectarianism: Organization and Ideology in Social and Religious Movements*. Edited by Bryan R. Wilson. London: Heinemann, 1967.
8. Michael Barkun. *Religion and the Racist Right*. Chapel Hill and London: The University of North Carolina Press, 1994.
9. David A. Gerber. "Anti-Semitism and Jewish-Gentile Relations in American Historiography and the American Past." In *Anti-Semitism in American History*. Edited by David A. Gerber. Urbana: University of Illinois Press, 1986, pp. 20–22.
10. See unknown author. "Gentile Fall Involved in Hope of Jewish Rule." *Dearborn Independent*, 1920, pp. 8–9.
11. Charles Roberts. *Race over Grace: The Racialist Religion of the Christian Identity Movement*. Lincoln: iUniverse, 2003, pp. 31–37.
12. Ami Pedahzur, and Arie Perliger. *Jewish terrorism in Israel*. New York: Columbia University Press, 2009.
13. Zvi Rannan. *Gush Emunim*. Tel-Aviv: Hakibutz Hameuhad, 1980.
14. Baruch Zisser, and Asher Coen. *From Reconciliation to Escalation. The Religious-Secular Division at the Start of the 21st Century*. Jerusalem: Schoken, 2003.
15. Arie Perliger, and Ami Pedahzur. "Counter Cultures, Group Dynamics and Religious Terrorism." *Political Studies*, 10 December 2014. Available online: http://onlinelibrary.wiley.com/doi/10.1111/1467-9248.12182/abstract (accessed on 25 August 2015).
16. Ricky Tessler. "Religious Radicalism between/in the Defensive Democracy, Defensive Politics and Defensive Citizenship." *State and Society* 1 (2003): 585–619.
17. Eli Don Yehiye. *The Politics of the Arrangement: Settling Disputes in the Realm of Religion in Israel*. Jerusalem: Floersheimer Institute for Policy Studies, 1997.

18. Nir Hasson. "Despite It All, Most Israelis Still Support the Two-State Solution." *Haaretz*, 7 July 2014. Available online: http://www.haaretz.com/news/diplomacy-defense/israel-peace-conference/1.601996 (accessed on 25 August 2015).
19. Chester L. Quarles. *Christian Identity : The Aryan American Bloodline Religion*. Jefferson: McFarland, 2004, pp. 133–34.
20. Uri Glickman. "Rebelion of the Rabbis." *NRG News*, 4 July 2005. Available online: http://www.nrg.co.il/online/1/ART/918/613.html (accessed on 25 August 2015).
21. Andrew Macdonald. "The Turner Diaries." 1978. Available online: http://www.jrbooksonline.com/PDF_Books/TurnerDiaries.pdf (accessed on 25 August 2015).
22. Betty A. Dobratz, and Stephany Shanks-Meile. *"White Power, White Pride!": The White Separatist Movement in the United States*. New York: Twayne Publishers, 1997, pp. 36, 192.
23. Kirsten Scharnberg, Evan Osnos, and David Mendell. "The Making Of A Racist." *Chicago Tribune*, 25 July 1999. Available online: http://articles.chicagotribune.com/1999-07-25/news/9907250249_1_hale-supremacist-young-man (accessed on 25 August 2015).
24. Stephen E. Atkins. *Encyclopedia of Right-Wing Extremism In Modern American History*. Santa Barbara: ABC-CLIO, 2011, p. 55.
25. Efrat Wiess. "Jerusalem: Professor Ze'ev Sternhell Lightly Wounded by Pipe Bomb." *Ynet News*, 2008. Available online: http://www.ynetnews.com/articles/0,7340,L-3601841,00.html (accessed on 25 August 2015).
26. Martha Crenshaw. "The Causes of Terrorism." *Comparative Politics* 13 (1981): 379–99.
27. Daniel Levitas. *The Terrorist Next Door, the Militia Movement and the Radical Right*. New York: St. Martin's press, 2003, p. 25.
28. Ami Pedahzur. *The Triumph of Israel's Radical Right*. Oxford: Oxford University Press, 2012, p. 71.

Entering the Mindset of Violent Religious Activists

Mark Juergensmeyer

Abstract: How can one enter the mindset of religious activists whose worldview and values are different from one's own? This is the challenge for analyzing contemporary violent religious movements and individuals around the world. This essay suggests guidelines, based on the author's interview experience, for entering religious minds through informative encounters, relational knowledge, bracketing assumptions, and constructing a view of the whole.

> Reprinted from *Religions.* Cite as: Juergensmeyer, M. Entering the Mindset of Violent Religious Activists. *Religions* 2015, *6*, 852–859.

1. Introduction

How can we enter into the mindset of religious activists, especially those with views that are quite different from our own? The problem is confounded when confronted with those who are engaged in acts of violence that appear to be justified by faith. This is the challenge for anyone who is trying to make sense of the religious-related violence that seems to be epidemic at the turn of the 21st century. One can explain the rise of the Islamic State in Iraq and Syria, Jewish extremism, or the outbreak of Christian Islamophobia by external factors, examining the political and social factors that lie behind them. Another option is that one can set them with the contexts of broad historical trends and relate them to similar phenomena at other times and places. However, as useful as these scholarly pursuits might be, these analyses seldom explain what role religion plays, and it does not help us understand the passion and commitment with which the activists are dedicated to their cause. For this we have to go inside the mindset of the activists themselves.

The benefit of doing this is that we can discover areas of understanding that we had not thought of before, and debunk assumptions and misconceptions about motives. Take the issue of religious beliefs, for instance. There is a common assumption among many observers that religious beliefs—and specifically tenets of religious scripture—motivate activists to undertake acts of violence. Whether it is the teachings of the Qur'an or the incendiary verses of the Hebrew Bible (the Old Testament), religious ideas and beliefs are often thought to be the problem. My own interviews, however, indicate that very few religiously-related activists frame their motivations in scriptural or theological terms. Most are woefully ignorant about the textual and intellectual aspects of their traditions. Instead, they talk about the defense of their community and their faith in general, and the threat of particular groups, including secular politicians, in particular. Religious beliefs and traditions are a part of their worldview, but only a part of it, even though it may be the vocabulary through which other social and political issues are enunciated. However, in order to discover this perspective of religion-related activists, one has to see the world as they see it. Entering the mindset of activists can open doors to understanding.

How can this be done? This is the challenge for anyone trying to make sense of people and groups that are different than themselves. It is a problem for textual and historical scholars, as well as those applying contemporary social and anthropological approaches. In addition, it is the question that I have had to face in a series of interviews with radical religious activists in a variety of religious traditions and locales over the last twenty years. In my own case, the interviews involved leaders of the Palestinian Hamas movement in Gaza, an activist in prison who was associated with the al Qaeda-related 1993 bombing of the World Trade Center, a Lutheran pastor convicted of bombing abortion clinics on the East Coast of the United States, Catholic and Protestant leaders during the "troubles" in Northern Ireland, Sikh separatists in India, Muslim insurgents in Iraq, and Buddhist activists in Sri Lanka, Myanmar, and Japan [1].

Despite the diversity of these cases, there were some common threads that tied together these activists from varied cultures and regions. All of them had supported or participated in public acts of aggression or violence, including acts that we would regard as terrorism. None of them regarded themselves as terrorists, however. Mahmud Abouhalima, the jihadi activist associated with the 1993 World Trade Center bombing, whom I interviewed in the Lompoc Federal Penitentiary in California, made a clear conceptual difference between terrorists—by which he meant people who simply wanted to kill indiscriminately—and soldiers who were fighting a defensive war. The latter described himself and his actions, and the same can be said of all of the other activists with whom I spoke. They all regarded themselves as soldiers in a grand battle, a cosmic war between right and wrong, truth and evil. That moral element of their vision is where religion came in: all of these activists were fighting for social or political reasons but they framed their efforts in religious terms. Though religion was only part of their stories, it was an important part, and it was the way in which many of them characterized their struggle.

Finally they all had in common one other thing: they wanted to talk with me. In all cases I had contacted them in advance and they had willingly—in many cases eagerly—agreed to the interviews, knowing that I would use the material in the books I was writing. Abouhalima insisted that my interviews with him be tape recorded to insure accuracy. A similar concern was expressed by a Buddhist monk in Myanmar, Ashin Wirathu, who *Time* magazine had labelled "the face of Buddhist terror" for his role in allegedly advocating violence against Muslims in his country [2]. Wirathu insisted on seeing the transcript of my interview before he would agree to my using it publicly. In fact, in all cases I sent transcripts or extensive notes of the interviews to the persons with whom I spoke. I wanted to make sure that I had accurately recorded their words and appropriately interpreted their meanings. This was a potentially dangerous approach, since any of them could deny that they had said such things and prohibit me from using the interview material. Fortunately none did, though the member of the Japanese movement, Aum Shinrikyo, whom I had interviewed in Tokyo was afraid that members of the movement would find him and punish him for what he had said. Though many leaders of the movement were in jail after their use of sarin gas to create a terrorist attack on the Tokyo subways, others were re-establishing the movement under a new name, Aleph. For that reason, I used a pseudonym for his name and obscured any information that might lead to his identity. Everyone else was agreeable to my using their interviews as I had recorded or made notes of them, and Abouhalima followed up the interviews with a number of letters to me adding additional information and ideas, some of which I used in the book.

However, all of this is preliminary to what I actually did when I interviewed them. How did I go about these meetings, and what were the salient methodological principles? My approach was based on established patterns of social and anthropological inquiry, adapted to the challenges of confronting world views quite different from my own. In general, I followed a distinctive approach that had several formative characteristics that in a general way replicated the guidelines that the Danish political scientist, Mona Sheikh, and I have formulated in our essay on how to do what we have termed epistemic worldview analysis [2,3]. These principles can apply to a variety of scholarly endeavors, including those where the subjects cannot easily be interviewed, including studies that are based on the analysis of a subject's writings and transcribed interviews, as well as textual and historical analysis. They apply to any attempt to enter into a mindset different from one's own, though in the case of religious extremists the challenge is particularly daunting.

2. Informative Encounters

The first task is to try to enter into the mindset of the subjects through direct engagement. Interviews provide that opportunity, of course, but so do analyses of the subjects' writings and transcribed interviews, and first-person narratives about them. Historical studies can bring to life figures who are centuries old in vivid detail. In my case, however, I was able to actually encounter my subjects through interviews. Then the issue was how to conduct these in a way that was most effective.

The problem with many scholarly interviews is that they follow a script of questions that are predetermined and that therefore limit the scope of what can be discovered. Even the best advice in the literature on doing interviews for qualitative research is goal-oriented, and suggests that the interviewer have specific subjects to pursue [4–6]. Since my motive was to get inside the mindset of the activists, I had to abandon the comforting script of questions, and engage in a more open-ended encounter. Hence most of my interviews appeared to be conversations. When I was in a mosque in Baghdad, talking with one of the leaders of the Association of Muslim Clergy of al Anbar province in Iraq, it may have seemed like were just chatting. To the casual observer, and mostly likely from the point of view of the subjects with whom I was speaking, there was nothing directive about the conversation. It was not random, however, since I had in mind areas of inquiry (though not specific subjects) that I wanted to discuss. However, I never posed questions in a didactic way.

Though one could conclude that these conversations were efforts at getting information through understanding the subject's point of view, they were not scientific surveys. At one point in my academic career I thought that that was indeed what social scientists were supposed to do. As a beginning graduate student doing field work in village India, I was determined to conduct a survey analysis among the lower caste workers of a Punjab village. To be properly scientific I devised a 60-question interview. It floundered with question #1 and totally collapsed with question #2. The first question was simple enough—"what is your name"? Yet among the lower caste members of North Indian villages they often had different names for different occasions: caste names, occupation names, religious names, and village names. The second question was "what is your religion"? This term, easy to understand in the West, could not be directly translated in Panjabi,

Hindi, or any other Indian language. The idea of one word that corresponds to a whole range of religious activity and identity did not exist. There was *dharma* for religious law, *qaum* for a religious community or nation, *mazhab* for religious beliefs, and *panth* for a religious fellowship ([7], pp. 1–7). Just what, the villagers wanted to know, did I have I mind?

The problem with social surveys is that they assume that we know what to ask before we ask the question. Instead, I began to experiment in an interactive approach, what one might call "informative encounters". These encounters were conversational in that they were not directive at the outset, though they were aimed at getting an understanding of how the subject viewed the world. In particular, I was concerned with the role of religious ideas and identity in the way that they framed political issues, and their justification for the use of violence in social conflict. However, rather than asking that directly, I usually began with a question asking them to provide some autobiographical background, to tell me how they came to their involvement in social activism. These accounts would often lead naturally to follow-up questions about religion, politics, and violence that probed the areas in which I was interested, but also illumined their view of the world and the way that these issues fit into the larger scheme of their personal concerns.

3. Relational Knowledge

Though I had a general idea of the areas of interest that I wanted to probe in my interviews, as I have said, I did not have a list of questions. When I was in Myanmar in September 2014, talking with the activist Buddhist monk, Wirathu, I began with questions about his involvement in the monastery and his interest in social issues [8]. When he said that Buddhists should be engaged in society, this naturally led to questions about how they should do it and whether violence is ever justified. "Buddhism is nonviolent", he would insist repeatedly. Clearly this line of discussion was closed, from his point of view. It did allow me, however, to reframe the question from his point of view. If Buddhism needed to be engaged, and needed to defend itself, I asked him, from what and where were the threats coming? Immediately Wirathu snapped back that Muslim extremists were the threat, and all that was distinctive about Burmese Buddhism was in peril. This allowed us to move into the area of Buddhist-Muslim relations and to ask him the degree to which Buddhists were justified in defending themselves—even, if necessary, defending themselves in a situation that might lead to violence. Wirathu allowed for Buddhist violence in this context, though the subject would never have come up if I were not able to switch the direction of the conversation and reframe my questions depending on his previous responses.

This is not just a matter of being adroit in one's line of questioning, but also a matter of learning from what was said. It requires one to change ideas about what to ask depending on previous answers, and to let the conversations move in whatever direction seems appropriate. This is neither inductive nor deductive reasoning. Inductive reasoning assumes that one has a general idea or principle from which one makes sense of particular data. Deductive reasoning tries to build up the larger picture from accumulating particular information. The approach that I use might be called "relational reasoning", a form of understanding that emerges from the give and take of points of view in an interactive conversation. It is *relational* in that what is discovered depends upon the relationship between the conversation partners, with questions changing in response to the way previous questions have been answered. It is *reasoning* in that it aims at understanding the point of view of the subject, trying to make sense of the logic that informs a person's actions, including especially those actions that seem so inappropriate and unjustified in normal relationships, acts of violence.

4. Bracketing Assumptions

The point of these conversations is to try to enter into the mindset of the interview subjects, to understand as best as possible how they see the world. This means that as much as possible we should try to bracket our own judgments about what is being said. It is a double bracketing in fact: we should try to reserve making value judgments, at least publicly, about the truth or falsity of what they are saying, and to avoid making judgments about the truth or falsity of our own points of view (though needless to say, we think that we are always right). Sometimes both of these are difficult, especially when the issue at hand is the moral sanction for violence, or the unequal treatment of other people on the basis of their ethnicity, religion, or gender. Yet for the sake of the interviews we should keep our judgment about these matters at bay. There will be ample opportunity in the future to reflect on the conversation and condemn the subjects, if we feel that condemnation is warranted.

However, in the heat of a conversation it is not easy to stay silent. I remember a conversation with the Israeli activist, Rabbi Meir Kahane, a cheerful character with a Brooklyn accent, who passed over the territorial claims of Palestinians as if they were trivial matters. From his point of view they were; after all, he believed that the Israeli claims over Eretz Israel—greater Israel, including the Palestinian West Bank of the Jordan River—were essential in order to lay the foundations for the coming of the Messiah. This is heady stuff in Jewish history, so it is understandable that if he fervently believed that the greatest moment of biblical prophecy was about to be fulfilled, territorial claims could seem to be a minor matter. Still, it was not a minor matter to Palestinians who were uprooted from their homes and who had their own claims to the region that Kahane thought was essential for Israel to occupy. "This is biblical land", Kahane told me, implying that the Palestinians did not belong there; "they should just leave", he said. It took all of my sense of self-control to keep from arguing with him, though I knew that there would have been no point to it if I did, his mind was closed on the subject. In a similar way, the Buddhist monk Wirathu in Myanmar was convinced that Muslims in his country were a corrosive force that would undermine Burmese culture and there would be no way to convince him otherwise.

My discussions with the Christian militant, Rev Michael Bray, probably involved the most give-and-take, since he was interested in talking about theology, and I knew the works of Reinhold Niebuhr and Dietrich Bonhoeffer that he admired. I clarified my own interpretations of their work, and Bray observed that they were different than his, which did not surprise him. He had already categorized me as a liberal Christian who would see scripture and theology differently from his point of view. So there, a tacit agreement to disagree, and there was no need to argue with him, he already knew my position. What I wanted to understand was his.

Perhaps the closest I came to getting into an argument in my interviewers was with the World Trade Center bomber, Mahmud Abouhalima. At one point in our discussion he was trying to make a distinction between his world of faith and the secular world around him. He pointed to me, and asserted that "you secularists" had no way of knowing what it was like to try to live faithfully in a secular society. I instinctively reacted, since I was raised in a churchgoing household, attended seminary before graduate school, and continued to be a regular member of a Protestant Christian congregation. Still, my protestations were brushed off by Abouhalima who insisted, "no, Mr. Mark, you are a secularist". And then he added, "I know your world, I've lived in it; but you haven't lived in mine" ([1], p. 70).

Abouhalima was right, in fact. My religiosity was one that was comfortable with the secular, multicultural modernity of the contemporary West. This was the world that he was projected into after leaving Afghanistan where he had been a part of the Mujahidin militia fighting the Soviet-backed government, and before that he was in his native Egypt, where he was a member of an extremist offshoot of the Muslim Brotherhood, the Gamaa i-Islamiya. The world of New Jersey was certainly different, as was Germany where he lived for some years after leaving Egypt. So he did know my world. Additionally, it is also true that I did not really know his, even though I lived for several years in India and have spent a considerable amount of time in Muslim-majority countries. However, I have never really been out of my secular modernist element, and Abouhalima was right to remind me that I did not know his world as he knew mine. That did not mean that I condoned his interpretation of the commandments of his faith, not did it alter my judgment that he was motivated as much by a kind of macho soldier-of-war adventurism as he was by piety. Still his point was well made, and I had to make the attempt to see the world as he saw it—or at least the way he wanted me to think that he saw it.

5. Entering Their Worldview

This brings up another point—was I really probing into his mindset, or was I simply uncovering a version of himself that he wanted to sell? The point of my informed conversations was to let the subjects reveal their perspective on the world around them, which is why I was careful not to dominate the conversations. One might object that this open-ended approach to interviews allowed the subjects to control the situation. Moreover, it would allow them to present themselves exactly as they would like to be presented. Especially since they were eager to talk with me, as I just mentioned, would they not be eager to present a carefully choreographed image of themselves for my sake?

The answer to this question is yes, most likely. However, even that is an interesting datum—it is useful to know how they would like to have themselves presented, and to contrast that with other information that I had gathered about their past and their social and political involvements. In every case I did not come to an interview cold, knowing nothing about the subjects; quite the opposite, I tried to learn as much as I could about what they had said and written, and how they had been perceived and described by others, before interviewing them. I kept all of this knowledge in the back of my mind as a kind of corrective to what they might be saying and as a reminder to push them in certain directions.

In the case of Abouhalima, for instance, he never admitted to being involved in the attack on the World Trade Center even though he was tried and convicted in a US court for exactly that crime.

Still, he was hoping to get out on appeal, and would not say anything that would implicate him directly in that incident. But in the course of the conversation I found that he was quite willing to talk about the Oklahoma City Federal Building bombing—after all, no one had implicated him in that crime, nor was there any possibility that he could have been involved in it since he was in prison at the time. This allowed me to ask him why some people, whoever they might be, would bomb buildings. He assured me that it was for a reason—Timothy McVeigh and his allies were not just bombing things for the sake of bombing them—they were trying to send a message. "What kind of message", I asked him, knowing that his answer would apply to his own convicted participation in the World Trade Center bombing as well as to McVeigh's Oklahoma City Federal Building attack. "They wanted to show you that your government is the enemy", he answered. He paused, and then added, "and now you know".

These are some of the guidelines that might be followed in attempting what Mona Sheikh and I have called "epistemic worldview analysis". They do not amount to a methodology, in the sense of a prescribed analytic approach. Rather they are general principles that are relevant in a variety of analytic situations—if one is involved in textual research, social survey studies or a more anthropological approach of entering into case studies. The greater involvement with the subjects of the study the better, though in the case of historical studies often the only evidence one has of their ways of thinking is in letters or writings or in others' commentary about them.

6. Conclusions

The degree to which scholars will want to immerse themselves in the milieu of their subjects depends in part on the purpose of the project: whether it is a broad comparative overview or a more intensive case study. Though I have done intensive case studies in other books, my project in *Terror in the Mind of God* was a broad comparative analysis of disparate activists in differing cultures and regions [1]. There I attempted to find patterns in their ways of thinking and to identify some similarities in their understanding of the relation of religious images and ideas to contemporary social and political situations. Of course it would have been a more thorough study if I had known the languages of all of my subjects—Arabic, Hebrew, Burmese and Japanese, as well as Hindi and Panjabi. As it was, I was reliant on translators for many of the conversations. It would have been a deeper study if I had spent more time in each locale, came to know others within their circle, and relied not on one or two interviews but on many. Yet this would have been a different book, or more likely a series of books. My purpose was to have comparative snapshots of a range of religious activists, and I feel fortunate to have had the remarkable conversations that I had. Though Abouhalima may still not believe it, I think that I was able to penetrate into his world and the worldviews of the many others with whom I spoke, for at least a bit, and that opening illumined much about why he and others did what they did, and why their worlds have been so very hard for us to understand.

Conflicts of Interest

The author declares no conflict of interest.

References

1. Juergensmeyer, Mark. *Terror in the Mind of God: The Global Rise of Religious Violence*, 3rd ed. Berkeley: University of California Press, 2003.
2. Juergensmeyer, Mark, and Mona Kanwal Sheikh, eds. *Entering Religious Minds*. Berkeley: University of California Press, 2015, submitted for publication.
3. Juergensmeyer, Mark, and Mona Kanwal Sheikh. "A Sociotheological Approach to Understanding Religious Violence." In *The Oxford Handbook of Religion and Violence*. Edited by Mark Juergensmeyer, Margo Kitts and Michael Jerryson. New York: Oxford University Press, 2013.
4. Brinkmann, Svend, and Steinar Kvale. *InterViews: Learning the Craft of Qualitative Research Interviewing*. London: Sage Publications, 2014.
5. Van Maanen, John. *Tales of the Field: On Writing Ethnography*, 2nd ed. Chicago: University of Chicago Press, 2011.
6. Weiss, Robert. *Learning from Strangers: The Art and Method of Qualitative Interview Studies*. New York: The Free Press, 1995.
7. Juergensmeyer, Mark. "Chatting with Myanmar's Buddhist 'Terrorist'." *Religion Dispatches*, 17 February 2015. Available online: http://religiondispatches.org/chatting-with-myanmars-buddhist-terrorist/ (accessed on 10 March 2015).
8. Juergensmeyer, Mark. *Religion as Social Vision: The Movement against Untouchability in 20th Century Punjab*. Berkeley: University of California Press, 1982.

MDPI AG
Klybeckstrasse 64
4057 Basel, Switzerland
Tel. +41 61 683 77 34
Fax +41 61 302 89 18
http://www.mdpi.com/

Religions Editorial Office
E-mail: religions@mdpi.com
http://www.mdpi.com/journal/religions

www.ingramcontent.com/pod-product-compliance
Lightning Source LLC
Chambersburg PA
CBHW061357010526
44107CB00012B/964